TRUTHFUL ACTION

TRUTHFUL ACTION

Explorations in Practical Theology

DUNCAN B. FORRESTER

T&T CLARK
EDINBURGH

T & T CLARK LTD
59 GEORGE STREET
EDINBURGH EH2 2LQ
SCOTLAND

www.tandtclark.co.uk

First published 2000

ISBN 0 567 08747 6

British Library Cataloguing-in-Publication Data
A catalogue record for this book is available from the British Library

Typeset by Waverley Typesetters, Galashiels
Printed and bound in Great Britain by Bell & Bain Ltd, Glasgow

Those who do what is true come to the light, so that it may be clearly seen that their deeds have been done in God.

John 3.21 (NRSV)

All thought exists for the sake of action. We try to understand ourselves and our world only in order that we may learn how to live.

R. G. Collingwood

Contents

Introduction

The subject of practical theology, sometimes misleadingly called 'applied theology', is increasingly popular and growing around the world. But in many ways it is like a teenager going through an identity crisis. Within the discipline there are many different understandings of what practical theology is about and how it should be handled; tricky issues of substance and methodology need to be faced and seldom are. In some contexts, practical theology is little more than a loose amalgam of skills-directed discussions, so that in a seminary or theological college the study of pastoral care, homiletics, liturgy, Christian education and so on are lumped together and labelled 'Practical Theology'. It is not always clear in what way this kind of practical theology is actually theological.

The old idea that practical theology is simply 'hints and tips' in ministry dies hard. Meanwhile, the rest of theology is sometimes assumed to have little or no bearing on practice, or what goes on in the world! 'Relevance' is left to the practical theologians, and it is often believed that one can get away with a kind of sloppy thought in practical fields which would not be countenanced elsewhere in the theological school. This is indeed a strange assumption. We would rightly worry if we believed that professional training in clinical medicine or social work, for example, was lacking in intellectual rigour or cohesion. Surely, in as far as practical theology is related to ministerial formation, it should be as emphatic as any form of professional education in its call for stringent standards.

I shall argue that practical theology will continue to be about ministerial formation. But it is about a great deal more. I shall attempt in these essays to argue and demonstrate that practical theology has boundaries, but these are wide and much important debate necessarily goes on across the fences. If practical theology is indeed public theology with a complex and daunting agenda, it is, I suggest, the best context within which to address the issues and challenges of ministry and the Church today. Christian ministry is not like acupuncture or osteopathy, an alternative form of therapy which works for some people and not for others. Like mainstream medicine and the National Health Service, the ministry of the Christian Church is responsible for the whole community and its health and flourishing. But it is not, of course, easy to see how such a form of ministry can be exercised in a secular age marked by church decline and a great deal of misunderstanding, suspicion and sometimes downright hostility to the Church as an institution, the figure of Jesus, and the Christian message. Several of the essays wrestle with aspects of this issue and suggest that new lessons about ministry can be learned from today's confusing situation.

Other essays examine practical theology as public theology and engage with some of the characteristic forms of practice in the public realm today. I am aware that this involves a considerable broadening of traditional notions of practical theology, but it is, I think, a necessary and allowable extension of the understanding of practice with which the book starts.

The final section presents three case studies of different forms of practice, on the general assumption that more general insights may be gathered from detailed and specific studies. Indeed, a serious practical theology demands such studies. The first examines a somewhat distinctive relationship between theology and radical practice that emerged in Scotland, and discusses its continuing relevance today. The second has to do with ecumenical practice in relation to ethics and understandings of the Church. The final study presents an imaginative strategy for mission in India which was developed and implemented in the early nineteenth century as a kind of model of responsible and rigorous practical theology. Initial successes were followed by significant failures. It is my contention that lessons for today can be learned from careful reflection on such instances from the past, and that this kind of reflection is one of the tasks of practical theology today.

This book does not claim to be a definitive or comprehensive account of contemporary practical theology: far from it. The various chapters represent soundings or explorations in practical theology that might contribute in due course to a new mapping of the subject. Just as in an English parish there is an annual 'beating of the bounds', or in a Scottish border town a common riding, in which the boundaries are inspected and the territory within surveyed from the frontiers, so in these essays I visit the boundaries and examine the heartlands from the frontiers. The essays are one man's view of the need to extend the boundaries and reconsider the ways of doing practical theology. I want to stress the importance of ensuring that practical theology is both seriously theological and also engaged in honest dialogue with other appropriate disciplines and with what is going on in the Church and in society. Above all, practical theology must attend to what God is doing and the practices to which God is calling us today.

Early versions of Chapters 5 and 6 were given as the Gilpin Lectures in the University of Durham, and Chapters 9 and 10 arose out of the Richard Hooker Lectures which I gave at the College of St Mark and St John in Plymouth and at the University of Exeter. I am grateful for the warm welcome I received in all three places, and for the helpful and constructive comments on my lectures. Chapter 12 arose out of my involvement in the Ecclesiology and Ethics project of the Faith and Order Commission of the World Council of Churches, and an early draft of Chapter 4 was given at the Berne meeting of the International Academy of Practical Theology.

Many people – students, colleagues and friends – have commented, questioned, argued and offered insights from their own experience and practice as these themes have been developed over the last few years in seminars, lectures and conferences. I am grateful to all of them. And I also want to give special thanks to Susan Sanders and my colleague and friend, David Lyall, who helped with the proofs and the index. But my greatest debt remains to Margaret, whose loving practice in ministry, home and marriage is constantly exhilarating, challenging and enriching.

DUNCAN B. FORRESTER

New College, University of Edinburgh

Epiphany 2000

SECTION ONE

❧

PRACTICAL THEOLOGY:
A CONTRADICTION IN TERMS?

1

What Is Practice?

What is practical theology about? All subjects must have a field, something they study. They need not monopolise this field; indeed, many fields of study are so complex that they need to be studied in several different ways or approached in an inter-disciplinary style.

The very name 'practical theology' suggests that it is con-cerned with practice. This, of course, does not imply that it is not concerned with the Bible, Christian doctrine, or church history, nor that other branches of theology are not practical. Indeed, an important part of justifying the existence of practical theology as a distinct discipline is to remind theology as a whole that it is practical.

But what does 'practice' mean? Wolfhart Pannenberg has declared that any fundamental consideration of the nature of practical theology requires a clarification of the concept of practice.[1] The *Oxford English Dictionary* gives as the first mean-ing of 'practice': 'The action of doing something; working, operation; method of action or working.' Practice, in other words, is patterned activity – not random or haphazard, but with an inner or outer coherence. It is a structure of behaviour. A shoplifter defends herself in court by saying she did it on impulse, she doesn't know why she did it; she has never done it

---

[1] Wolfhart Pannenberg, *Theology and the Philosophy of Science*. London: Darton, Longman & Todd, 1976, p. 435.

3

before; it is quite uncharacteristic behaviour; it is not her practice to shoplift.

The second dictionary meaning is: 'The habitual doing or carrying out of something; usual, customary, or constant action; ... conduct.' Practice, in other words, is a regular pattern of repeated behaviour. Jesus, we read in Luke 4.16, went to the synagogue in Nazareth 'as his practice was'. Our habits, our regular patterns of activity, reveal the sort of people we are. The story goes that the citizens of Königsberg used to set their watches by the passing of the philosopher Immanuel Kant, so regular were his habits! That is an extreme case, and there is something almost mechanical about it, if it really happened that way. But this story reminds us that practice involves some kind of consistency and reliability in our behaviour. And it warns us about the danger of becoming obsessive, unable to break free from an established pattern of practice to respond to human need, the unexpected call to do the unprecedented, or to take risks.

The third *OED* sense is this: 'The doing of something re-peatedly or continuously; exercise in any art, handicraft, etc., for the purpose, or with the result of attaining proficiency; hence the practical acquaintance with or experience in a subject or process so gained.' In other words, practice is the basis of a skill. In music, dancing, athletics or swimming, the beginner needs to practise in order to attain proficiency, as does the most skilled performer in order to maintain excellence in competition or in work. Practice is the necessary preliminary to performance; but performance is the same behaviour under conditions of special stress and challenge. Only those who have been faithful in practice as preparation can excel in practice as performance, practice 'for real'. Practice thus often means sweating blood. The athlete practises until her whole body aches and every muscle cries out. Then, suddenly, you are through the pain barrier, you get the movement right, you are fluent, confident in the foreign language or the game of tennis. The great performer has achieved apparent effortless-ness and grace as a result of gruelling practice and not going stale. The musician – or athlete, or what-have-you – must still practise tirelessly even when, through practice, she has a knowledge of, a responsiveness to, and an involvement with her music which is only partly communicable in words. Paderewski, the great pianist, was reputed to have said: 'If I don't practise for a week, my audience knows it. If I don't practise for three days, my family notice. If I don't practise for a day, I am aware that I am not performing as well as I feel I can.'

There is, of course, the problem of trying too hard, of going stale. Great practitioners tend to go through a 'pain barrier', from suffering to exaltation. Really good practitioners can often relax and let the 'inner game' take over, so that performance flows through them graciously, as it were, without conscious effort. The performance of the great skater seems so natural and apparently easy that the untrained observer thinks, 'I could do that'. But the grace and style conceal the gruelling preparation and practised skill that lie behind this beautiful and graceful performance.

In theology this process is known as a *habitus*, a disposition of the mind and heart from which action flows naturally, in an unselfconscious way. The righteous in the story of the sheep and the goats in Matthew's Gospel have a spontaneous tendency, a *habitus*, to reach out to help and assist their neighbours, to respond to need without calculation, setting aside their own interests. The *habitus* means that action springs not from rational calculation of interests or possibilities, but from the depths of the personality, where the *habitus* has been slowly formed from early childhood. The 'goats' say that they would have helped had they known that it was the Lord coming to them in the form of the needy, but they were inherently callous rather than responsive, calculating rather than spontaneous.

The fourth and final dictionary sense of practice is this: 'The carrying on or exercise of a profession or occupation, especially of law, surgery, or medicine; the professional work or business of a lawyer or medical man.' Here practice is the behaviour of a class of professionals in accordance with a professional code and under the discipline of 'the profession'. The ends or goals of a profession are generally agreed, if in rather general terms: physicians' practice is to maintain or restore health; lawyers are concerned with the proper observance of the law. Each 'practice' has inherent and specific notions of excellence. Professionals jealously guard their practices against unqualified interlopers. I cannot set up as a lawyer or a surgeon even if I want to, because I have not been trained, accepted and initiated into the professional guild, the craft, or what used to be called sometimes in the past the 'mystery'.

This last term is a useful reminder that there is still a mystique surrounding the practice of professionals. The profession safeguards its practice from others and rarely allows its proceedings to be scrutinised by outsiders. It prefers to regulate its practices and discipline its members itself. Hence suspicious outsiders constantly echo George Bernard Shaw's epigram: 'All professions are conspiracies against the laity.' And with good cause, for professions can indeed act in a selfish way; practice can be abused for the benefit of the practitioner at the expense of the client or patient.

Later in this book we shall return to questions of professional practice. Meanwhile there are a few points to note. Patterns of practice with their own inbuilt standards of excellence are useful for the community as a whole, although professionals sometimes defend their own interests against the common good. Practice is not an isolated matter; it takes place in fellowships, in solidarity with others. And any practice has various inbuilt norms and excellences. A dentist, for example, must know the right way to fill a cavity, how to extract a tooth, and so on. Behind this technical skill lies knowledge of more than technique – anatomy, physiology, and so forth. But the dentist must also obey norms of conduct towards his patients; he must have a precise kind of personal integrity as part of his professional identity. If he is incompetent, or makes sexual advances to patients, he is disciplined, struck off the register and not allowed to practise. A practice thus has standards of excellence built into it, as Alasdair MacIntyre argues in *After Virtue*:

> By a 'practice' I ... mean any coherent and complex form of socially established cooperative human activity through which goods internal to that form of activity are realised in the course of trying to achieve those standards of excellence which are appropriate to, and partially definitive of, that form of activity, with the result that human powers to achieve excellence, and human conceptions of the ends and good involved are systematically extended.[2]

---

[2] Alasdair MacIntyre, *After Virtue*. London: Duckworth, 1981, p. 175.

When the term 'praxis' is preferred to 'practice', the emphasis is on the reflective or meaning content of behaviour, the integral interaction between theory and practice. Praxis usually refers to transformative practice. Praxis involves making things (*poesis*) and changing things. Thus we can speak about prophetic praxis, which is concerned with challenging established orders or procedures which oppress, exploit and dehumanise, judging them by the standards of the Reign of God. Or we can speak about the praxis of discipleship, meaning by this the way in which faith is necessarily embodied in a way of life in which we come to encounter the truth of God more deeply.

Modern theologians sometimes speak of the necessity for orthopraxis and orthodoxy to go together; behaviour and belief, they suggest, cannot be separated into different compartments. 'Theology', writes Elaine Graham, 'is properly conceived as a performative discipline, in which the criterion of authenticity is deemed to be *orthopraxis*, or authentic transformatory action, rather than *orthodoxy*.'[3]

The practical theologian is concerned with various modes of practice. As theologian she is necessarily concerned with the practice of the triune God, with discerning what God is doing in the world; with human behaviour considered theologically and with what God is calling us to do and be today; with the being and activity of the Church; with the practice of Christians; and finally with what virtually monopolised the interest of practical theologians for far too long, the activities of the ordained ministry and other ecclesiastical agents.

The Practice of God

Karl Barth is right to say, 'God is who He is in His works'.[4] But how do we know the practice of the triune God, what James Fowler calls 'the characteristic patterns of God's involvement in and providential guidance of the processes of our evolving universe, including God's interaction with human-

---

[3] Elaine Graham, *Transforming Practice: Pastoral Theology in an Age of Uncertainty*. London: Mowbrays, 1996, p. 7.

[4] Karl Barth, *Church Dogmatics*, II/1. Edinburgh: T&T Clark, 1957, p. 260.

kind'?[5] The answer, in simple and direct language, is by attending to the communicative practice of Jesus.[6] The Bible speaks of a God who acts, creating, sustaining and redeeming, a God who gives the law to God's people and enjoins them to be perfect as God is perfect – and that involves acting in the style or manner that God acts. This is not the remote, apathetic god of the Stoics or the Deists, who is a detached lawgiver, but a God who is involved.

The theme of the practice of the triune God is developed particularly clearly in John's Gospel. 'My Father is working still', declares Jesus, 'and I am working' (John 5.17). The works of Jesus are dependent on the Father and his works, and derivative from them. Jesus does nothing of himself: 'He who sent me is with me; he has not left me alone, for I always do what is pleasing to him' (John 8.28–29). Jesus does the work that his Father gave him to do (John 17.4) and on the cross cries '*tetelestai*', 'It is finished', the work is perfectly completed in suffering, love and obedience. The work of the Father and the Son are continuous with one another. Jesus' activity in healing, teaching, forgiving, loving and suffering shows the nature and activity of God: 'the work my Father has given me to do and to finish, the very work I have in hand, testifies that the Father has sent me' (John 5.36).

The Spirit is sent to comfort, strengthen and reinforce, to enable the practice of Christians: 'Whoever has faith in me will do what I am doing; indeed he will do greater things still, because I am going to the Father. Anything you ask in my name I will do' (John 14.12f.). The Christians' work is therefore a participation in the work of the Holy Trinity, and in doing this work, the knowing will come (John 3.21 and 7.17). The Trinity is thus a model of action-in-fellowship, whose activity is

[5] See James Fowler's discussions of the Praxis of God in *Weaving the New Creation: Stages of Faith and the Public Church* (San Francisco: HarperCollins, 1991), and *Faithful Change: The Personal and Public Challenges of Postmodern Life* (Nashville: Abingdon, 1996, chap. 12).

[6] Two recent publications pursue what I am trying to say here in very different ways and much more complex fashion: Edmund Arens, *Christopraxis: A Theology of Action* (Minneapolis: Fortress, 1995), borrows the conceptual structure of his book from Habermas; Andrew Purves, 'The Trinitarian Basis for a Christian Practical Theology', in *The International Journal of Practical Theology*, II/2 [1998], pp. 222–39, adopts a Barthian structure for his argument.

not limited to the Church or to believers. This is the God of all nations, who uses Cyrus the unbeliever as his Anointed and speaks to and through the boy Samuel even when 'he did not yet know the Lord'. We must have an adequately broad understanding of God's continuing activity in the world, as broad as that of the prophets and the apostles. God's action concerns not just individuals but nations and peoples and structures, both the claims of the neighbour and the challenges of the 'principalities and powers' and the 'elemental spirits of the universe' which are to be brought into subjection to Christ.

Human Practice

A theology of practice must first ask questions about God's activity and consider the practice of other agents within the horizon of the divine practice and as actual or potential participation in God's activity. This proper theological interest in God's activity in history and nature implies that, at the level of human agency, practical theology cannot be concerned exclusively with the activity of Christians or the Church. It applies a theological critique and analysis to the practice of people as such – people-in-relationship rather than artificially isolated individuals who are assumed to be free from all social ties and forms of conditioning. But with these provisos, practical theology is also concerned with the practice of Christians. At this level it might take as its motto the saying of Kierkegaard that the real problem is not so much what Christianity means as how to be a Christian, adding that in striving to be and act as a Christian one learns what Christianity is.

The specific danger here is to regard the Christian as agent in unduly individualistic terms either of pietistic individualism, where there is little reference to the Christian fellowship, or of possessive individualism in which the individual is seen as owning herself and defined in terms of what she can gain and what she possesses, in terms of things rather than social relationships. Christian practice, Christian being and Christian relationships must always be understood in the context of the Church and the Reign of God, and cannot therefore be understood in narrowly individualistic terms.

A concern for ministry is surely a necessary and significant part of the agenda of practical theology, but it is far from being the whole or the heart of that agenda. The understanding of ministry should be broad and theologically well-grounded. Nothing is worse than the acceptance of a narrow and outdated understanding of ministry as a pattern of practice to which students are taught to conform. But practical theology still has a concern for critical and responsible professional formation. It is right that the ordained ministry should have fully professional skills and standards of responsibility, but if the ministry regards itself simply as 'a profession' it relegates the other members of the Church, who share in the royal priesthood of the whole people of God, to the status of clients or patients, recipients of ministry rather than participants in ministry.

Practice and Passion

When we explore the place and significance of passion, emotion, feeling and suffering in our understanding of practice, in particular the practice of the presence of God, it may be good to start with the contrasting position of the Greeks. They saw a duality, two poles between which one had to choose or for ever oscillate between them. The two poles were represented by the gods Apollo and Dionysus (or Bacchus).[7] Dionysus represented the affective life and was associated with strong emotions of joy, fear, pain, delight, love, lust and so on. The dominant philosophical tradition looked askance at the Dionysian element in life, often regarding intense emotion as dangerous, unpredictable, irrational, meaningless and brutish. For later thinkers such as Descartes or Kant, emotions were often seen as 'blind animal reactions, like or identical with bodily feelings, that are in their nature unmixed with thought, undiscriminating, and impervious to reason'.[8] Emotions might

---

[7] This duality is developed by Nietzsche particularly in *The Birth of Tragedy*. Nietzsche's *Ecce Homo* concludes with these words: 'Have you understood me? Dionysus versus Christ.' Nietzsche's project has generally been understood as an attack on an unduly Apollonian Christianity. For further discussion now see Alistair Kee, *Nietzsche against the Crucified*. London: SCM Press, 1999.

[8] Martha Nussbaum, *Love's Knowledge: Essays on Philosophy and Literature*. New York: Oxford University Press, 1990, p. 40.

need some outlet, some relatively harmless discharge, even among educated and enlightened people. Hence Plato's Guardians were allowed strictly controlled opportunities for sexual activity, for instance. Sexual desire in itself was seen as a distraction from serious practice, a disturbance of the inner tranquillity required in order to know and do the Good. Emotions were understood as requiring control if they were not to become destructive of a balanced understanding, wisdom and a stable social order. In the Apollonian world-view the head should rule the heart, reason must regulate the emotions. Hence Socrates, the quintessential Apollonian, is depicted as a man who dies without fear, regret or distress, secure in the intellectual conviction that death is unimportant and that it is unseemly for a philosopher to be emotional. Xanthippe, Socrates' wife, gave way to sobbing and so had to be removed for disturbing the equanimity appropriate to a philosopher and his disciples in face of death!

This duality, of course, not only uses gods – Dionysus and Apollo – as types, but reflects differing understandings of God. The highest God, the God of the philosophers, Apollo, is *apathetic*, impassable, detached, uninvolved; and this god's disciples should shape their lives accordingly. Dionysus or Bacchus, on the other hand, is pure emotion, uncontrolled, unpredictable, uninhibited; his devotees express emotion without restraint in ecstasy and orgy. For the Dionysian, the heart must rule the head; for the Apollonian it is the other way round.

From the beginning Christianity found it hard to live at ease with this duality, although an Apollonian emphasis has penetrated deep into the Christian tradition, as shown in the repeated suggestions that feelings and emotions are things to be controlled and the deep ambivalence about sexuality, to say nothing of certain strands in the Christian ascetic tradition. 'Any action, thought or word which involves passion is out of harmony with Christ and bears the mark of the devil, who makes muddy the pearl of the soul with passions and mars that precious jewel', wrote Gregory of Nyssa. In Christ is to be found the overcoming of passion, for he is 'the source of tranquillity'.[9]

[9] Gregory of Nyssa, *On Christian Perfection.* PG 46.283–6.

This Apollonian attitude was still powerful in my student days, when we were encouraged to read a book by Leslie Weatherhead with the significant title, *The Mastery of Sex*. For the Apollonian, even if a Christian Apollonian, sexuality is something to be controlled, mastered, repressed, sublimated or brought into subjection because it is essentially dangerous, unruly and inimical to an Apollonian Christianity. It is not something to be delighted in, the heart of love.

But an Apollonian Christianity in which, in Gregory of Nyssa's terms, 'the godhead is purity, freedom from passion, and separation from all evil'[10] sits uneasily with the gospel story. Here the Greek duality must be transcended. Thus John's Gospel starts by applying to Jesus a term much loved of the Stoics, the Logos, the rational principle of the universe dwelling in serenity to all eternity. But this Logos acts, and his activity amounts to a practice. Like Dionysus (a similarity emphasised by Rudolph Bultmann), he went to a wedding party. He expressed throughout his ministry strong feelings of compassion, concern, anger and even, at the end, desolation and despair. His life, his practice, was a strange unity which culminated in suffering, in a death very different from the orderly, dispassionate death of Socrates. His male disciples, unlike those of Socrates, betrayed, denied and deserted him in face of death; the women stayed by and were the first witnesses of the resurrection. Pain, agony and forsakenness were the climax of Jesus' redemptive activity.

I am not here making an apologetic point about practical theology, but rather affirming the centrality of passion, in both the senses of that word (as intense emotion and as suffering), to an adequate christology, and consequently the importance of passion in the Christian life. The Christian God is not apathetic; neither should that God's disciples be.

The Passionate Priesthood of Jesus

From the beginning of his ministry a multitude of ordinary folk, the *ochlos*, followed Jesus around wherever he went. They gave

---

[10] Gregory of Nyssa, *Homilies on the Beatitudes*, Or. 6.

him no tranquillity. They pursued him when he sought time for rest and prayer. They were unrelenting in their demands on him. They thronged around him. They were thrilled and astounded at his healings of ordinary folk just like them. He was amazingly generous with his time. He never seemed to be too busy or too tired to have time for them. He listened to them, talked to them and taught them. The way he treated them made them feel they were worth something. Thronging around Jesus, they felt valued. When they were hungry, he fed them. Jesus had time for the mob, the multitude. No one else did. Harassed, helpless and leaderless, they turned to Jesus. And we read that the sight of the crowds moved him to pity; they were 'sheep without a shepherd'.[11]

The word rendered as 'moved with compassion' or 'moved with pity' (*splangnidesthai*) is an interesting term. It means literally that Jesus felt the condition of the people who drifted around the fringes of decent society 'in the guts'. He felt their anger and frustration, their confusion and uncertainty, their self-contempt and aggression in the depths of his being. He entered into their condition and their feelings, even into their despair.

It is significant that the Letter to the Hebrews sees the compassion, the empathy, the ability to enter into the condition and feelings of others, as well as the dying passion of Christ, as central to its understanding of his priestly work: we may 'boldly approach the throne of grace, in order that we may receive mercy and find grace to give us timely help' because we have a high priest who is able 'to sympathise with our weaknesses' because he 'has been tempted in every way as we are'.[12] Christ our High Priest shares our feelings, our sufferings, our uncertainties, even our despair. Only so can he be our great High Priest. And Christians, as a royal priesthood, need to learn to share in the pain, anger, grief and confusion, as well as the joys, of our fellows if we are to bring these things to God for healing. That priestly work is surely a central dimension of Christian practice.

---

[11] Matthew 9.36.
[12] Hebrews 4.14–16.

Loving and Knowing

There is a further way in which the Christian tradition rejects the Apollonian emphasis without embracing the Dionysian. Knowledge of God and of our fellows is not a matter of detached Apollonian cerebral activity. We know God in loving; truth is revealed in love and in loving. 'Everyone who loves', we read in 1 John, 'is a child of God and knows God, but the unloving know nothing of God, for God is love.'[13] And further: 'he who dwells in love is dwelling in God, and God in him'.[14] Lovers, and only lovers, can know God; love is at the heart of personal knowledge. This emphasis is deeply entrenched in the biblical record. The same Hebrew verb (*yada*) can be translated as knowing or loving (in the sense of sexual intercourse), so that we read that Adam *knew* Eve his wife, and they had a son.[15] To know God is to respond to God in the loving practice of discipleship or, as the liberation theologian Miranda constantly emphasises, knowing God in the Old Testament is the doing of justice, which is, of course, closely integrated with love. Of the one who upholds the cause of the poor and lowly we read: 'Did not this show he knew me? says the Lord.'[16] The biblical record suggests that we come to know the truth in loving action and in the doing of justice, not in standing back in detachment and passivity, not in seeking objectivity through disengagement, certainly not in experimental probing of the data, torturing the facts to make them reveal their secrets.

In a complicated sermon on John's Gospel, St Augustine, I suspect, saw a glazed and sleepy look creeping over the faces of his congregation. So he cries out:

> Show me a lover and he will understand what I am saying. Show me someone who wants something, someone hungry, someone wandering in this wilderness, thirsting and longing for the fountains of his eternal home, show me such a one and he will know what I mean. But if I am talking to someone without any feeling, he will not know what I am talking about.[17]

---

[13] 1 John 4.7–8.
[14] 1 John 4.16.
[15] Genesis 4.1, 17, 25; 38.26, etc.
[16] Jeremiah 22.16.
[17] Augustine, *Homilies on St John's Gospel*, 26.5.

Ordered and Disordered Passions

In seeking to reaffirm the place of passion, emotion, feeling in Christian life, practice and understanding, I am not to be understood as proposing a sort of Dionysian celebration of emotion as such, an affirmation of passion to correct the still dominant Apollonian stress in modern theology and in many understandings of the Christian life.

There are, to use the language of Augustine, ordered and disordered passions. The difference has to do with the goals at which passions are directed. It is not as if some passions – love, generosity, meekness and so on – are acceptable to God and may find expression in prayer and worship, while other passions – anger, despair, confusion, doubt – are unworthy and ought to be excluded. It is to the infinite impoverishment of our spirituality that we are today so often expected to leave at the church door feelings of lamentation, uncertainty, anger and even hatred, all passions that bulk large in the Bible and in real life. Denise Ackermann, a South African feminist theologian, has powerfully explored the role of lamentation as both protest and healing in the days of apartheid.[18]

Passions which are just a discharge of emotion and nothing more do not deserve commendation, although Aristotle was right to suggest that *catharsis*, the discharge or purging of emotions of anger, rage and so on without damage to others, can have its place. No less than any Stoic, Augustine recognises that emotions directed at self-aggrandisement or the fulfilment of purely selfish purposes are harmful and evil. Emotion that is turned in upon itself is sinful and destructive. As C. S. Lewis tells us in his remarkable autobiography, *Surprised by Joy*, as a young man he was obsessed with his own inner workings, turned in on himself; with conversion he found he was set free to be open to God and his fellows. Ordered passions seek a goal outside the self and find their ultimate fulfilment in God. Our hearts are restless until they find their rest in God and pass into the serenity of eternity. Goals matter, and ordered emotions are directed towards their ultimate satisfaction in God.

[18] ' "A voice was heard in Ramah": A feminist theology of praxis for healing in South Africa.' In Denise Ackermann and Riet Bons-Storm (eds), *Liberating Faith Practices: Feminist Practical Theologies in Context.* Leuven: Peeters, 1998, pp. 75–102.

God draws us through our passions to himself, the ultimate, all-fulfilling goal; it is not simply a matter of our own choices and motivations, as St Augustine comments in the sermon from which I have already quoted:

> 'No one can come to me unless the Father draws him.' You must not imagine you are being drawn against your will, for the mind can also be drawn by love . . . It is not enough to be drawn of your own free will, because you can be drawn by delight as well . . . If, then, the things that lovers see as the delights and pleasures of earth can draw them, because it is true that 'everyone is drawn by his delight', then does not Christ draw when he is revealed to us by the Father? What does the mind desire more eagerly than truth? For what does it have an insatiable appetite, why is it anxious that its taste for judging the truth should be as healthy as possible, unless it is that it may eat and drink wisdom, righteousness, truth and eternal life?[19]

In the Christian life, and especially through the pastoral care that is exercised in the Church, the passions are not constrained or denied but directed to their true goal, to their ultimate fulfilment and completion. This is the true therapy of the passions. The ordered passions of which Augustine speaks are not like soldiers on drill parade. He is not suggesting that the head must rule the heart. Within the Body, believers are like the members of an orchestra from whom the maestro freely elicits passionate harmony which gives the hearers as well as the musicians the music of eternity.

Dwelling in Truth

Passion, feeling, emotion are at the root of theological endeavour. In words from John's Gospel which should be the motto of any department of Practical Theology: 'Those who live by the truth come to the light so that it may be clearly seen in all that they do.'[20] The truth encountered in loving activity is also something to be lived in, indwelt. Christian practice is dwelling in truth, not simply applying the truth, putting the truth to work, or verifying the truth in action. Christian practice does

---

[19] Augustine, *Homilies on St John's Gospel*, 26, 4–6.
[20] John 3.21.

not exist in fits and starts; it is a settled orientation, a way of life, a coherent life-style, a *habitus*. Christians are not obsessed with the need to follow a detailed regime meticulously and well; they are passionate enough to take risks, break free, trust and, above all, love.

The theme of dwelling in truth has been developed in our day with startling relevance by Václav Havel, former dissident and now President of the Czech Republic.[21] He tells the parable of a greengrocer during the communist dictatorship, who one week puts in his window, among the carrots and tomatoes, the slogan 'Workers of the World Unite!', and the next week, 'Struggle Together for World Peace!'. Why does he do it?

- Because the slogan has been delivered to him from the wholesalers along with the fruit and vegetables;
- Because everyone else does it;
- Because he has done this sort of thing for years;
- Because if he refused there would be trouble; he would be accused of disloyalty;
- Because this harmless action ensures a tranquil life for him.

The greengrocer is not very interested in what the slogans actually say. He certainly does not feel he is communicating some exciting new truth to his customers. The reflex action, week by week, of putting up the slogan in his window simply means, 'I am dependable and obedient, and I want to be left in peace'.

The words of the slogans in the greengrocer's window, Havel suggests, not only conceal the degradation of his condition, but also hide the realities of the system behind a façade of respectability, morality and high aspirations. They suggest that the system is in harmony with the moral order, that power and truth are at one.

But that is not true. The greengrocer is living a lie. And most of the time his life is more comfortable that way.

---

[21] Václav Havel, *Living in Truth*. London: Faber, 1987. The parable of the greengrocer is to be found on pp. 41ff.

Now, suppose that one day something snaps in our green-grocer. He refuses any longer to put up slogans so that he can have a quiet life. He starts to speak his mind in public. He seeks out and befriends other dissidents. He no longer plays by the rules of the game. He steps out of living the lie. He begins to live in the truth.

His bill is not long in coming. He loses his job. Old friends shun him in the street. His children can't get places in college. He has to move house and take a job sweeping the streets.

His little dissent radically shakes the assumption that truth and power are one. His tiny protest is an earthquake: what is foolish in the world has shamed the wise, what is weak in the world has shamed the strong. The powerless find power when they live in truth. They do not live in truth in isolation but together, in solidarity. The very notion of living in truth is inescapably concerned with others. This community is respon-sible for the world and for those who are not its members. It cannot be introverted, turned in upon itself, concerned only for itself.

Christians also believe that the truth is something to be lived and loved within the fellowship of the Church and reach-ing forward to the coming Reign of God. It is not just a matter of thought, systems of ideas and propositions. Unlike the great systems of thought so effectively denounced by Søren Kierkegaard, the truths that emerge from the endeavour to live in truth are usually in fragments, hints, clues, cries, questions, pointers. These are the 'puzzling reflections in a mirror' of which 1 Corinthians 13 speaks. This truth cannot be mani-pulated, comprehended or controlled; nor is it oppressive and coercive, as most grand systems are. This truth can only be loved, lived in, reverenced and worshipped. And only at the end will the dimness and distortion of the mirror be replaced with a face-to-face personal encounter with the truth.

From a very different standpoint from Havel's, the philo-sopher–scientist Michael Polanyi makes a similar affirmation: religion is

> an indwelling rather than an affirmation. God cannot be observed, any more than truth or beauty can be observed. He exists in the sense that He is to be worshipped and obeyed, but not otherwise;

not as a fact – any more than truth, beauty or justice exist as facts. All these are things which can be apprehended only in serving them.[22]

God's truth can only be apprehended in the practice of discipleship, and discipleship involves passionate commitment.

---

[22] Michael Polanyi, *Personal Knowledge*. London: Routledge & Kegan Paul, 1958, p. 279.

2

Theory and Practice

'Divinity', said Martin Luther, 'consists in use and practice, not speculation and meditation. Everyone that deals in speculations, either in household affairs or temporal government, without practice, is lost and worth nothing.'[1]

But can theology be practical? The conventional stereotype of theology in the modern world is as the most unpractical of all disciplines, the very epitome of irrelevance. And in a theological context, practical theology is often despised as no more than a bundle of pastoral outcomes of theological truth discovered elsewhere.

Harold Wilson, the former British Prime Minister, was voicing the pragmatic prejudices of the age when with derision he denounced attempts to discuss political principles as just 'theology' – in other words, an unproductive luxury which is a distraction from the serious business of seeking efficiency, success, economic growth and all the unexamined and often conflicting values of our society. It was Pilate, sitting in judgement upon Jesus, who, according to John's Gospel, asked the question 'What is truth?', only to brush it aside in order to proceed to action. Pilate may have felt that pursuing the issue would have been an act of academic self-indulgence which might land him in a morass of profitless verbal polemics; certainly it

---

[1] *The Table Talk of Martin Luther*, trans. William Hazlitt. London: Bell, 1895, p. 179.

would inhibit him from the immediate and decisive action for which the people were clamouring and to which expediency counselled him. As only too often, before and since, the refusal to take the question of truth with ultimate seriousness leads to practice which is ill-considered and dangerously responsive to the pressures of the moment. And so we may start with a preliminary definition of practical theology as a study which is concerned with questions of truth in relation to action.

G. K. Chesterton tells a parable about a controversy in the street concerning a lamp-post, which many people desired to pull down. A monk, personifying theology, is approached for advice and in dry scholastic style commences by saying, 'Let us first consider, my brethren, the value of light. If light be in itself good . . .' At this point he is rudely knocked aside, a rush is made at the lamp-post, which is down in a moment, and the people 'go about congratulating each other on their unmedieval practicality'. That is only the start of the trouble, for

> some people have pulled down the lamp-post because they wanted the electric light; some because they wanted old iron; some because they wanted darkness, because their deeds were evil. Some thought it not enough of a lamp-post; some too much; some acted because they wanted to smash municipal machinery; some because they wanted to smash something. And there is war in the night, no man knowing what he strikes.

So gradually they come round to the belief that the monk should have been heeded at the beginning; what might have been debated by gaslight must now be discussed in the dark.[2]

It is a comforting parable for the theologian in a pragmatic, activist age; perhaps too much so, for it most dangerously over-simplifies the relation between theology and action. Chesterton is defending theology against charges of irrelevance to practice, and this point is well taken. But we cannot accept too easily the notion that the detachment from action and the devotion to contemplation which the figure of the monk suggests enable the theologian, given time, to produce from his meditations sure guidance for behaviour in the world. There is, as we shall see more fully later, a deeper reciprocity between theory and

---

[2] G. K. Chesterton, *Heretics*. London: Bodley Head, 1911, pp. 23–4.

practice, whereby theological understanding not only leads to action but also arises out of practice and involvement in the life of the world.

Practical theology as a distinct theological discipline is comparatively young, but the idea that theology as such is a practical science has been there from the beginnings of Christian theological reflection. In the gospels there are repeated reminders that disciples are to be 'doers' as well as 'hearers', that Christianity is far more than theory or speculation – it is a way of life. Particularly in the Johannine writings we find a stress on doing the truth, and that those who love and do the truth are the ones who know God: 'He who does what is true comes to the truth' (John 3.21). The truth is not regarded primarily as something to be contemplated or examined in a detached way; it is to be encountered, lived out, related to and, above all, loved, if it is to be truly known. Theology, therefore, must be concerned with the doing of the truth and the encounter with truth in action, with what Roger Garaudy calls 'the active nature of knowledge'.[3]

The Roots of Practical Theology

Most of the discussion concerning what it means to be a practical science and whether theology is a practical or theoretical discipline has been dominated, not altogether helpfully, by the classical Greek duality between the active and the contemplative lives and the corresponding distinction between the practical and theoretical sciences. The Greek understanding of this duality was not, however, uniform; the Platonic and Aristotelian traditions differ profoundly in the way they delineate the two poles. For Plato the contemplative life, the life devoted to an engagement with theory, with pure thought, is so much more attractive and fulfilling than the life of action that his Guardians, who have encountered truth and reality as a result of a long and strenuous training in contemplation, have to be induced against their will to engage in the only form of practice to which Plato accords real significance, that is, ruling. For Plato the task of these *illuminati* is to reshape society and human nature to

[3] Roger Garaudy, *The Alternative Future*. Harmondsworth: Penguin, 1976, p. 89.

conform to the pattern they have uncovered through contemplation. Practice, action, is to be made to conform to theory; it
does not in itself in any way constitute truth. The Guardians,
because of their education, know what is good for people better
than they know themselves. For Plato, most action, particularly
menial, technical or mechanical activity, is denigrated as
necessary for society but having no real relationship to theory.
The Guardians are the theorists *par excellence*. Their vision of
the Good authorises them to rule for the good of all. Their
mandate is to remake society and the human soul in the light
of the vision they have received.

Aristotle, on the other hand, placed alongside pure theory
what he called *phronesis* or practical wisdom, something that
was more the fruit of reflection upon experience than detached
contemplation and which related far more directly to action.
Despite the fact that Aristotle when pressed continues to assert
the superiority of the contemplative over the active life and of
theory over practice, it is from him that the distinction derives
between two kinds of theory and two kinds of science – a pure
theory directed towards the unchanging Reality and a practical
wisdom oriented towards action and virtue in a world of change
and decay. Thus a strictly Aristotelian theology, like a Platonic
theology, which regards God as ultimate unchanging Reality,
must give priority to theory over action.

The Christian tradition was seldom wholly at ease with this
Greek duality. In particular it was uncomfortable with the
denigration of action which runs through it. Christianity has
consistently tried to affirm that understanding and doing,
theory and practice, contemplation and action, and especially
knowing and loving, are integrally related and interdependent.
Accordingly, if theology was compelled to choose between
regarding itself as a 'pure' theoretical science or a practical
science in the Greek sense (and it often and properly resisted
the terms in which the choice was presented) it usually opted
for the latter. For Christian theology understood itself not so
much as a detached, dispassionate endeavour to comprehend
the things of God, but rather as the coming to know God in
striving to do God's will.

Among the medieval schoolmen, Duns Scotus and Occam
were particularly insistent in stressing that theology was a

practical science concerned with the ultimate goal of life – God
– and how to attain this goal. The Reformers developed this
emphasis. Luther, for instance, declared that 'true theology is
practical; speculative theology belongs with the devil in hell'.[4]
And Luther's emphasis on true theology being a 'theology of
the cross' serves to remind us of two important modifications
which had to be made to accommodate the classical notion of
a practical science to Christian usage: theology must concern
itself with the activity of God as well as with human practice,
and the concept of practice, as we saw in the previous chapter,
must be broadened to include passion, in both its senses as
suffering and as emotion. Pietists, concerned centrally with
religious experience, and Evangelicals, committed to 'practical
Christianity' and social reform, both affirmed in their different
ways that theology must be practical or it is nothing.

Theory and Practice

We must first of all rule out a simple linear relationship between
theory and practice: either you get your theory straight and
then allow theory to mould practice, or theory emerges more
or less spontaneously out of our practice. The first possibility is
characteristic of Plato and his disciples. It allocates to the
theorists, the philosophers and intellectuals, the insight,
intelligence and capacity to decide what is good for others and
then determine how to implement this good. It continues to be
influential in the modern world, for instance in the theory of
Karl Mannheim that intellectuals could rise above sectional
interests and take a detached and objective view of things from
above the fray, as it were.[5] Nineteenth-century philosophical
idealism and Fabian socialism are good examples of this
tendency in Britain. In the Church it shows itself particularly in
centralised structures of hierarchical authority and in the still
widespread conviction that first you get your understanding of
the Bible and theology right, and then you proceed to apply
this truth discovered in the speculations and exegesis of the
academy.

---

[4] Martin Luther, *Werke*, Weimarer Ausgabe, TR1 no 153.
[5] See Karl Mannheim, *Ideology and Utopia*. London: Kegan Paul, 1946.

The opposite tendency, to give an absolute priority to practice, is still influential in a pragmatic and activist age. Theologians such as J.-B. Metz or Jürgen Moltmann affirm that 'the new criterion of theology and of faith is to be found in praxis'. 'Truth', Moltmann continues, 'must be practicable. Unless it contains initiative for the transformation of the world, it becomes a myth of the existing world.'[6]

Behind this kind of thinking there is the powerful influence of Marxism. It was Marx himself who wrote in the *Theses on Feuerbach* (1845):

> The question of whether objective truth can be attributed to human thinking is not a question of theory, but a practical question. In practice man must prove the truth, that is the reality and power, the this-sidedness of his thinking . . . The philosophers have only interpreted the world, in various ways; the point, however, is to change it.[7]

But sometimes theologians to whom such sentiments are congenial assert the primacy of practice in a rather simplistic way, as if understanding and theory emerged spontaneously and effortlessly out of immersion in activity. In fact a productive and serious dialectical relationship between theory and practice of the sort that Marx was advocating is far from easy to establish or sustain; but it is essential if theology is indeed to be a practical science. Theory and practice belong together; separation distorts each. Like the philosophy Marx attacks, too much theology has been an interpretation, and by implication a justification, of the world as it is. But theology surely has to do with changing the world, with transformation, conversion, the mission of the Church and the attempt to understand reality within the perspective of the coming Reign of God. Out of this kind of faithful involvement the understanding comes.

In a notable passage, Lobkowicz compares Aristotle with Hegel and Marx:

> Aristotle philosophises out of 'wonder', out of intellectual curiosity which is half awe, half the desire to adjust man's existence to the

[6] Moltmann, cited in A. Kee, *A Reader in Political Theology*. London: SCM Press, 1974, p. 54.

[7] Marx, *Theses on Feuerbach*, 1845, xi.

order of being, to the cosmos. Both Hegel and Marx, on the contrary, philosophise out of unhappiness and dissatisfaction, out of the 'experience' that the world is not as it ought to be. Accordingly, while Aristotle primarily aims at understanding, at discovering structures and laws to which man's thought and actions have to adjust, Hegel and Marx aim at 'reconciling' and/or 'revolutionising'. In Aristotle nothing is or even can be wrong as it is in its natural state. The problem for Aristotle does not consist in correcting the universe or in making it rational; it consists in discovering its inherent order and rationality and in adjusting oneself to it. In Hegel and Marx almost everything is wrong and consequently has to be *aufgehoben*, transfigured, transformed, revolutionised. In this respect, the only truly important difference between Hegel and Marx is that Hegel is still enough committed to the Greek philosophical tradition to believe it possible to reconcile man with the universe by teaching him adequately to understand it, while Marx, disappointed with Hegel's speculative transfiguration, has lost all faith in the healing and reconciling power of mere thought.[8]

Christian practical theology also believes that realities need to be transformed, transfigured, revolutionised, converted, transfigured. And this transformation is not a matter of human effort alone, or something to be awaited passively, or effected by a change of understanding alone. The significance of action that changes things is emphasised by Gustavo Gutiérrez:

> Truth, for the contemporary human being, is something *verified*, something 'made true'. Knowledge of reality that leads to no modification of that reality is not verified, does not become true . . . The praxis that transforms history is not a moment in the feeble incarnation of a limpid, well-articulated theory, but the matrix of authentic knowledge and the acid test of the validity of that knowledge. It is the place where human beings recreate their world and shape themselves. It is the place where they know the reality in which they find themselves, and thereby know themselves as well.[9]

The 'reflective practitioner' is involved in an ongoing dialogue between theory and practice in which, if it is effective, under-

---

[8] N. Lobkowicz, *Theory and Practice: History of a Concept from Aristotle to Marx.* Notre Dame: University of Notre Dame Press, 1967, pp. 340–1.

[9] G. Gutiérrez, *The Power of the Poor in History.* London: SCM Press, 1983, p. 59.

standing is deepened and practice improved. Another way of describing the process is as a hermeneutic circle or, rather, spiral.

The Hermeneutic Spiral

It is quite inadequate to depict the relation between theory and practice as a uniform, one-way linear movement, suggesting that either theory must shape and determine practice, or that theory flows effortlessly out of practice. The interaction between theory and practice, between understanding and action, is in real life more complex and interesting than that. Recent radical theology, particularly liberation theology, has borrowed from modern philosophy the concept of the hermeneutic circle as a useful model for construing and understanding the relation between theory and practice. The liberationist version of the hermeneutic circle starts from a commitment to the gospel and the poor, and subjects received understandings of the tradition, the scriptures, patterns of practice and discipleship to suspicion. In this way our ability to understand the world, read the Bible and develop patterns of relevant discipleship are deepened and often radically altered. The process is not really a circle; if you move around a circle you come again and again to the point from which you started. It is rather a spiral, in the process of which we ascend to higher levels of understanding and more appropriate and faithful practice through a constantly moving process of radical questioning. Liberation theologians are not shy of accusing academic theology of 'going round in circles' by generating artificial and unimportant questions which have little if any bearing upon life in the 'real world' and produce answers which have little relation to action or bearing on life.

Juan Luis Segundo, in his classic study *The Liberation of Theology*, argues that an authentic hermeneutic circle or spiral must meet two preconditions. The first is that

> questions rising out of the present be rich enough, general enough, and basic enough to force us to change our customary conceptions of life, death, knowledge, society, politics and the world in general. Only a change of this sort, or at the very least a pervasive suspicion about our ideas and value judgements concerning these things,

will enable us to reach the theological level and force theology to come back down to reality and ask itself new and decisive questions.[10]

The second precondition is an openness to the possibility that received interpretations of the Bible or doctrinal formulations might need to be altered if they are indeed to be bearers of the gospel in a radically new situation. Without such openness to reformulation one cannot progress through the hermeneutic spiral, and the new questions will either go unanswered, or will receive irrelevant, unconvincing and hackneyed answers.

The liberationists' way of doing theology starts from engagement; commitment comes before understanding, as in Anselm's account of the nature of theology, '*fides quaerens intellectum*' (faith seeking understanding). This is the point of insertion into the hermeneutic spiral, the place from which the effort to deepen understanding and improve faithful practice begins. The issues that are central to liberation theology arise out of the conviction that the God with whom we are engaged is the living God, active in today's world, One who can only be encountered in particular contexts and is to be responded to in quite specific ways. God is implicated in history and it is there, in the world, as well as in Scripture and worship, that we meet him. For the liberation theologians the pressing and interesting questions are what faith in God means today, in this specific context. Faith in God, as the Bible teaches, is inseparable from commitment to the neighbour. And there should be a special care for the needy and poor neighbour. Thus faith in God is seen as inseparable from commitment to the poor; not to an abstract, general idea of the poor, or a spiritualised notion of the 'humble poor', but to the poor as they are around us in our society and in our world today.

This option for the poor has various important implications. We should, for instance, expect to learn from the poor of the things of God. And we can only hear them if we are close, alongside, in solidarity. So theology should be done in solidarity with the poor. And that means taking sides. Furthermore, in

---

[10] J. L. Segundo, *The Liberation of Theology*. Dublin: Gill & Macmillan, 1977, pp. 8–9.

order to understand and respond to the poor, we have to have recourse to social analysis. The poor belong to a class, within a class system which is at least in part the cause of their poverty. Theology not only listens to the poor but it asks why they are poor and what can be done about it.

In the hermeneutic spiral, understanding results from the suspicions and the questions generated by engagement and praxis. Our experience of faithful commitment in the world makes us ask new questions, or pose the old questions in a new way. We question ourselves, our behaviour, the way we understand and affect our world and the people around us, and the way we understand the tradition of faith and its formulations. New questions are asked about social forces and social conflicts, enquiring about the balance of power, who benefits and who loses, and what can be done to change things. The role of ideology has to be examined to see how far it is used as a cloak to disguise what is in fact happening, how far it is an instrument of social control, and how far it illumines reality and shows what is going on. Received interpretations of the tradition and theological orthodoxies need to be reassessed: have they been watered down so that we can live with them more comfortably? Whose interests do they serve?

In the hermeneutic spiral, engagement, action and understanding interact with one another to seek a strengthening of commitment, a reform of the Church, and a more just and caring social order, which all reflect the coming Reign of God.

Modifications or adaptations of the hermeneutic spiral as it has been developed in liberation theology have proved very popular as a model for the relation of theory and practice in practical theology. What they call the 'pastoral circle' is the central concept in Joe Holland and Peter Henriot's influential *Social Analysis: Linking Faith and Justice*.[11] Here the major concern is relating the Church's social concern to a rigorous analysis of the social context and a radical rethinking of theology. More recently, Paul Ballard and John Pritchard have advocated a form of the pastoral circle on the grounds that it allows both flexibility and diversity in the development of a serious and

---

[11] Revised edition, Maryknoll: Orbis, 1983.

methodologically rigorous practical theology.[12] Liberation theology has provided a powerful stimulus to relevance and rigour in the doing of practical theology. It has broadened the scope of the subject beyond the narrowly ecclesial to encompass the whole field of practice, and it has suggested and pioneered a way of relating theology, social analysis and practice which is mutually fruitful and does not fall into either the trap of idealism or the barrenness of materialism.

[12] Paul Ballard and John Pritchard, *Practical Theology in Action: Christian Thinking in the Service of Church and Society*. London: SPCK, 1996, especially chap. 6.

3

Practical Theology
As an Academic Discipline

The question whether practical theology is a distinct academic discipline within theology is a modern question, really dating only from the Enlightenment and the nineteenth-century reorganisation of the European university which brought a fresh understanding of the university's task. Here the question was, first, whether theology, the old 'Queen of the Sciences', was still entitled to any place at all in the university; and if it was, how theology was internally organised, what kind of 'science' it was, and how it related to the other disciplines in the university.

Pre-modern Times

Christian theology had, of course, existed before the Enlightenment; indeed, its origins go back to the very beginnings of the Christian faith. Prior to the Middle Ages, theology was studied by scholars and monks, mainly in monastic settings. It was reflection on faith – in Anselm's terms, *'fides quaerens intellectum'*, faith seeking to understand itself, the critical exploration, appropriation and commending of faith. The ultimate goal of this study was the beatific vision, fellowship with God, wisdom and, at a more mundane level, the equipping of clergy and the people of God for their tasks. Inasmuch as faith involved discipleship and was an orientation of the whole person rather than a simple act of intellectual assent, theology was understood as a practical matter. Contemplation could not be separated from action, any more than faith could be separated from the Church, the community of faith.

In the Middle Ages universities developed in Europe and provided a new setting for the study of theology. Dr Gillian Evans has traced the medieval development of theology as an academic discipline. In the twelfth century theology as '*speculatio*' was understood as a 'gazing on the divine' which was seen as 'essentially a devotional exercise'. By the late twelfth century, Dr Evans argues, speculative theology had been stripped of all such elements: it became 'an activity of the mind in which religious emotion had little or no place . . . the divorce of contemplation from abstract thought of an academic kind was complete'.[1]

Throughout the Middle Ages, theology was generally re-garded as the Queen of the Sciences in universities which were, almost without exception, ecclesiastical foundations and whose primary task was the training of clergy and the critical formulation of church teaching. But was theology as such a theoretical science in the Aristotelian sense or a practical science – again as understood by Aristotle? Thomas Aquinas endeavoured to demonstrate that theology was a theoretical science, a *sophia* in Aristotle's sense, because it is an end in itself, whereas practical knowledge is directed towards other ends and other goods.[2] Other medieval theologians, such as Duns Scotus and the nominalists who were so influential in the Protestant Reformation, taught that theology was a form of *phronesis*, a practical wisdom that was close to Aristotle's understanding of that term. Scotus taught that theology was concerned with God as the supreme good and therefore the ultimate goal of human life. Objective knowledge of this goal was necessary for believers engaged in the way of discipleship, to aid them in moving towards their true goal and destiny.[3] The Protestant Reformers tended to follow in the Scotist tradition,

---

[1] Gillian Evans, *Old Arts and New Theology: The Beginnings of Theology as an Academic Discipline*. Oxford: Oxford University Press, 1980, p. 93.

[2] W. Pannenberg, *Theology and the Philosophy of Science*. London: Darton, Longman & Todd, 1986, p. 232.

[3] Pannenberg, *Theology and the Philosophy of Science*, pp. 232–3.

regarding theology as a practical science with central pastoral and existential elements.

Theology in the Early Modern University

Post-Reformation and Enlightenment universities continued to have theology at the heart of their enterprise and to see the task of theology in the university as essentially a practical one, particularly concerned with the education of ministers for the service of the Church. The theological faculty stood along-side medicine and law as one of the three 'higher faculties', with explicit remits for the formation of professionals. The university as such was concerned with struggling with truth and also educating for good practice. The university under-stood its concern with theory as directed towards the goal of practice.

In Scotland, for instance, an Enlightenment tradition developed which insisted that at the heart of the academic enterprise there was a theologically informed moral philo-sophy which had as one of its central concerns the education of good practitioners.

The foundation of the University of Berlin in 1809 was a notable turning point in the development of the modern university.[4] Berlin became a model for other German univer-sities and, increasingly, for higher education outside Germany on both sides of the Atlantic. In this tradition the university is properly concerned only with *Wissenschaft*, a scientific com-mitment to relate everything to universal rational principles. Theology had to justify its place in such a university, and the scholar who did this most effectively was the eminent theologian, Schleiermacher.

Schleiermacher

Theology, Schleiermacher taught, is both scientific and has a practical task which should be pursued within the university – the preparation of leadership for the Church. In justifying the

---

[4] On this see Hans Frei, *Types of Christian Theology*. New Haven: Yale University Press, 1992, pp. 95–116.

place of theology within the university, Schleiermacher suggested that there are three levels in theological study. The foundation is philosophical theology, which establishes and examines the first principles of Christian theology on the unquestioned assumption that Protestant Christianity is the crown and epitome of all religion. Then comes historical theology, which examines the development of the Christian tradition. Finally, as the 'crown of theological study' comes practical theology, which is the 'technique' of church leadership. Ministers and church leaders should combine a 'scientific spirit' and what is called 'ecclesial interest', or a commitment to serve the Church. Those who are most successful in combining ecclesial interest and the scientific spirit are aptly to be called 'princes of the Church'! The scientific and the practical endeavours interpenetrate, for 'Even the especially scientific work of the theologian must aim at promoting the Church's welfare and is thereby clerical; and even those technical prescriptions for essentially clerical activities belong within the circle of the theological sciences.'[5] Theology, for Schleiermacher, is a function of church leaders, not the whole people of God. Accordingly, it is equipment for clergy, just as medicine or jurisprudence are the studies necessary for physicians or lawyers.

Schleiermacher tends to take as a given the existing structures of church and ministry; it is not part of the responsibility of theology, or of practical theology, to criticise them. His thought thus becomes 'a blueprint for the clerical church, and almost its apologia'.[6]

Although at first glance it may be flattering for practical theologians to have their subject described as the crown of theological study, on closer examination it turns out that Schleiermacher's position means little more than that practical theology is the last stage of theological education. Furthermore, it seems that practical theology is really nothing more than *applied* theology. After the more 'scientific' endeavours of philosophical and historical theology, nothing seriously

    [5] F. Schleiermacher, *Brief Outline of Theology as a Field of Study*. Trans. T. T. Tice. Lewiston, NJ: E. Mellen Press, 1990, p. 8.
    [6] W. Jetter, cited in Pannenberg, *Theology and the Philosophy of Science*, p. 429.

theological needs to be done. Practical conclusions may be drawn from the philosophical theological roots and the historical theological body; practical theology's task is no more than to put them to work. Practical theology is thus basically a kind of technology. Practice has no influence on the way philosophical or historical theology is studied, or on their conclusions.

Despite problems such as those we have outlined above, Schleiermacher's vindication of the right of theology to a place in the modern academy and his account of the internal organisation of theology still have influence today, although many people believe he produced a radically unsatisfactory resolution of the still continuing tensions between what he calls 'ecclesial interest' and the 'scientific spirit'. These issues are still with us, as are questions about the proper place, context and content of education for ministry.

We now move on briefly to consider some alternative, more recent accounts of the nature and claim of the academic study of practical theology.

Karl Barth

The liberal German university modelled on the University of Berlin was a state institution, granted intellectual freedom by the state and ultimately responsible to the state. To the amazement of those who looked to the German university as the bastion of the best in the Western intellectual tradition, in the early 1930s the German university capitulated almost without a fight to Nazism. This posed a major problem for academic theologians in Germany, many of whom now felt that they had to choose between loyalty to a university that had embraced Nazism and fidelity to the Christian faith and to the Church. Some of the most distinguished felt compelled to give priority to their place as doctors of the Church, which meant in most cases committing themselves to the Confessing Church and to what Schleiermacher had called 'ecclesial interest'. Some, like Bonhoeffer, moved to teach at a Confessing Church seminary and finally died a martyr's death; others, like Karl Barth or Paul Tillich, emigrated from Germany and took part in the struggle from a distance.

Such moves out of the university did not involve abandoning a belief that theology was in a sense a 'science' and had a proper claim to a place in the academy. Barth, for instance, refused to allocate theology to some universally valid idea of what constituted a science, but claimed that theology, like other sciences, had a way of understanding which was appropriate to its own subject matter. Theology is not a science like geology or geometry, but it has its own proper path to understanding the things of God. Theology, for Barth, is about God, not about 'religion', human piety, or exalted emotions; only God can reveal Godself; and theology is a function of the Church before it is a subject in the university.

The place Barth gives to practical theology in his immensely influential system is clearly laid out in his little book, *Evangelical Theology: An Introduction*.[7] Here, in a section entitled 'Theological Work', there are four headings: Prayer, Study, Service and Love. It is as if Barth has abandoned the task of justifying the place of theology in the university in order to have time for the doing of a very practical theology. Study – *wissenschaftliche* study! – has its place, it is true, but in a context which starts by affirming the Anselmian suggestion that theology is a kind of praying, an interaction or conversation between the believer and God, and ends by setting up the principle that true theology must be done in love and for love. If it is authentic, theological study flows into service and ultimately into love.

In this context, Barth suggests that the specific remit of practical theology concerns the transition to the work and witness of the believing community, that is, to the proclamation of the gospel. The key problem for him is how the Word of God may be served by human words, how the message may be conveyed with faithfulness, truth and power. Practical theology is thus a hermeneutical subject. It is concerned with the translation of the message from the 'language of Canaan' to the language of today, the language of Egypt or Babylon. A central question for the practical theologian is thus the psalmist's cry, 'How can we sing the Lord's song in a strange land?' The message, Barth suggests, is 'taught its content by

---

[7] Karl Barth, *Evangelical Theology: An Introduction*. London: Collins Fontana, 1965, pp. 169–71.

exegesis and dogmatics, and it is given its form through the experiences of whatever psychology, sociology, or linguistics may be most trustworthy at a given moment'.[8]

In a real sense Barth sees all theology as practical theology. And at the heart of his theology is proclamation, the Word, communication. This concern for words and the Word should not be seen as a narrowing of the agenda; it is in fact a constant reminder that at the heart of reality is the Word made flesh, who should be worshipped and attended to by theologians and believers. And although his presentation suggests a linear progression from the language of Canaan to the language of today, and a message which receives its content from 'academic theology' and is then simply transmitted by practical theology drawing on insights from the social sciences, in fact there is clearly a circular movement in Barth's theology whereby theological discoveries and rediscoveries are stimulated by discerning the work and Word of God in the struggles and problems of the day.

Barth's close friend and associate Thurneysen also saw practical theology as the application to the life of the Church of the insights realised by systematic and biblical theology. Within this general understanding of practical theology as to do with the communication of the Word, Thurneysen, in his *A Theology of Pastoral Care*, sees pastoral care as the 'specific communication to the individual of the message proclaimed in general in the sermon to the congregation'.[9] For Barth and Thurneysen, practical theology, like all theology, focuses centrally on the proclamation of the gospel. It is clearly for them a theologically based discipline which is none the less permitted to seek help and borrow insights from secular disciplines as appropriate. And it is an *ecclesial* discipline, devoted to serving the Church and, above all, the Church's preaching.

Karl Rahner

Despite all the assertions down the centuries that theology as such must be practical, it was only in the late eighteenth century

---

[8] Barth, *Evangelical Theology*, p. 170.
[9] E. Thurneysen, *A Theology of Pastoral Care*. Atlanta: John Knox Press, 1962, p. 15.

that we see the gradual emergence of a distinct theological discipline called 'Practical Theology', among both Protestants and Roman Catholics. Practical or pastoral theology was recognised as an academic discipline in Vienna in 1774 and in Tübingen in 1794. Initially the subject was regarded as a kind of technical training for the priest's fulfilment of his role (apart from the confessional, where moral theology provided the help and guidance required). Most of the subject's problematic was derived from the minister or priest's activities in the parish, so that the discipline had a narrowly clerical focus and tended to proceed on pragmatic rather than critical theological premises.

The radical German Roman Catholic theologian, Karl Rahner, wrote extensively on practical theology,[10] which he saw as 'an original science' which has responsibility for 'a theological analysis of the present situation in which the Church is to carry out the special self-realisation appropriate to it at any given moment'. He has been much concerned with defending the subject's credentials as a theological discipline in its own right, not simply 'a mere hotchpotch of practical consequences' following from other disciplines. Practical theology is the 'scientific organisation' of the Church's reflection on its task. Its interests are not, for him, as closely confined to the ecclesiastical realm as they are in Barth and Thurneysen; it is, Rahner believes, concerned with asking what God is doing both in the Church and in the world, and with how believers and what he calls 'anonymous Christians' alike should respond. Because its subject is the Church's self-realisation in all its aspects, '*everything* is its subject-matter'.[11] But as an 'original science' it cannot fulfil its task without giving very serious and critical attention to the other theological disciplines and the human sciences. As an essentially ecclesial discipline, it has an obligation to adopt a critical and prophetic stance towards the Church as well as 'the world'.

More recently, disciples of Rahner like J.-B. Metz and Latin American theologians influenced by his thought have extended his understanding of practical theology so that it becomes a

[10] E.g., Karl Rahner, 'Practical Theology within the Totality of Theological Disciplines', *Theological Investigations* Vol. IX. London: Darton, Longman & Todd, 1972, pp. 102–4.

[11] Rahner, 'Practical Theology', p. 104.

theology of practice as such, relating to the basic Christian communities and political movements of liberation as much as to the formal hierarchical structures of the institutional Church, and stressing the Reign of God and the necessity of a preferential option for the poor.[12]

Seward Hiltner

Seward Hiltner represents an influential school of mainly American theologians who see practical theology as centring on the pastoral activity of the Church.[13] Hiltner examines the life of the Church from what he calls 'the shepherding perspective' and believes that this study will produce theological wisdom. His analysis is informed by insights from the social and human sciences, particularly psychology and psychiatry. But, as Alastair Campbell points out,[14] there is in Hiltner's scheme no place for the concept of revelation, and his tendency to regard the contemporary shape of the Church and the exercise of ministry as 'given' makes his thought rather conservative and inflexible. Another American, Tom Oden, has launched a devastating critique of the whole school of pastoral theology of which Hiltner was a guru. It lacks, he argues, theological seriousness and gives almost canonical status to the latest fashions in psychology and psychiatry.[15]

Wolfhart Pannenberg

The contemporary German Lutheran ecumenical theologian, Wolfhart Pannenberg, has produced an important and influential modern account of practical theology.[16] Theology

---

[12] See, for instance, J.-B. Metz, *Faith in History and Society: Toward a Practical Fundamental Theology*. London: Burns & Oates, 1980; *A Passion for God: The Mystical-Political Dimension of Christianity*. New York: Paulist Press, 1998; or any of the key works of G. Gutiérrez.

[13] See especially, Seward Hiltner, *Preface to Pastoral Theology*. Nashville: Abingdon, 1958.

[14] A. V. Campbell, 'The Nature of Practical Theology', in D. B. Forrester (ed.), *Theology and Practice*. London: Epworth, 1990, p. 15.

[15] Thomas C. Oden, *Contemporary Theology and Psychotherapy*. Philadelphia: Westminster Press, 1967.

[16] Pannenberg, *Theology and the Philosophy of Science*.

as a whole has a proper concern with 'the praxis of life', but among the theological disciplines, practical theology has a special concern with praxis. It is more than a theory of the practice of ministry, or even the practice of the Church. Essentially it is a search for truth, and

> the question of the truth of Christianity cannot be enquired into without also enquiring into the question of the truth of all areas of human experience . . . Theology can do justice to Christianity only if it is not a science of Christianity but a science of God. As a science of God its subject matter is reality as a whole.[17]

And as a subject which examines the practice of the Church it should have a special concern for the horizon of mission. It was mission that brought the Church into being and mission is 'the ultimate horizon on which the whole life of the church must be understood'.[18] A serious practical theology will understand the Church as reaching forward to its fulfilment along with humankind and the whole creation in the coming Reign of God. Eschatology and hope are therefore key themes in practical theology.

In both Protestantism and Roman Catholicism the issues raised in this chapter continue to be discussed and debated today. Volume after volume of good advice to ministers, hints and tips on how to perform the traditional functions of ministry, with little or no critical theological reflection or suggestion that the subject is or may be a systematic and rigorous discipline, continue to appear under the heading of practical theology. F. D. Schleiermacher's suggestion that practical theology was the completion and 'crown of theological study' indicated the possibility of a better integration between practical theology and the other theological disciplines, but this has not always been easy to achieve. Schleiermacher saw practical theology as essentially the craft of church management, the channel through which the theories of biblical and systematic theology flow to nourish the life of the Church. The present structures of church and ministry were accepted uncritically, as was the assumption that the subject addressed itself exclusively to the

---

[17] Pannenberg, *Theology and the Philosophy of Science*, pp. 264–5.
[18] Pannenberg, *Theology and the Philosophy of Science*, pp. 238–9.

practice of clergy. This position is generally viewed with suspicion today.

But Schleiermacher's account of the relation of 'ecclesial interest' and the 'scientific spirit' remains a key issue. If ecclesial interest is abandoned, academic theology loses its roots in a particular community of faith in 'the real world', and with that it often abandons a concern with relevance. If the scientific spirit is set aside, theology becomes the in-house discourse of small and declining Christian communities, without sustainable claims to being public truth with something to offer in the public square. The balance or tension needs to be maintained for the sake of responsible and relevant theology, to save the Church from becoming a ghetto incapable of communicating with the culture and society in which it is embedded, and for a healthy and lively university which does not dodge or marginalise fundamental issues which are admittedly difficult to handle and almost impossible to resolve. Perhaps the task of theology in the university is to be like the grit in the oyster around which the pearl may gather, by asking the hard, unfashionable questions which are often a productive irritant, by affirming the continuing significance of the tradition of faith, and by reminding the intellectual power structures of their responsibility for the weak and the poor.

4

❧❧❧

Practical Theology
and Christian Ethics

In the University of Edinburgh in the 1930s a chair was allocated
to practical theology only on condition that it was linked with
Christian ethics. Christian ethics was seen as a 'respectable'
discipline, entitled to a place in the academy on the basis of
an established methodology and intellectual track record;
practical theology was still regarded as an uncritical hotchpotch
of hints and tips for ministers – at best (as students occasionally
amended the heading on the departmental notice board by
adding two letters) 'Practical*ly* Theology'; at worst, the tedious
presentation to students by an ageing former minister of his
pattern of pastoral practice of some decades before as a model
of ministry.

This suspicion of practical theology was particularly strange
in a Scottish university where the tradition has been constantly
maintained, against the theoretical thrust of Oxbridge, that
higher education is primarily directed to professional *practice*.
This distinction between Scotland and England is captured in
an intriguing difference in linguistic usage: in Oxbridge one
'reads' a subject, even if it is engineering or social work; in
Scotland one 'does' a subject, even if it is metaphysics or
literature! It used to be said that the English believed that if a
student had read Plato and Thucydides, Homer and Euripides,
he (hardly ever she!) was perfectly equipped to govern a colony,
command an army, lead a gentlemanly life of leisure, or become
a bishop – which last was sometimes regarded as the explanation

why some bishops seemed to understand the state of the Church on the analogy of the siege of Troy, and any innovation as a Trojan horse!

Although the link between Christian ethics and practical theology at Edinburgh was originally adventitious, it is now felt to have been almost providential, allowing a focus on practice, approached both analytically and normatively. Christian or theological ethics draws on Scripture and the Judaeo-Christian tradition and unashamedly possesses the classical conviction that ethics is concerned with goodness and character, and with helping people to be good, with 'the embodiment, in the actions and transactions of actual social life' of Christian insights.[1] Although for decades many moral philosophers in the English-speaking world, under the influence of the movement of linguistic analysis, devoted themselves to language games and denied that they had any concern with helping people to be good or societies to be just, *Christian* ethics on the whole successfully resisted being sucked into this cul-de-sac, and remained an engaged normative study of action, rooted in a particular tradition, narrative and community of shared faith. At Edinburgh, and in some other places as well, practical theology for a time simply piggy-backed quite happily on the back of this kind of Christian ethics.

Although such a linkage between practical theology and Christian ethics has clear advantages and opens a range of positive possibilities, it also presents dangers. What happens, for instance, if ethics is detached from systematics? Is it possible that systematics might then lose its ethical seriousness and integrity and become increasingly pure *theoria*? And Christian ethics linked to practical theology of a certain kind might sacrifice critical theological rigour, becoming narrow, no more than ethics at the service of ministerial practice, a professional ethics for clergy. On the other hand, what happens when Christian ethics is treated more or less as an independent discipline, with a real hegemony over other theological disciplines, as in some institutions in the United States? These are issues of the relationships between the theological disciplines, and other

---

[1] MacIntyre, *Three Rival Versions of Moral Enquiry.* Notre Dame: University of Notre Dame Press, 1990, pp. 80, 175.

disciplines (for the purposes of this discussion primarily moral philosophy and the human sciences), to which I now turn.

The Academic Encyclopaedia and Its Limits

The modern university and even (with appropriate qualifications) most seminaries reflect and reinforce the increasing specialisation and fragmentation of modern life. The tidy ordering of the medieval university, with theology as the Queen of the Sciences, is unrecoverable, but we are faced today with various and conflicting endeavours to give some kind of coherence to the academic enterprise as a whole. The way the definition and relations of disciplines are arranged, the way a university is structured, express implicitly or explicitly an ideology, a world-view, an overarching interpretation. In pre-modern days the general effort was to locate specific studies within a biblical grand narrative;[2] in modern times the Bible, religion, the Christian faith, theology and ethics are to be fitted into the project of an 'encyclopaedia', ordering all knowledge in terms of some more or less secular principle. Alasdair MacIntyre argues that the Ninth Edition of the *Encyclopaedia Britannica* (1873ff.) pointed towards a time when 'The Encyclopaedia would have displaced the Bible as the canonical book, or set of books of the culture'.[3] Accordingly, the Bible (and all thinking rooted in the Bible), 'is judged by the standards of . . . modernity in a way which effectively prevents it from standing in judgement upon that modernity'.[4] It is here, I think, that central problems lie: is it possible for practical theology and Christian ethics to be *in* the university, but not domesticated or tamed by the university? How can they maintain a distinctive critical distance from the increasingly secular and confused values of the university so that they can play a specific sort of constructive role? Is a dual responsibility, to church and to the academy, any longer viable?

I come from a particular Enlightenment encyclopaedic tradition in which a theologically informed and practically orientated moral philosophy was the keystone of the academic

---

[2] So Hans Frei and others.
[3] MacIntyre, *Three Rival Versions*, p. 19.
[4] MacIntyre, *Three Rival Versions*, p. 179.

edifice, as it were. I encountered the warm afterglow of this tradition in the teaching of the moral philosopher John Macmurray in Edinburgh in the 1950s. The same tradition was for long enshrined in the old American colleges influenced by the Scottish academy, where the President, normally a theologian or philosopher, lectured to the whole student body on moral philosophy. A theologically informed moral philosophy was assumed to give coherence to the educational process and guidance for living life well.[5]

MacIntyre suggests that in the nineteenth century there was a mounting tendency to ascribe priority to morality and to ethics or moral philosophy, on the assumption that there was a 'social agreement, especially in practice, on the importance and the content of morality', which none the less 'co-existed with large intellectual disagreements concerning the nature of its intellectual justification', although almost everyone concurred in the belief that such justification was in principle possible.[6] General consensus about the nature of right conduct and a bracing degree of difference about the philosophical foundations of morality were believed to give coherence to the academic enterprise.

Elsewhere MacIntyre suggests that there is a kind of tragic inevitability in the collapse of a consensus on metaphysics gradually eroding the confidence that disputes about morality may be resolved, so that we entered a stage when we had nihilism in metaphysics co-existing with a liberal consensus on morals and politics. But this liberal consensus, MacIntyre suggests, is fragile and without roots; it is already disintegrating. Yet in the nineteenth century there was still great confidence in the encyclopaedic enterprise.

An alternative encyclopaedic project to that outlined above was contained in Schleiermacher's *Brief Outline on the Study of Theology*.[7] This was a sophisticated and creative application of the encyclopaedia principle to theology. Although, in a much abused phrase, Schleiermacher referred to practical theology

[5] On this see especially George E. Davie, *The Democratic Intellect*. Edinburgh: Edinburgh University Press, 1961.

[6] MacIntyre, *Three Rival Versions*, p. 26.

[7] F. Schleiermacher, *Brief Outline on the Study of Theology*. Trans. Terence Tice. Richmond, VA: John Knox Press, 1966.

as the 'crown' of theological study, the real crown or capstone of his theological encyclopaedia lay outside theology, in 'science'; theology itself was not a science, but a discipline or set of disciplines which deploy the results of science for the sake of the leadership of the Church. Theology is thus almost parasitic upon science. It is itself a 'positive' science, 'an assemblage of scientific elements which belong together not because they form a constituent part of the organisation of the sciences, but only in so far as they are responsible for a practical task'.[8]

Unlike theology, ethics is a true science for Schleiermacher, but it has no pre-eminent role in relation to theology in general, or to practical theology in particular. Schleiermacher is therefore to be distinguished from the Scottish tradition in the more exalted place he allocates to scientific *theoria*, and his consequent somewhat Platonic downgrading of those disciplines which deal with practice – Christian ethics and practical theology in particular. Karl Barth tells the story of finding a bust of Schleiermacher in the ruins of Bonn University after the war and reverently restoring it to its plinth.[9] At least in relation to his encyclopaedia project, I believe that Schleiermacher's position is irretrievable. Today we do not have agreed maps of the academy, and I do not believe that practical theologians should spend their time and energy asserting a claim to a place in a non-existent atlas. After all, if the university throws us out, we can operate quite happily in the Church – only, as I shall argue, the university would be the poorer for it. I think MacIntyre is right in suggesting that the encyclopaedia is a failed project with which we should not now get entangled.

Theology and Ethics Today

The position both of theology and of ethics in the academy has been much challenged in recent times. MacIntyre is surely right in suggesting that moral and theological truths became

[8] *Brief Outline*, p. 19; See Richard R. Osmer, 'Rhetoric, Rationality and Practical Theology', typescript, 1993, pp. 4–11; and John E. Burkhart, 'Schleiermacher's Vision for Theology', in Don S. Browning (ed.), *Practical Theology*. San Francisco: Harper & Row, 1983.

[9] Karl Barth, *Dogmatics in Outline*. London: SCM Press, 1949, 0.7.

increasingly regarded as belonging in the realm of privatised and arbitrary belief: 'Questions of truth in morality and theology – as distinct from the psychological or social scientific study of morals and religion – have become matter for private allegiances, not to be accorded . . . formal badges of academic recognition.'[10] Ethics has accordingly been moved to the periphery of academic life, and has with increasing nervousness stressed its autonomy, from theology in particular. This has left an ominous vacuum at the heart of the academy. As a consequence, academics interested in issues of public policy or social responsibility have sometimes begun to look with expectation towards theology, and in particular theological ethics, for help and a sense of direction. We are therefore at a time of particular opportunity for a practical theology and a Christian ethics which interpenetrate and inform one another.

Although there are special difficulties today in constructing an acceptable and coherent intellectual map of the university, it is still necessary to say something about why practical theology and Christian ethics continue to claim a place in the academy, and what that place might be. When I was appointed to a chair of Christian Ethics and Practical Theology some of my colleagues in the very secular university in which I then taught thought that the term 'practical theology' was a joke or an oxymoron: theology, they said, cannot be practical, and practice cannot be theological – after all, theology is now commonly used as a term for irrelevant theorising! If we are to claim that the two subjects with which we are concerned are entitled to a place in the university and have a contribution to make to the endeavours of the university, we have to spell out something of the remit, method and contribution of the subjects. If MacIntyre and others are right in suggesting that the post-encyclopaedic university in a postmodern world is in a crisis, confronted on all sides with questions that it lacks the resources to answer, perhaps an ethically informed practical theology can suggest some possible ways forward towards a greater relevance and a better sense of being a community of shared purpose.[11]

[10] MacIntyre, *Three Rival Versions*, p. 217.
[11] MacIntyre, *Three Rival Versions*, p. 271.

Professor David Donnison, a leading British social scientist concerned particularly with issues of public policy, despairs of the capacity of the modern university to provide the wisdom that society requires. At the root this is because, in a culture where most people believe that God is dead, moral judgements have become regarded as 'little more than approving or dis-approving noises – expressions of personal preference or taste, much like the words we use when choosing between vanilla and strawberry ice-cream'.[12] Since there is no academically acceptable way of resolving conflicts about moral judgements, the commonest strategy is to side-step the issue. Academics are concerned with weighing evidence and assessing logical coherence; because morals are now regarded as arbitrary matters of taste and prejudice they are pushed to the margins and deprived of intellectual dignity:

> As for moral dispute – that has been banished from the lecture rooms altogether, for it leads people to say things like, 'You ought to be ashamed of yourself', and this is not the kind of things you say in a seminar. To make the distinction unmistakably clear, politicians and priests are brought into such academies from time to time to conduct moral debate; but on a one-off basis, usually at the invitation of student societies, speaking from a different kind of platform – thereby exposing to everybody the unscientific status of their pronouncements.[13]

This, Donnison concludes, leads to a narrowing and distortion of academic life, which is in many cases condemned to irrelevance or irresponsibility.

Practical Theology

In such a situation the relation of practical theology to Christian ethics assumes a fresh importance. Getting this relationship right may be significant for the academic enterprise as a whole, and helpful to a range of other disciplines.

Practical theology exists in the academy to affirm that all theology is practical, just as biblical studies reminds theology of the centrality of Scripture and systematic theology points to

---

[12] David Donnison, *A Radical Agenda*. London: Rivers Oram Press, 1991, p. 42.
[13] Donnison, *A Radical Agenda*, p. 44.

doctrine as an unavoidable element in the theological enter-prise.[14] And if theology is a practical science, in the Aristotelian or any other sense, it cannot be detached from ethics. As MacIntyre writes:

> In moral enquiry we are always concerned with the question: what **type** of enacted narrative would be the embodiment, in the actions and transactions of actual social life, of this particular theory? For until we have answered this question about a moral theory we do not know what the theory in fact amounts to; we do not as yet understand it adequately.[15]

And a similar point was made by the English moralist and social thinker, R. H. Tawney, when he said, 'To state a principle without its application is irresponsible and unintelligible.'[16] For theology to be a practical science in the classical sense first developed by Aristotle, it must be a form of *phronesis*, which is 'a reasoned and true state of capacity to act with regard to human goods'.[17] The person of practical wisdom is able to deliberate well on what is good for the individual, and on the good life in general.

If practical theology is wisdom or knowledge orientated towards action and thus inevitably pervaded with the ethical, it is important also to affirm that it is *theology*. But what is theology? In the excellent brochure about the University of Berne with which we were supplied when this chapter was first delivered as a paper, we read that there are two faculties of theology in the university. The account of the Old Catholic Faculty declares that 'Old Catholic Theology is concerned with the question of God'; the Protestant Faculty announces, 'Theology is con-cerned with religion, Christianity, and the history of the church as well as its present status.' But here lies a central problem for us all. If theological discourse is primarily about religion, it is always in danger of dissolving into study of the context and becoming a kind of sociology or psychology of religion.

[14] On this see especially W. Pannenberg, *Theology and the Philosophy of Science*. London: Darton, Longman & Todd, 1976, pp. 231–41 and 423–40.

[15] MacIntyre, *Three Rival Versions*, p. 80.

[16] R. H. Tawney, *'The Attack' and Other Papers*. London: Allen & Unwin 1953, p. 178.

[17] Aristotle, *Nicomachean Ethics*, vi.5; D. Ross (ed.). London: Oxford University Press, 1954, p. 43.

But if theology is discourse about God in the presence of God, and discourse with God, we are engaged with something totally other. We cannot talk about God or talk to God while setting aside, even temporarily, the ethical or normative question: What is God calling us to do? How should we respond? We are also involved simultaneously in doxology, for, in the familiar saying of, I think, Dietrich Bonhoeffer, 'You may not chant the psalms unless you stand up for the Jews.'

Karl Barth was, I think, a paradigmatic practical contextual theologian.[18] He sought to speak of God, to listen to God's command and to discern the signs of the times. And he addressed the context of his time in two principal ways: first, by producing tracts for the times, declarations (most notably that of Barmen) and manifestos; and, secondly, by taking fundamental theological work with a new seriousness because of his conviction that bad, untrue, sloppy theology leads to unjust, idolatrous, murderous practice, and vice versa. Like any contextual theologian of discernment, he provided insights of validity far beyond his immediate context and fairly quickly came to see that the primary issue posed by God at that time was what Hitler was doing to the Jews, not the freedom of the Church.

Karl Barth was, I believe, right to speak of dogmatics as ethics, and ethics as dogmatics. He refused to set an independent and separate church ethics alongside church dogmatics, let alone an autonomous or free-floating ethics established on an entirely non-theological foundation. 'Dogmatics itself and as such', he affirmed, 'is ethics as well.'[19] It is also true, in Barth's view, that ethics *is* dogmatics, that ethical activity and reflection inevitably imply beliefs and fundamental assumptions. Ethics and dogmatics, ethics and theology, cannot be divorced; they are inseparably bound to one another. The modern tendency to subordinate theology to ethics, or to separate them, leads to serious distortions. If Barth is right that 'Dogmatics itself is ethics; and ethics is also dogmatics',[20] Christians should be suspicious of the distinction between the theoretical and the

---

[18] See Tim Gorringe's splendid study on Barth as a contextual theologian: *Karl Barth: Against Hegemony*. Oxford: Oxford University Press, 1999.

[19] Karl Barth, *Church Dogmatics*, I/2. Edinburgh: T&T Clark, 1956, p. 783.

[20] Barth, *Church Dogmatics*, I/2, p. 793.

practical, especially as it developed in the Greek and Enlightenment traditions. For the practical theologian there should be
no ugly ditch between 'is' and 'ought'. You cannot name God
without recognising God's claim and God's command.

This means that theologians should be very cautious about
buying into a sharp cleavage between fact and value, as if
there were such a thing as a naked fact and values were
merely cultural constructs. Christian theology is characteristically uncomfortable with the positing of a gulf between 'is'
and 'ought', or a sharp disjunction between fact and value,
as suggested famously by Max Weber. Weber promoted an
ethically neutral social science based on the assumption of
an unbridgeable and tragic ditch between the 'is' and the
'ought'. Leo Strauss, in attacking Weber, argues that a
refusal to entertain the possibility of true value judgements is
intellectually and morally spurious; it actually distorts reality,
for it

> would lead to the consequence that we are permitted to give a
> strictly factual description of the overt acts that can be observed in
> concentration camps and perhaps an equally factual analysis of
> the motivation of the actors concerned: we would not be permitted
> to speak of cruelty. Every reader of such a description who was not
> completely stupid would, of course, see that the actions described
> are cruel. The factual description would be a bitter satire. What
> claimed to be a straightforward report would be an unusually cir-
> cumlocutionary report. The writer would deliberately suppress his
> better knowledge, or, to use Weber's favourite term, he would
> commit an act of intellectual dishonesty.[21]

'Facts' are not part of the givenness of things; our values and
our beliefs play an indispensable role in the way we construe
reality, discern the signs of the times and respond. A central
academic responsibility is to be critically aware of our values
and their roots, because these things deeply shape both our
logic and our empirical work, the way we see reality and the
way we respond to it. Although I believe that practical theology
today must have the social sciences as its principal dialogue
partners and feel that John Milbank's cautions are exaggerated,

---

[21] Leo Strauss, *Natural Right and History*. Chicago: University of Chicago Press,
1953, p. 52.

there are real dangers if a practical theology buys uncritically into a Weberian understanding of social science.[22]

If Alasdair MacIntyre is right that the modern university is fragmented and lacks the resources to deal with the questions that confront it, partly because it has become incapable of co-herent and rigorous moral inquiry, is it possible that a practical theology which is effectively integrated with Christian ethics might offer a major contribution towards a renewal of academic integrity and responsibility? It is at this point that I think Don Browning's project of a 'strategic practical theology', and his successive studies of ways in which theory-laden practices relate to norms and values, are so important.[23] He constantly sees practical theology as an exercise in theological ethics and Christian ethics as a central dimension of practical theology. In however tentative a way, this approach bridges the ugly ditch between 'is' and 'ought', fact and value, in order to enable reflected and effective practice. Could this be our gift to the whole academy, in its post-modern disarray and uncertainty?

An Ecclesial Discipline

Both practical theology and Christian ethics are rooted in, and have responsibilities towards, two communities – the academy and the Church. Schleiermacher famously spoke of the relation between the 'scientific spirit' characteristic of the university and the 'ecclesial interest' which marked off theology as concerned with leadership in the Church. He was right to see the subject as having two homes and to discern a creative tension between them and their expectations and standards. But Schleiermacher's distinction is in some ways too neat. Perhaps theology can contribute significantly to the recovery of a true scientific spirit in the university. And ecclesial interest can provide both motivation and material for scientific investigation.

[22] John Milbank, *Theology and Social Theory: Beyond Secular Reason.* Oxford: Blackwell, 1990.

[23] See especially Don S. Browning, *The Moral Context of Pastoral Care.* Philadelphia: Westminster, 1976; *Religious Ethics and Pastoral Care.* Philadelphia: Fortress, 1983; *A Fundamental Practical Theology.* Minneapolis: Fortress, 1991.

It is surely significant that Barth, in a context in which theology was firmly embedded in the university, found it necessary to speak not simply of *Christian* dogmatics, but of *church* dogmatics and *church* ethics, in order that theology might recover its integrity, fulfil its vocation and grapple with the issues of the day. In facing a modern situation in which he feels that Christian ethics is in danger of losing its distinctiveness and dissolving into academic ethics in general, Stanley Hauerwas has developed Barth's point by arguing that the Church not only *has*, but *is* a social ethic. The primary ethical task of the Church, he argues, is to be the Church as a community of faith, worship and service.[24] In expounding John Howard Yoder, Hauerwas suggests that 'Practical reason is not a disembodied process based on abstract principles but a process of a community in which every member has a role to play.'[25] Even in its sinfulness, such a community of character is both a community of moral discourse and an exemplification of the moral orientation sustained by the biblical tradition. For Hauerwas, the only theology and the only ethics that matter are rooted in the life of the Church and serve the development of Christian character and faithful practice, participating in the Church's function of witnessing to the truth.

This does not mean that Hauerwas sees theology as a kind of in-house discourse, the language game of the Christian community which has no claim to truth in a more general sense. He engages in his writings with issues on the public and the academic agenda, with medical ethics, war and peace, the position of the handicapped, and many others. He comes at these questions from an unashamedly theological and Christian angle and in so doing often brings a strange freshness to tired controversies, directing the attention to commonly forgotten dimensions and neglected resources.

Hauerwas has been accused by James Gustafson and others of 'sectarian withdrawal' from engagement with the moral tensions and ambiguities of what some people call 'the real world'. The charge does not, I think, stick, although I am more

---

[24] S. Hauerwas, *The Peaceable Kingdom*. London: SCM Press, 1984, p. 99. The phrase is repeated frequently in Hauerwas' writings.

[25] S. Hauerwas, *Christian Existence Today*. Durham, NC: The Labyrinth Press, 1988, p. 73.

sympathetic to the suggestion that Hauerwas tends towards a rather romanticised understanding of the Church. His position might be strengthened if he spoke more clearly of how a sinful church in a fallen world can nevertheless be a sacramental sign of God's love and truth. Hauerwas is determined not to allow Christian ethics to dissolve into a general ethics of Americanism, and his increasing concentration on the churchliness of Christian ethics has led him more and more to address the traditional problematic of practical theology. Hauerwas is a further sign of the welcome erosion of the boundary between practical theology and Christian ethics, as he both affirms the crucial significance of the Church and remembers that God's purposes and God's practice encompass the whole creation.

Practical theology and Christian ethics are both together ultimately concerned with discerning God's activity in the world and learning how to respond faithfully and well.

SECTION TWO

ISSUES IN CHURCH
AND MINISTRY

5

❧

Transforming Ministry

Few people in the West would deny that there is today a crisis in ministry, except perhaps those who are so totally immersed in the struggle to be effective and adequate ministers that they echo Henry Kissinger's famous remark in 1969, when he was Secretary of State: 'There cannot be a crisis next week. My schedule is already full.' The crisis in ministry is real. It needs to be analysed with care so that we may understand and respond more adequately.

A crisis is, of course, a turning point, a *dénouement*, full of possibilities of good or ill. As its etymology suggests, it is a decisive moment, a time for decision, for judgement. In a crisis, the issues and priorities suddenly become clearer than they were before. We can, if we will, discern what is going on, and in a crisis we are confronted with stark choices. A crisis is a turning point. Things are unlikely ever to be the same again.

A crisis is, then, a time of judgement and of testing, when past events are reviewed and assessed and decisive action may be taken to remedy or heal the defects of what has taken place and confirm and strengthen what has been good. A crisis therefore looks forwards as well as back. And although a crisis presents special opportunities of faithful discernment of 'the signs of the times' and calls for human judgement and action, the primary judgement, unveiling and action are God's. A real crisis, regarded theologically, is a *kairos* for the Church. As the South African *Kairos Document* of 1986 put it:

A crisis is a judgement that brings out the best in some people and the worst in others. A crisis is a moment of truth that shows us up for what we really are. There will be no place to hide and no way of pretending to be what we are not in fact. At this moment in South Africa the Church is about to be shown up for what it really is, and no cover up will be possible.[1]

A *kairos*/crisis thus provides the context for a discerning of the truth and is a summons to renewed practice and the kind of theological reflection which is firmly rooted in life and addresses real issues, not artificial and abstract questions which only concern an in-group of academics or clergy. A *kairos*/crisis may evoke insight and action, tied together inseparably; it is, despite appearances (to quote the *Kairos Document* again), 'the moment of grace and opportunity, the favourable time in which God issues a challenge to decisive action'.[2] A crisis, accordingly, is the stimulus which enables us to hear the Word of God and distinguish it from the noise which surrounds it. This discernment is not, of course, of a purely momentary and fleeting truth, or an insight which only has bearing upon the moment of crisis in which it first emerged. It continues to have significance and reality long after the immediate crisis is passed and in contexts very different from that in which it originally arose. Thus Augustine's response to the crisis of the collapse of the Roman empire, *De Civitate Dei*, has become a classic text, and Reinhold Niebuhr's Gifford Lectures, *The Nature and Destiny of Man*, delivered in Edinburgh in the opening months of the Second World War, have an enduring significance far beyond the immediate crisis to which they were initially addressed.

This kind of theology must look facts in the face. It must struggle to understand what is going on, analysing the situation and probing the problem in all its complexity. And for this purpose it must judiciously use the human sciences and be attentive to the ways the situation is being understood through the best available tools of social analysis. But theology should

---

[1] In Charles Villa-Vicencio (ed.), *Between Christ and Caesar: Classic and Contemporary Texts on Church and State*. Cape Town: Philip and Grand Rapids: Eerdmans, 1986, p. 251.
[2] Villa-Vicencio (ed.), *Between Christ and Caesar*, p. 251.

also be aware of the limits and dangers of such tools. They are sometimes so insensitive to what one might crudely call 'the religious dimension of life' that they fall victim to a range of avoidable distortions; they often operate with a very narrow and unbalanced understanding of human beings and human motivation; sometimes they have an inbuilt and largely unconscious hostility to religion which makes some of their 'scientific' conclusions mere wishful thinking. But, despite such cautions, I would suggest that such analytic tools, discerningly used, are indispensable today.[3]

Social analysis, however, does not and cannot ask or answer theological questions. Christians must ask theological questions: at their simplest, what God is saying and doing, what words of judgement and hope there are for us in a present crisis. Otherwise we easily get locked into some kind of deterministic bondage to statistical trends or psychological processes, with little place for grace, newness, forgiveness, or freedom.

It is also important when we are discussing matters of ministry and church life that we understand ourselves to be discussing real questions of broad significance, not petty in-house issues generated by the community of faith but of no conceivable significance to anyone else. We are not addressing ecclesiastical idiosyncrasies, like Monsignor Ronald Knox's obsession with the right way of ironing a surplice! Churches and theology have shown themselves peculiarly adept at avoiding the real issues of the day. But sometimes issues which appear at first glance to be entirely domestic concerns of the Church are in fact of immense long-term significance. For example, the controversy in the early Church about whether Gentile and Jewish Christians might eat together was certainly not a trivial matter, although it initially concerned a tiny number of not very significant people in a remote corner of the civilised world. In fact, it involved key questions about the nature of the Church, what it is to be a Christian and the social reality of the reconciliation wrought in Christ. And beyond that it raised profound issues about community, relationships and the nature

---

[3] It should be clear that I counsel caution in relation to the radical hostility towards modern social theory represented by John Milbank in his magnificent *Theology and Social Theory*.

of human beings. The resolution of that controversy in a tiny new religious community in an insignificant corner of the Roman Empire had repercussions which are still reverberating around the world. Max Weber saw the outcome of that argument in Antioch as a proclamation of human equality which profoundly shaped the evolution of Western society.[4]

The *Kairos Document* reminds us also that a crisis cannot be adequately understood from outside, or analysed with Olympian detachment. Those in the eye of the storm, those engaged and committed in the situation, have insights which are not available elsewhere and are indispensable parts of a proper discernment. So the call is for active practical involvement and the goal is a transformation of practice. It follows that we cannot expect to interpret or understand the crisis in ministry today without attending very intently to the experience of those in ministry, including their frustrations, anger and uncertainty. We must probe ministerial exhaustion, disillusion and burnout as well as experiences of fulfilment, enthusiasm and delight. One of the lessons to be learned from liberation theology is that there is a kind of privileged insight to be found among those involved in transformative practice, people not content simply to keep the existing system running, but awaiting and working for the Reign of God, expectant people, open to the future. Ministry, in other words, is not to be renewed or transformed by social scientists or academic theologians viewing the crisis from outside, but by people involved in and committed to ministry, seeking help as appropriate for the deepening of understanding and the renewal of practice. Both our understanding and our practice need renewal; they can only be transformed together; and in this process there must always be an eye to the demands and possibilities of our particular context and historical situation.

Interlocking Crises

We cannot sensibly treat the crisis in the practice and understanding of ministry in isolation. In fact, it relates very closely

---

[4] Max Weber, *The Religion of India: The Sociology of Hinduism and Buddhism.* New York: Free Press, 1958, pp. 37–8.

to the crisis about the place of the Christian faith and the function of the Christian Church in our society, and to a whole series of pressing and complex issues about the integrity, cohesion and viability of secular pluralism.

There is, first of all, the issue of *ministerial identity*. There is today to be found at every turn a profound uncertainty about what ministers are for. More than fifty years ago Daniel Jenkins, the Congregationalist theologian, wrote of the embarrassment the presence of a minister commonly evoked; many people did not know how to respond or what to talk about, because the minister represented a dimension of life with which they no longer had contact. The typical person, he said, is 'grateful . . . when the minister turns out to be as embarrassed as himself about the gulf between them and keeps the conversation when he calls safely on the level of the football prospects and the weather and polite enquiries about the family's health'.[5] In the media, ministers commonly appear as figures of fun – if they appear at all. It is seldom that we see a minister as a person with a recognised role and function in the community – except in programmes about small rural communities such as *The Archers*. It is true that church dignitaries and individuals of evident holiness, like Mother Teresa or Archbishop Desmond Tutu, still attract positive media attention, but despite that there is a pervasive embarrassed uncertainty about the place and functions of the clergy. G. K. Chesterton once said, 'A clergy-man may be as apparently useless as a cat, but he is also as fascinating, for there must be some strange reason for his existence.'[6] For many people today the fascination has faded and the emphasis is on the puzzling uselessness.

Within the churches the situation appears at first glance to be far different. The Vatican, for example, continues to present a confident and highly traditional view of the priestly role and to discount any fundamental questioning of this as illegitimate. But perhaps the nervous rebukes to theologians who ask awkward questions betray a degree of uncertainty even there. It is not only traditionalist church authorities and conser-vative theologians who present clear, rigid and old-fashioned

[5] Daniel Jenkins, *The Gift of Ministry*. London: Faber, 1947, pp. 8–9.
[6] G. K. Chesterton, *Orthodoxy*. London: John Lane, 1943, p. 269.

understandings of ministry as timelessly valid; many congregations in sharp decline have precise, excessive and old-fashioned expectations of their minister which have little or no relation to the present age with its demands and opportunities. They attempt to force their ministers willy-nilly into this mould, with or without some kind of theological justification.

Ministers on the ground are at the receiving end of a whole range of conflicting messages and expectations from theologians, their congregations, the broader society and church authorities. It is not surprising that they are often uncertain and confused, having internalised many of the expectations and attempted to make some sense of the conflicting messages about who they are and what they are for. The confusing situation has been well outlined by a Dutch Roman Catholic theologian, Jan Kerkhofs:

> Any one who reads surveys and statistics about ministers in our Western countries at all carefully will note an apparent contradiction. On the one hand numerous declarations indicate satisfaction about the ministry . . . on the other hand we find countless frustrations and restrictions, and sometimes desperate fatalism. There is a very great deal of good will and idealism and almost as much disillusionment . . . However, the question is whether there may not also be problems which are specifically connected with the ministry, and whether the church, in particular, as the sphere of freedom and love, cannot and indeed must not be different if the gospel is to be credible both outside it and within. *The current view of the ministry frustrates the community of faith and is the cause of much suffering among clergy.*[7]

In this situation of much confusion and suffering the minister, according to a major study of English clergy, is particularly vulnerable because he or she is the person 'who most acutely experience[s] the frustrations of the churches' questionable relevance in the modern world'.[8] The mainline churches are all seriously hit by numerical decline and consequential problems of human and material resources. But the central

---

[7] In L. Grollenberg et al., *Minister? Pastor? Priest?* London: SCM Press, 1980, p. 5. My emphasis.

[8] Ranson, Bryman and Hinings, *Clergy, Ministers and Priests.* London: Routledge, 1977, p. 169.

problems, and they are complex and intractable, are to do with how to *be* the Church in a post-Christendom situation in which the Church is a minority and has no inherent right to be at the centre of things. Adaptation is difficult, and there is an ever-lurking temptation to settle into being a sect or a kind of religious club for those who like that sort of thing, abandoning any serious claim to be guardians of public truth with responsibility in and to the public realm. It is not easy to find a new identity and a renewed sense of purpose. And internal uncertainties, conflicts and disagreements within the churches severely hamper their ability to play a distinctive and constructive role. Furthermore, there is a tendency for ecclesiastical divisions to reflect and exacerbate conflicts in society, as contemporary events in Northern Ireland and the former Yugoslavia demonstrate. The search for vital and relevant forms of ministry is inseparable from the search for a renewed and authentic identity for the Church.

There has been no lack of theologians who have seen the secular pluralism of our society and culture as something to be celebrated and embraced. And, on the other hand, Lesslie Newbigin, Stanley Hauerwas and others have suggested that the churches in the West have done more than accommodate themselves to the dominant secular pluralist viewpoint, they have assimilated and internalised the values and views of secular pluralism in such an unguarded and syncretistic way that they can no longer see any distinction between the Christian gospel and the values of our culture. This analysis is perceptive and points towards the need to recover a sense of Christian distinctiveness if the Church is to be able to minister in any effective way to the tensions that lie at the heart of modern secularism.

This has been pinpointed most effectively by Michael Ignatieff in his remarkable book, *The Needs of Strangers*.[9] 'A decent and humane society', he argues, 'requires a shared language of the good.' But this is precisely what is lacking in our kind of society. Indeed the very question is excluded as part of a package of ultimate issues:

[9] Michael Ignatieff, *The Needs of Strangers*. London: Chatto & Windus, 1984, pp. 18–19.

> We are . . . the only species to ask questions about the purposes of
> our existence which our reason is unable to answer. Contemporary
> politics is largely silent about this need for metaphysical
> consolation and explanation, but, next to love, it is one of our
> strongest promptings and one which is utterly unreconciled to the
> limitations of our ignorance.[10]

A secular pluralist society's politics cannot satisfy this need for
ultimate meaning, or provide a true sense of belonging: 'We
can no longer offer each other the possibility of metaphysical
belonging: a shared place, sustained by faith, in a divine
universe. All our belonging now is social.'[11] Can the Church in
our kind of secular society provide a sense of belonging and
satisfy the perennial longing for ultimate meaning?

Social belonging itself is under constant threat for two
reasons – it lacks religious or metaphysical grounding, and
there is no longer a public theology or philosophy to bind
people together and provide constraints to private or group
interest and aggression. Thus 'secularism today simply implies
a generalised silence in culture about the whole category of
man's spiritual needs'.[12] There is a vacuum at the core; secular
pluralism is a predicament rather than a solution.

Such is the context in which the Church must minister today.

Responses

Two general lines of response to these interlocking crises are
discernible in the churches today. In the first place, there is
much nostalgia spiced with panic. As alarm spreads at the
various indices of decline, many Christians look back wistfully
to the past and seek to recapture the imagined 'great days'
when everyone went to church, and the Church was at the heart
of things, a powerful, respected and often feared institution.
There is a longing for the restoration of Christendom, rolling
back the tide of decline, restoring the old order of things.
Pope John Paul II's frequently reiterated project for the 're-
evangelisation of Europe' seems to be just this kind of

---

[10] Ignatieff, *The Needs of Strangers*, p. 99.
[11] Ignatieff, *The Needs of Strangers*, p. 78.
[12] Ignatieff, *The Needs of Strangers*, p. 99.

revivalism. And similar Christendom assumptions undergird the thought of those who put their energy into defending ecclesiastical establishments and who present Christianity as an effective civil religion whose place is still at the power centres of the nation rather than among the marginalised, weak and forgotten. In many congregations the Christendom view is prominent among those who see no possibility other than the restoration of the past.

The Christendom view has its own associated models of ministry – the chaplain to the powerful, the parson of high social status who is the moral exemplar to society, the core of Coleridge's 'clerisy',[13] the highly conservative minister who sees the task as simply 'keeping the show on the road'. Perhaps the most devastating and acute critique of such understandings of ministry long ago was Søren Kierkegaard's devastating *Attack upon 'Christendom'*, with its call to clergy to be witnesses to the truth rather than social functionaries.[14] Writing in a Denmark pervaded with Christendom assumptions – that everyone, more or less, was a Christian and belonged to the established Church, that the Church was the guardian of national identity, and that clergy were respected and powerful officers of state – Kierkegaard discerns a radical dilution of the Christian faith and a fundamental distortion of the understanding and practice of ministry. In place of martyrs, disturbing prophets and ministers who make a costly witness to the truth, we have, says Kierkegaard, prosperous ministers, 'a highly respected class in the community whose *métier* is to transform Christianity into the exact opposite'.[15] The modern clergyman is, writes Kierkegaard,

A nimble, adroit, lively man, who in pretty language, with the utmost ease, with graceful manners, etc., knows how to introduce a little Christianity, but as easily, as easily as possible. In the New Testament, Christianity is the profoundest wound that can be inflicted upon a man, calculated on the most dreadful scale to collide with everything – and now the clergyman has perfected

[13] S. T. Coleridge, *On the Constitution of the Church and State*. London: Dent, 1972, chap. 5.
[14] Søren Kierkegaard, *Attack upon 'Christendom'*. Trans. Walter Lowrie. Princeton: Princeton University Press, 1968.
[15] Kierkegaard, *Attack*, p. 222.

himself in introducing Christianity in such a way as it signifies nothing, and when he is able to do this to perfection he is regarded as a paragon. But this is nauseating! Oh, if a barber has perfected himself in removing the beard so easily that one hardly notices it, that's well enough; but in relation to that which is precisely calculated to wound, to perfect oneself so as to introduce it in such a way that if possible it is not noticed at all – that is nauseating.[16]

Our situation, however, is radically different from Kierkegaard's in that, save for isolated pockets, Christendom has collapsed and with it the old certainties about the minister's role and responsibilities. It is, for ministers, confusing and perplexing to face such widespread uncertainty, within and without, about what ministers are for. But it is also a time of opportunity, for ministers are not, as once they were, confined securely in socially recognised roles; today, in a more plural and secular age, they are set free to be themselves and witness to the truth in fresh and exciting ways.

The second type of response sees the crisis as a *kairos,* as a time for asking fundamental questions about church and ministry, a time for renewal and reformation, a time for the recovery of authenticity and a new, confident openness to God's future. A good instance of this sort of response is the project of Edward Schillebeeckx and his colleagues which resulted in *The Church with a Human Face.*[17] This was sparked off by a quite specific crisis in the Dutch Roman Catholic Church – a colossal decline in the number of vocations to the celibate priesthood, so that many large parishes could not have their own priest and the sacramental life of the Church was severely endangered. This stimulated Schillebeeckx and his colleagues to ask fundamental questions: What is a priest for? What is the relation between the corporate priesthood and the priesthood of ordained individuals? Is there any reason why women should not be ordained? And so on. As a consequence, they were pushed back to Scripture and the early Church and emerged

---

[16] Kierkegaard, *Attack,* p. 258 [from the *Journals*], xi 1A 69.
[17] London: SCM Press, 1985. Cf. his *Ministry – A Case for Change* (London: SCM Press, 1981) and L. Grollenberg et al., *Minister? Pastor? Prophet?* London: SCM Press, 1980.

with an understanding of ministry which shared many insights with the churches of the Reformation and suggested that the most relevant models of ministry for today were also close to the patterns and understandings of ministry in the early Church. In a way the crisis of ministry was recognised first in the Roman Catholic churches of Western Europe in the 1960s, and many people regarded it as essentially arising from the issue of celibacy. Churches of other traditions which have more recently recognised that they face a crisis in ministry could learn much from the radical and constructive responses of the Dutch Roman Catholic theologians – and meditate on the implications of the fact that this reconsideration of ministry with all its practical implications was effectively nipped in the bud by the Vatican.

Again in the Roman Catholic Church, an acute shortage of priests in Latin America was the occasion for much radical rethinking of the shape of the Church and the patterns of ministry. Liberation theologians were characteristically critical of the hierarchical structuring of the Church and saw the dearth of priests as enabling a new practice of the corporate priesthood of believers. Theologians such as Leonardo Boff argued, historically correctly, that the structure of the Church had from early times reflected the structure of the social order in its context. And the same, he suggested, was true today: the Church which was called to be a 'sacrament-sign' and a 'sacrament-instrument' of liberation and give 'concrete historical embodiment' to the gospel was nevertheless liable to mirror and reinforce the power structures of class society. But in the Base Christian Communities or Popular Church, Boff suggested, there is a new Church emerging which is allied to the weak and the poor rather than the dominant classes. In this process of 'ecclesiogenesis' new possibilities for the Church and its ministry are presenting themselves. But once again ecclesiastical authority did not allow this new movement to show its full potential.[18] Latin America, like the Netherlands, is a

---

[18] See Leonardo Boff, *Church, Charism and Power* (London: SCM Press, 1985) and his essay in S. Torres and J. Eagleson (eds), *The Challenge of Basic Christian Communities*. London and Maryknoll: Orbis, 1981. The best recent study is Manuel A. Vásquez, *The Brazilian Popular Church and the Crisis of Modernity*. Cambridge: Cambridge University Press, 1998.

reminder that in the post-Christendom situation there is a range of possibilities for recovering authenticity in ministry.

For all its uncertainties and dangers, today's crisis/*kairos* is a time of extraordinary freedom and opportunity. Ministers no longer need to fit neatly into roles and stereotypes defined for them by society. They can explore ways of discerning and responding to the Spirit's guidance. And in doing this they are following the way of Jesus. He came into a situation unlike ours in that there was a clear model in people's minds of what a holy man, a minister, a priest was like, and what a rabbi's relation should be to the disciples. A holy man was treated with reverence by everyone. He maintained his purity by scrupulous observance of food rules and by care about the company he kept. His disciples were there to attend to his teaching and perform every menial task for him.

Jesus came and turned this accepted pattern upside down. He shocked people and perplexed his disciples. They expected him to behave like a traditional holy man, to fit into the accepted pattern, to nurture and defend his purity and authority against pollution or questioning.

But Jesus touched lepers, sat at table with notorious sinners, mixed with quislings and prostitutes. And then he took a towel and washed his disciples' dusty feet – menial service, degrading work, a trivial task, but a new pattern of ministry: simple, unpretentious humble service of the needs of women and men, humble self-giving which was at the same time a challenge to the principalities and powers and an exemplification of the authentic nature of Christian ministry.

It is this that we have an opportunity of recovering today: a pattern and a practice of ministry which is profoundly challenging to the dominant values and attitudes of today, and constructively transformative.

6

❧❀❧

Power and Pastoral Care

I want in this chapter to address some questions about the relation between issues of power and pastoral care. I do this for various reasons. In the first place, I think it is necessary to question the romanticism of powerlessness and the negative image of power which is endemic in much modern theology. Only too often people speak as if we had a powerless Church set free to attend to the needs and problems of the world, purified from the temptations of power. Now, there is some truth lurking behind such statements. There is no doubt that the Church as an institution and clergy as pastors have less power than once they had. I also have some sympathy with Alasdair MacIntyre's suggestion, in his famous conclusion to *After Virtue*,[1] that the barbarians have taken over power and as a consequence have done all they can to exclude the Church from power and influence, although always hoping to have ecclesiastical endorsement for their purposes and policies. And I think MacIntyre is also right that in such a situation the Church should reassess its role and refuse to devote its energies to shoring up the *imperium*, legitimating and blessing existing secular power structures.

But note that in MacIntyre's scenario the Church is *excluded* from a close and clearly defined relationship with the political

---

[1] A. MacIntyre, *After Virtue: A Study in Moral Theory*. Notre Dame: University of Notre Dame Press, 1981, pp. 244–5.

authorities, the *imperium*. It does not choose to wash its hands
of the responsibilities of power. It does not seek to distance
itself from questions of power and its deployment. It does not
regard issues of power, or questions of what the powerful do
with their power, as unimportant or irrelevant to the gospel. It
does not disengage from such matters – it simply comes at them
from a different angle and with perhaps greater possibility of
wrestling with questions of power on the basis of its own
distinctive insights.

Nor is the Church itself in fact powerless today. It may have
less *secular* power than once it had, but it would be naïve and
dangerous to suggest that it does not continue to have power,
which it should exercise in a Christian and responsible way.
Its new relationship with power involves new dangers and
new opportunities. Its new situation is not one of powerlessness,
but one which may well enable the Church to take the position of the poor and powerless with more understanding and
seriousness, and to appreciate more acutely the temptations
and dangers involved in the exercise of power. There is, then, a
sense in which the new relationship to power can enliven and
enable pastoral care of both the powerful and the weak,
precisely by recognising that issues of power are inescapably
involved.

The second reason why we must keep questions of power in
focus when we are discussing pastoral care is that the gospel
addresses persons-in-community, not that artificial intellectual construct which has penetrated so deeply into the modern
psyche, the isolated autonomous individual. A person-in-
community is in fact part of a web of power relationships which
may heal or harm, support or destroy. Care and service are not
alternatives to the exercise of power, nor ought they to be (as
they sometimes are) disguises for rather unsavoury and
manipulative uses of power, but rather they are activities which
require the proper use and deployment of power.

Pastoral Care and the Church

Not only does pastoral care address persons-in-community; the
primary agent of pastoral care is the Church, the community
of faith, and the individual pastor operates as the agent of that

community. Effective pastoral care may be provided by the community as a whole and by a variety of individuals on behalf of that community. In the case of a family in the congregation where great damage is being caused by the alcoholism of the father, for example, the congregation may give support, guidance, direction and encouragement in a whole variety of ways. The situation is much more difficult when, as increasingly happens today, the family as such is not related to the life of the congregation and the only pastoral care that can be offered is on an individual to individual basis. Much pastoral distress is caused when people find that the sinews of community are frayed and they are, as it were, floating free. The feeling, common in the past, that the individual is oppressed by the family or the community with their rules and standards seems to be gradually being replaced by the problems of isolation and loneliness.

I would wish to argue that Christian pastoral care is essentially ecclesial and in necessary conflict with the pervasive individualism of our society. We urgently need a British or European equivalent of Robert Bellah's *Habits of the Heart*.[2] I suspect this would show that we are well down the same road as the United States, already a collection of people with tenuous ties of solidarity and floating free of any but the blandest and vaguest structures of meaning and identity. 'Today', Bellah writes, 'religion represents a frame of reference for the self as conspicuous in its absence as in its presence.' Although American statistics of belief and churchgoing are far higher than in Europe, dominant forms of religious belief live at peace with the values of modern secular society:

> Liberalised versions of biblical morality tend to subordinate themes of divine authority and human duty to the intrinsic goodness of human nature, since 'God did not make junk', as a liberal pastor puts it.[3]

A stress on self-acceptance and 'positive thinking' is pervasive. *Habits of the Heart* contrasts this bland individualising of religion, and the undemanding sense of identity as 'a child of the

---

[2] Robert Bellah et al., *Habits of the Heart*. London: Hutchison, 1988 and Berkeley: University of California Press, 1985.
[3] Bellah et al., *Habits*, p. 63.

Universe' that goes with it, with the more astringent and communitarian views that initially shaped the United States. John Winthrop, a leading Puritan and first Governor of the Massachusetts Bay Colony, for example, in a sermon delivered just before landing at Salem in 1630, spoke of the kind of community they sought to establish, in which a Christian and moral life could be lived:

> We must delight in each other, make others' conditions our own, rejoyce together, mourn together, labor and suffer together, always having before our eyes our community as members of the same body.[4]

If there are resonances between the American scene as depicted in *Habits of the Heart* and the European situation (and I am sure there are), pastoral care which seeks to be Christian must resolutely resist enrolment in the dominant individualised and fragmented world-view, and seek to root itself in the fellowship of the Church and the tradition of rigorous and serious Christian theology. Otherwise it would be simply collusion in the damaging trivialisation of the age, when a British Prime Minister, Margaret Thatcher, could proclaim, 'There is no such thing as society. There are only individuals and families.' We need to recover some of the old solidarities if we are to care for people and structures aright.

One of the most dangerous implications of the domestication of pastoral care in middle-class religion, its privatisation and separation from serious theology, is this: it now has much difficulty in relating to the victims of injustice and oppression. This is partly because modern pastoral care's dominant concern with subjectivity and inter-personal processes makes it hard for it to relate constructively to the disease and distress which are rooted in systemic disorder and social conflict. But more of that later.

A Pastoral Theology of Power

Another reason for pastoral care taking power seriously is in a way the most obvious of all – the Christian tradition nurtures a distinctive and important understanding of the nature of

---

[4] Bellah et al., *Habits*, p. 28.

power, its dangers and its opportunities.[5] Let me suggest very briefly what this is.

Some years ago, as part of the Apostolic Faith Study, the Faith and Order Commission of the World Council of Churches was discussing the phrase from the Nicene-Constantinopolitan Creed: 'I believe in one God, the Father, the Almighty.' A leading German theologian was discoursing in learned and abstract fashion on the omnipotence of God when an Ethiopian Metropolitan, with a huge beard, a kind of black pancake of a headdress and several elaborate pectoral crosses – a thoroughly exotic figure – rose to his feet with great dignity and interrupted the German theologian in full flow. '*Pantokrator* does not mean omnipotent', he said, and sat down abruptly. The German theologian tried to dismiss him with a few patronising remarks about *pantokrator* being the Greek equivalent of the Latin *omnipotens*. The Ethiopian rose to his feet again, this time visibly angry. He clasped his arms in front of his chest like a mother cradling a baby and swayed gently from side to side as he said, '*Pantokrator*, as all the Greek Fathers affirm, means that God holds the whole world lovingly in his arms and protects it, as a mother her child. God has the power he needs to care for the world. God is not an arbitrary despot.' When he sat down there was silence. No reply was possible.

And now in the Faith and Order text, *Confessing the One Faith*, these words are to be found:

> Authority and dominion belong to the Fatherhood of God. The Father God is the one who rules and wields authority over all creation, 'the Almighty'. The term used in the Creed is Pantokrator, literally, 'the one who holds and governs all things'. It does not mean 'one who can do anything he wants' in an unqualified way, but rather 'one in whose hands all things are'. It is less a description of absolute omnipotence than of universal providence. To call the Father Pantokrator is to affirm that the whole universe is in his grasp, that he does not, and will not, let it go. At the same time it brings with it (at least in principle) the dethroning of all other claimants to universal sovereignty, to

[5] Among recent studies on the theology of power see especially James P. Mackey, *Power and Christian Ethics.* (Cambridge: Cambridge University Press, 1994) and Walter Wink's trilogy, *Naming the Powers* (1984), *Unmasking the Powers* (1986), *Engaging the Powers* (1992). Minneapolis: Fortress.

government and mastery over the world and its history and destiny
. . . Faith in God's omnipotence gives confidence that 'the powers
of the present age' – whether political, economic, scientific,
industrial, military, ideological or indeed religious – do not control
and will not have the last word concerning the destiny of the world
and humankind. The Lordship of the Almighty relativises and
judges them all; it confronts all other claims to sovereignty, it is a
challenge to every form of enslaving bondage . . . To confess the
Lordship of the Almighty is to celebrate the liberating strength of
the Creator and to proclaim hope for each individual and for the
whole universe . . . The confession of God's omnipotence does not
mean that he is to be conceived as a coercive and all-powerful
tyrant. Rather, God's power is the power of creative love and of
loving concern for creatures.[6]

Such a linking of power and care through rooting it in the very
nature of God is surely suggestive and helpful. Karl Barth
reminded his listeners in Bonn just after the end of the Second
World War that Adolph Hitler had characteristically referred
to God as 'the Almighty'. But that, said Barth, is a fundamental
distortion. If God is power in itself, then he must be bad. We
cannot and must not understand God in the light of an
otherwise determined understanding of power; we must
rather understand power in the light of what we know of God.[7]
We should start, perhaps, with Jesus' reinterpretation and
reinforcement of the tradition of the good shepherd king when
he finds the disciples squabbling about precedence. In the
Marcan narrative the male disciples were obsessed with status,
as Ched Myers and his associates point out;[8] in this context it is
significant that at the beginning (1.31) and end (15.41) of
Mark's story it is women who demonstrate the quality of
servanthood advocated here by Jesus:

You know that those who are supposed to rule over the Gentiles
[*ethne* = nations] lord it over them, and their great men exercise
authority over them. But it shall not be so among you; but whoever
would be great among you must be your servant [*diakonos*], and
whoever would be first among you must be slave [*doulos*] of all. For

[6] *Confessing the One Faith*. Faith and Order Paper 153. Geneva: World Council of
Churches, 1991, p. 33.
[7] Karl Barth, *Dogmatics in Outline*, 1949, pp. 47–9.
[8] Ched Myers et al., '*Say to this Mountain': Mark's Story of Discipleship*. Maryknoll:
Orbis, 1996, p. 133.

the Son of Man came not to be served but to serve, and to give his life as a ransom for many.[9]

Such passages suggest a linkage between care and power which is essential to the proper nature of each and rooted in the heart of the gospel. Care without power is sentimental and ineffective; power without care is arbitrary and oppressive. Care, love, qualifies and redefines power. Care with power is liberating and effective. Power is for the sake of care. Care needs power; power ought to be directed towards care. Only the two together can provide an authentically Christian way of responding to individual and collective needs. In saying this I am consciously reaffirming that the care of the individual and the care of society are inseparable from one another, that the exercise of power must be shaped by love and justice, that the process of pastoral care is directed to growth in the Body and in the person towards 'the measure of the stature of the fullness of Christ'.

In the light of this, I want to say something about three issues: the deployment of power within the Church; the empowerment of the powerless; and ministry to power structures and those with special influence within them.

Power in the Church

It is almost a commonplace in the work of historians and sociologists to suggest that the Church, in its structures and organisation and in the way it deploys power, usually mirrors the world around it, either as it is today or as it was in the past. This may be positively harmful, when the Church is seen as reflecting and even exacerbating social divisions and conflicts or abusing ecclesiastical power.[10] Often enough the Church, by the way it structures and uses its own power, is seen as providing an endorsement or even a sanctification of a specific political order, an analogical relationship between heavenly and earthly power providing mutual support and legitimation.[11] What I

[9] Mark 10.42–5.

[10] Mackey, in *Power and Christian Ethics*, discusses detailed instances of the abuse of ecclesiastical power.

[11] On this see the late David Nicholls' brilliant *Deity and Domination: Images of God and the State in the Nineteenth and Twentieth Centuries*. London: Routledge, 1989.

want to suggest is this: the Church, in the way it allows the gospel to shape its common life, its deployment of power and its care, should provide an exemplary community which suggests a new and better way of human flourishing, and should manifest in its own life a little of that alternative to the way of the world.

This has happened in the past. Why should it not happen again today? The American political philosopher, Sheldon Wolin, has argued that Christianity in late antiquity revivified political thought by living out 'a new and powerful ideal of community which recalled men to a life of meaningful partici-pation'. This community contrasted sharply with late classical and Hellenistic ideas on how human beings ought to relate to one another, and because of that injected fresh and key ideas into Western social thinking.[12] Michael Mann, in the first volume of his ambitious *The Sources of Social Power*, suggests that the congregations of the early Church were unintentionally subversive because 'they were a rival social organisation to the empire', offering a better sense of meaning and belonging, and better care and discipline than did the political and social institutions of the Empire with which the Church was in unavoidable tension.[13] In the Church, women, men and people from excluded communities – children, pagan soldiers, notorious sinners, foreigners and the ritually impure – were 'made at home in the universe'.[14] 'The "home"', writes Mann, 'was a social home, a community, but one that had universal significance in relation to ultimate meaning and morality. It fused the sacred and the secular, the spiritual and the material to produce a transcendent *society*.'[15] The Church offered a resolution of the profound crisis of social identity by mani-festing an *oikumene* which was open to all and transcended lesser loyalties. The Church was a place where in principle everyone was at home.

And so it might be today, in a society which is highly fragmented and where, as Michael Ignatieff reminds us, there

[12] Sheldon Wolin, *Politics and Vision*. London: Allen & Unwin, 1961, pp. 96–7.

[13] Michael Mann, *The Sources of Social Power*, vol. 1. Cambridge: Cambridge University Press, 1986.

[14] A. D. Nock, *Early Gentile Christianity and its Hellenistic Background*. New York: Harper & Row, 1964, p. 102.

[15] Mann, *Sources of Social Power*, p. 325.

is little sense of 'metaphysical belonging'.[16] Such a faith community, such a church, must pose a standing challenge and an alternative way to an increasingly divided, individualist society. It does this above all by its openness to, and care for, those whom society rejects or forgets. The Church is called to be a kind of active denial of the world's ranking of significance and usefulness and the world's deployment of power. It is sad that only too often the Church's use of power mirrors and magnifies the power structures of the secular sphere and demonstrates no distinctiveness.

Empowerment

The special openness to, and care for, those whom society rejects or forgets, those who are powerless, of which I have been speaking, needs to be given some 'cash value'. For them the problem is essentially lack of power. One way of responding is suggested by Stephen Sykes when he writes:

> The only credible option for the Christian church is to distribute and exercise power in such a way as to empower the marginalised and powerless. It may do this partly by deliberate interference in zero sum analysis to redress a balance in dog-eats-dog environment; and partly by the promotion of collective theories of power, in which the resources inherent in the marginalised and powerless are valued so as to contribute to a greater and more whole community.[17]

Even today the Church has an unusual level of contact with some of the marginalised. Sykes cites people struggling to care for a frail elderly parent, or a dementing spouse, or a son with schizophrenia. There is also the fact that the Church – particularly the established churches and the Roman Catholic Church – is *there* among the poor, in Urban Priority Areas and slums and areas with a high population of ethnic minorities. Although we often, quite rightly, deplore the frailty of that presence and the opportunities and responsibilities not taken

[16] Ignatieff, *The Needs of Strangers*, p. 78.
[17] Stephen Sykes, 'Power, Sex and Money', in M. Northcott (ed.), *Vision and Prophecy: The Tasks of Social Theology Today*. Edinburgh: Centre for Theology and Public Issues, Occasional Paper No. 23, 1991, p. 41.

up, at least there is some presence, some communication, and the Church is not entirely in an affluent, bourgeois captivity. Sykes goes on to say that there are things in relation to the powerless and the marginalised in Britain on which the Church can and must speak with authority because no one else is able to do this. When the powerless and inarticulate come to the new market-place to buy health care or welfare assistance, who, asks Sykes, is there to help them? Who is to protect their rights? We must not, he suggests, be paternalistic, regarding the powerless as people to be helped simply out of a sense of obligation. 'To be with the powerless', he writes, 'is the way of Jesus Christ, undertaken out of joy and love and gratitude, and elicits their inherent gifts as persons without patronage or condescension.'[18] This kind of caring can be hard and deeply testing:

> It is a direct invitation very often to a life of prayer, as one speedily confronts the limits of our high-tech medicine, which glamorises certain problems relieved by miracle drugs or remarkable surgery, and condemns the intractable, chronic problems of mental illness, dementia or terminal illness to financial starvation and the last efforts of under-supported relatives. It is when we see that there is nothing we can do to improve the situation that one speaks of a God who embraces human powerlessness from within, a gracious God who takes the human cause in its depths of loneliness and abandonment, from whose love nothing whatever can separate us.[19]

One needs, I think, to push Sykes' argument further. Christian care involves concern for policy as well as people. It often involves taking sides in a partisan and political way.[20] A proper pastoral concern for people can, and often must, involve taking their side and standing with them. And this is a place where the sort of discernment and understanding which may deeply influence policy for the better are possible.

A number of years ago a young woman with a fresh sociology PhD was employed to research what kind of accommodation would be most appropriate for homeless men in Edinburgh.

---

[18] Sykes, 'Power, Sex and Money', p. 42.
[19] Sykes, 'Power, Sex and Money', p. 42.
[20] On this see, for example, Peter Selby, *Liberating God*. London: SPCK, 1983, pp. 86ff.

The expectation was that this would be some kind of hostel in the centre of the city with an effective social work support structure. The researcher started her interviews with homeless men, and at the beginning everything went according to plan. The men on the whole gave her the answers they thought she would expect. This, they thought, would be the most painless way of getting rid of yet another alien researcher seeking to make a living out of asking them questions. Then, in one interview, the researcher found herself getting angry as a homeless man spoke of the treatment he had received in the Social Security office and in the night shelter where he was a regular. He told her how he felt degraded and patronised by everyone in authority. And the researcher knew as she listened to him that, through inefficiency or malice, he was being denied benefits and opportunities to which he was entitled. She swept him with her into the Social Security office and acted as his angry advocate. The researcher was treated with the respect that had been denied to the homeless man and she secured a range of additional benefits for him.

Word spread quickly among homeless men in Edinburgh about what had happened. The young researcher was now regarded as 'on our side', not just a detached scientific inquirer. She found a new honesty and openness in her interviews. Now the men spoke frankly, and a new and quite different picture emerged of what they wanted and what they believed they could cope with. Hardly anyone wanted city-centre hostel accommo-dation. Most wanted a small council flat with basic furniture and a simple support network on which they could rely. Given this, they believed they could reintegrate into the community – and this was their deepest wish. Only a committed, *engagé*, approach from someone recognised to be on their side was capable of eliciting data that was essential if policy on homelessness was to be wise and effective. Homeless men were being empowered to take hold of their own destiny. An academic inquiry only bore fruit when the researcher was bold enough to take sides. Care involved empowerment and this fed effectively into policymaking, the deployment of power.

Churches too should be in the business of empowerment and politics precisely because they are concerned about pain and distress. This is why they are involved in issues of justice and policy. As David Donnison, the distinguished specialist in social policy, has argued, pastoral concern for people necessarily leads to involvement in questions of poverty and power:

> If you are concerned about pain ... then you must also be concerned about poverty, because the poor suffer more than their fair share of pain. You must be concerned about power, too, because the poor are not excluded from the benefits of an affluent economy by accident ... Poverty is most heavily concentrated among the groups whom the powerful can most readily neglect. If we do not find ways of remedying their powerlessness we are unlikely to remedy their poverty.[21]

And in this task surely the Church of Jesus Christ has a central role to play. It is sad that so often it is reluctant to engage with real issues of power and empowerment, or sees them as having no relation to its pastoral task.

Pastoring the Powers

Down the years the churches – particularly, but not exclusively the established churches – have developed a great deal of expertise in ministering to the powerful and to power structures. Many of the powerful and influential are still in the Church, seeking to live in truth as they exercise power, seeking perhaps forgiveness, encouragement, guidance – or, possibly, ecclesiastical endorsement and the recruitment of support for sometimes dubious activities. At the height of the repression during his dictatorship in Chile, General Pinochet was as regular as always in his attendance at mass.

Much pastoring of the powers clusters around the various kinds of chaplaincies, or what are sometimes called 'sector ministries' – to the armed forces, Parliament, hospitals, schools and colleges, industry, and so on. First of all, it is good to affirm the importance of these forms of ministry and the significance of what has been learned in and from them for the life and witness of the whole Church. Chaplains, unless they understand their role as simply fishing for souls in a particular pool, are in a privileged position to understand the dynamics, possibilities

---

[21] David Donnison, *A Radical Agenda*, pp. 27 and 88.

and problems of a complex institution, for example the National Health Service, and the subtle interplay between the structure and the people who are involved either in working the structure or in receipt of its services. At its best, chaplaincy is a real engagement with the 'principalities and powers' and a way of opening communication and understanding between the institution and the wider society it is meant to serve. The chaplaincy approach can help the Church to take the social, economic and political structures of society seriously, proclaiming the manifold wisdom of God to the principalities and powers.[22]

But, having noted the significance, indispensability and effectiveness of chaplaincy engagement with social structures, it is surely necessary also to recognise the ambiguity often involved in the chaplaincy role. Michael Northcott has argued rather sweepingly that industrial chaplaincies in the 1960s and 70s were simultaneously sucked into both an increasingly secular understanding of the world and a sharp and sometimes uncomprehending separation from the mainstream life of the Church. This, he suggests, involved a 'capitulation to secularism'.[23] Stephen Pattison, after reminding us of the degrading, offensive and horrifying things that can go on in some psychiatric hospitals, raises the awkward question why chaplains failed to 'recognise and act against the palpable structural evils which diminished all those living and working in psychiatric hospitals'. He suggests, correctly, that the chaplains were not evil, callous or uncaring people. But they took the institution and its ways of working for granted as a context within which they could care for individuals and remain neutral in conflict situations, 'Whose side are the chaplains on?' he asks. The answer is that they often claim to be on neither side, but are perceived as being unqualifiedly on the side of the system within which they minister. Pattison instances the chaplain in a high-security psychiatric hospital, where large-scale systematic abuse of patients by nursing staff had been proved to be going on, who was asked on a radio programme,

[22] Ephesians 3.10. I have discussed chaplaincies in my *Beliefs, Values and Policies: Conviction Politics in a Secular Age*. Oxford: Clarendon Press, 1989, pp. 66–9.
[23] M. S. Northcott, *The Church and Secularisation*. Frankfurt am Main: Peter Lang, 1989, pp. 188–9.

'How do you see your role in the hospital in the light of these events?' 'I do not see my role, I just do it', was his reply.[24]

Similar issues can arise in prison chaplaincy work. It has been asked in recent times why prison chaplains, who must have more than an inkling of the degrading and brutalising things that happen in some of Britain's prisons, have made no public protest or complaint. If the answer to that is that in many cases prison chaplains are employees of the state and bound by the Official Secrets Act, the question must then be asked whether ministers of the gospel should agree to serve under such conditions. But to be fair, such institutional settings can and do allow abundant scope for effective personal pastoral work while often disallowing or discouraging prophecy.

And military chaplaincy is no different. I remember very vividly a debate in the Church of Scotland General Assembly during the Gulf War, when members of the Forces' Chaplains Committee launched a vigorous attack on the Moderator at that time and others, who had taken a critical stance towards the Gulf War. The argument was that this disturbed the troops and made the chaplains' work more difficult. Prophetic and critical voices, the argument went, should be silent in time of war lest they threaten the morale of the troops. Contrast this attempt to get the Church to gag its own prophets with the British government's attempts in 1943 to conceal from the churches that German civilian residential areas were being targeted in blanket bombing attacks, lest the targeting policy should be criticised. The Secretary of State for the Air at the time, Sir Archibald Sinclair, defended the policy of concealment in a memo to Sir Charles Portal: 'Only in this way could he satisfy the enquiries of the Archbishop of Canterbury, the Moderator of the Church of Scotland and other significant religious leaders, whose moral condemnation of the bomber offensive might disturb the morale of Bomber Command.'[25]

---

[24] Stephen Pattison, *A Critique of Pastoral Care*. London: SCM Press, 1988, pp. 1 and 99. Pattison's more substantial treatment of this theme is his *Pastoral Care and Liberation Theology*. Cambridge: Cambridge University Press, 1994.

[25] Cited by Tony Carty in Howard Davis (ed.), *Ethics and Defence: Power and Responsibility in the Nuclear Age*. Oxford: Blackwell, 1986, p. 121.

But even allowing for such problems, which have their equivalents in every form of pastoral ministry, chaplaincy work, ministry to structures, systems and organisations as well as to the individuals involved in these structures, is vitally important and has major lessons to teach the Church as a whole about its mission in tomorrow's world. For pastors are engaging in chaplaincy work with sectors of society which are already far more secularised than the congregation or domestic suburban life. The struggle to communicate, minister and care in contexts where there is little pretence of religious belief, a great plurality of commitments and an almost complete absence of basic Christian formation has lessons for the whole Church.

The same issues with which chaplains have been struggling for years are now arising in the congregation and the parish: how to communicate the gospel and care in the name of Christ in situations where there is both ignorance and profound mis-understanding of the Christian tradition. This is, of course, an opportunity as well as a problem. If well and properly told, the Christian narrative may still be heard with freshness and excitement. But chaplaincies must be cautious lest they allow themselves to be sucked into the system in such a way that they can no longer exercise a free Christian pastoral and prophetic ministry in and to the system; and they must be bold enough to venture into territory which is both a field of mission and a place where people are hurting and needing help. Chaplains treading the corridors of power should beware lest they inhale the sweet smell of power. Yet chaplaincies have pioneered forms of inclusive and open ministry that are effective when we no longer assume a Christian society or indeed a religious context.

Professional Power

While the minister or religious functionary has a good claim, contested only by one other occupation, to be the oldest profession in the world, it is only in modern times that a clearly defined professional model of ministry has emerged. A pro-fession is a way of validating and forming, channelling and constraining, power over others. Professionals 'possess a specialized skill in applying general theoretical principles to particular problems'.[26] This skill and knowledge is a form of power, and professionals are often accused, sometimes with justice, of reluctance to share their skills and knowledge or negotiate with others about the solution to particular problems.

A profession guards its portals and oversees the education and formation of its members so that it can be sure of a requisite degree of knowledge and skill, so that power may be used aright. A profession disciplines its members and protects against abuse of power. And professions maintain a mystique and act collectively to safeguard or enhance the status and emoluments of the profession – to say nothing of their self-interested endeavours to protect their monopoly and exclude others from usurping their functions. The collective self-interest of a major profession such as medicine or the law, is evident, and government or the public sometimes see a responsibility to control and limit professional power, recognising that it is not infrequently in conflict with the common good or the public interest.

The professional model is today extremely attractive to many clergy. Professionals, in the popular view, have an identifiable body of skills useful to the community; these they are expected to exercise in accountable ways for the achievement of identifiable goods for people. In addition, professions are good at claiming status for their members and they exercise power – things very attractive to clergy in a situation that is often confusing and disconcerting for them.

Now, there are things in the professional model which I feel should be strongly affirmed – the need for ministers to have an identifiable body of skills, regularly updated, and the need for accountability and supervision, to name two important features of the professional model. But this model is also peculiarly dangerous because of its concern with power and status, and because what adopting it for the Christian ministry would imply for the nature of the Church. It was George Bernard Shaw who said famously that all professions are conspiracies against the laity,[27] and more recently Ivan Illich has demonstrated that many professional practices are disabling rather than enabling,

---

[26] Bill Jordan, *The Common Good*. Oxford: Blackwell, 1989, p. 163.
[27] In the Preface to *Mrs Warren's Profession*.

creating dependency rather than freedom.[28] The professional model of ministry is in danger of making the members of the Body of Christ 'patients' or 'clients', dependents on the professional clergy rather than active participants in ministry. It erodes the need for pastoral care to be mutual and reciprocal within the Body, and it builds up again a mystique of ministry from which the majority of Christians are excluded. We should be cautious about the professional model of ministry because it distorts the relation between power and care to which we have been pointing in this chapter.

Far better is the late Bob Lambourne's account of pastoral care as 'a pattern of corporate, responsible, sensitive acts motivated by a compelling vision', which should be 'lay, voluntary and diffuse in the community' and 'motivated as much by a struggle for corporate excellence as by a struggle against defects'.[29] And perhaps a better model for ministry than the professional is that of the 'reflective practitioner'.[30] Here the task is more an art, or perhaps a practical wisdom (*phronesis*), exercised in close consultation with all involved and with constant honest scrutiny of the practice with a view to its improvement, rather than the application of a theory or a body of established knowledge. It is often based more on a feel for what should be done and accumulated experience constantly reviewed, than upon rules or formal norms.

Ministry is for the whole people of God, not just for the 'experts'. It is a vocation rather than a profession, a way of life rather than a job, a way of loving that is realistic but not hard, a shared responsibility rather than a task for prima donnas. And the power that is involved in Christian ministry should be radically reconceived in the light of the teaching and practice of Jesus Christ, who came not to be ministered to but to minister and to give his life as a ransom for many.

[28] Ivan Illich, *Disabling Professions*. London: Boyars, 1978.
[29] Cited in A. V. Campbell, *Paid to Care?* London: Darton, Longman & Todd, p. 38.
[30] As developed by Donald Schön in his book, *The Reflective Practitioner: How Professionals Think in Action*. London: Temple Smith, 1983, and others.

7

Liberating Worship

Three general affirmations about worship need to be held together in tension:

- The cult is the nourishing heart of Christian practice, central to any proper understanding of Christian discipleship and identity. Enactment of the liturgy – both Word and Sacrament – is the place where the Church is most fully church. This is perhaps most clearly seen in the Jewish Passover rite, but it is present in all authentic worship. In the Passover, the youngest child present, representing those who are not yet formed, who have not received an identity, who have not yet heard and re-enacted the story often enough or in sufficiently different ways for it to have shaped their self-understanding, asks the key questions: 'What do these strange and unusual actions *mean*? Why do we do these things?' The answer is oblique: the story is retold and re-enacted ritually, for this is the story that makes us who we are, a story which is replete with clues as to how the people of this story should behave and what their orientation in life should be.

- The second affirmation seems in sharp contrast to the first. It represents a position which is found in many places in the New Testament, but particularly clearly in the Letter to the Hebrews. This is that the cult has been fulfilled, completed, superseded by the work of Christ.

Worship continues in heaven in the constant intercession of Christ for us, but on earth the cult has now become superfluous, redundant. Indeed, carrying on the cult in any traditional sense impugns the adequacy and efficacy of Christ's work, which is his worship. What is left to us, as 'true worship', is the offering of our very selves, the life of the community, poured out in service to others. The emphasis here rests not on the cult as something we do, but on what Christ has done and what Christ continues to do for us in heaven. Vigen Guroian has stressed that worship involves 'remembering the future', experiencing the eschatological future, encountering the heavenly reality now, and appropriating the past.[1] Christian worship in this understanding is shot through with moral and behavioural assumptions; true worship is the joyful offering of the whole of life in response to Christ (Rom 12.1); we participate through service and love in the constant self-offering of Christ.[2]

- My third affirmation is not so much theological as empirical. It is that worship often becomes frozen, like a fly in amber, in such a way that it appears to be a relic of a dead past without life or bearing on today's world or today's demands. When worship deteriorates in this way, the Church is deprived of a necessary tool for discernment and resources for practice. But the reality of worship today is rather complex. It is, I suppose, encouraging that communist regimes regarded even worship that seemed rather moribund as a continuing threat to their systems, a kind of question mark against totalitarian regimes and a challenge to the moral formation they attempted to impose. And it is strange how often, even in avowedly secular societies, intelligent but unbelieving people seek to recruit Christian worship as an instrument of consolation, challenge or encouragement. It would be rash to reject almost any form

---

[1] See Vigen Guroian, *Ethics After Christendom* (Grand Rapids: Eerdmans, 1994); *Incarnate Love* (Notre Dame: University of Notre Dame Press, 1989); *Life's Living Toward Dying* (Grand Rapids: Eerdmans, 1996).

[2] On service and love as participation in the self-offering of Christ, see especially R. J. Daly, *The Origins of the Christian Doctrine of Sacrifice*. London: Darton, Longman & Todd, 1978.

of liturgy as *entirely* moribund and lacking in ethical force. For many people the Anglican funeral service for Diana Princess of Wales in Westminster Abbey provided a relevant and central focus for an extraordinary outpouring of national grief. After all, one of the functions of liturgy, as of Scripture, is to preserve images, insights, perspectives and memories, which sometimes seem to have spent their force and to belong to a past age, in the hope (which has been proved true time and again) that some of them may be reborn and show themselves relevant to the context of a new age. But that is no excuse for failure to reform and renew liturgy. Indeed, the modern liturgical movement has opened up a whole range of fresh ideas for mobilising the formative possibilities of liturgy.

Holding these three affirmations in tension is necessary if we are to avoid an archaeological or moralistic account of worship. Our worship is a response – necessarily fragmentary and incomplete – to what has been done for us, what is being done, and the destiny prepared for us. There is not, and should not be, a clear mark or frontier between the cult and the life of the community, between the liturgy and the liturgy after the liturgy, between the Lord's Table and the common table. There should not be too sharp a distinction between church and world. Salt and yeast penetrate and work anonymously, invisibly; one sees and tastes their effects without tasting them directly. But salt must have its savour and yeast must be alive and pure. And here the renewing and liberating dimensions of liturgy are important.

It is good to understand liturgy as sustainer of memory and hope. Both memory and hope are under threat today. In an age of neophilia the past has, in many people's view, been superseded. Sustaining memory is a resource for growth and morality. But the memory of Jesus is a disturbing memory, which resists constant endeavours to domesticate and tame it. Many kinds of mariology, for example, present a rather bland icon which has little place for the Mary of the *Magnificat*. Images of the Holy Family seldom take account of the sometimes stormy relation of Jesus to his natural family. Hope, like memory, is in crisis today. For those in the 'culture of contentment' it is a threat to be disposed of. If you stand at the 'end of history', there is nothing left to hope for. Liturgy as sustaining both memory and hope is oddly, but constructively, anomalous in the modern world.

Let us now consider the two central acts of Christian worship – baptism and the eucharist, or Lord's Supper. These, in Stanley Hauerwas' memorable words, are

> the essential rituals of our politics. Through them we learn who we are. Instead of being motives or causes for effective social work on the part of Christian people, these liturgies *are* our effective social work. For if the church *is* rather than has a social ethic, these actions are our most important social witness. It is in baptism and eucharist that we see most clearly the marks of God's kingdom in the world. They set our standard, as we try to bring every aspect of our lives under their sway.[3]

Baptism

The rite of baptism is a celebration of grace, a recognition of God's choice, and also a re-centring of life, a re-orientation, a new beginning. It is a turning to God from idols (1 Thess 1.9), so that now we must 'live lives worthy of the God who calls you into his kingdom and glory' (1 Thess 2.2). Repentance, conversion, baptism thus give a new identity, a new orientation, a new goal. Baptism is, in Wayne Meeks' terms, a process of decentring and recentring, with which is associated a resocialisation. Within this new community and new orientation formation takes place.

Baptism is not simply a rite; it is a life lived to God, which finds its fulfilment only at the end, as Jesus' baptism found its fulfilment in the cross. It therefore has an inevitable connection with growth and formation, for it is a redirection of life in community towards true maturity, 'the measure of the stature of the fullness of Christ' (Eph 4.13). Baptism is entry into a community of forgiven sinners, a fellowship of reconciliation, not a company of moral heroes.

Yet actual baptismal practice sometimes denies the forgiveness and reconciliation proclaimed and assumes a narrow and

---

[3] Hauerwas, *The Peaceable Kingdom*, p. 99.

distorted understanding of the Church into which one enters at baptism. The Irish theologian, Enda McDonagh, has made this point sharply:

> Baptism in a particular Church, Protestant or Catholic, expresses integration into a particular historical community of Christians with its own cultural and political traditions which set it apart from and against another community of Christians. Affiliation to the Unionist or Nationalist community is the other side of the baptism event in Northern Ireland, which is in opposition to and sometimes in deadly conflict with integration into the Body of Christ.[4]

Baptism which is understood as entry into some ethnically or culturally defined community which is not the Church, the *una sancta*, and which encourages the formation of attitudes and the adoption of practices which are less than Christian, is in danger of becoming a parody. The easy solution in a context like that of Northern Ireland, McDonagh suggests, would be to stop baptising. But that would be to lose 'the challenge and the empowerment' which baptism offers Christians in hard days as in fair. So he suggests that both the great branches of the Western Christian Church should be represented at every baptism as a sign of the fullness of the Church and a reminder that the Church is a community of reconciliation, for 'in the one Spirit we were all brought into the one body by baptism' and have 'all put on Christ like a garment' (1 Cor 12.12–13; cf. Gal 3.27–28). Baptism is properly, and indeed necessarily, understood as the initiation of a process of moral formation. That is, of course, not all it is, but it is an essential dimension of any adequate understanding of baptism.

Eucharist

> Like the new-born infants you are, you should be craving for unadulterated spiritual milk so that by it you may *grow* towards salvation; for surely you have *tasted that the Lord is good*. (1 Peter 2.2–3; my italics)

The eucharist may be understood as nourishment for moral growth and formation. Like all worship, this central liturgy has

---

[4] Enda McDonagh, *Between Chaos and New Creation*. Dublin: Gill & Macmillan, 1986, p. 85.

an important function of edifying, building up the community and its members. Individualistic worship, like speaking in tongues without an interpreter, does not edify and should be discouraged, as should the modern extremes of individualistic worship.

The Lord's Supper thus has an important formative role, both in relation to the community and the individual. As at Jesus' table there was an open invitation, and deeply entrenched suspicions, divisions and hostilities were overcome, so at the eucharistic table Jew and Gentile, rich and poor, weak and strong come together and experience a new and challenging depth of community. When the poor are despised, the sacrament is invalid (1 Cor 11.20); in the eucharistic sharing the divisions of the world are challenged and a better way is shown. The eucharist involves a commitment (*sacramentum*) to sharing with the needy neighbour, for Jesus said, 'The bread that I shall give is my own flesh; given for the life of the world' (John 6.51). It is not bread for believers, but for the life of the world (*kosmos*). The reverent use and sharing of the sacramental elements likewise involve a commitment to this as the proper use of the natural environment, a necessary component of a eucharistic lifestyle. In and through the eucharist we are called to be holy people in a world that is being made holy.

The eucharist is also food for a journey and an anticipation (*antepast*) of the coming heavenly banquet. We find in the eucharist an authentic but partial expression of the conviviality of the realm of God, the taste of the future, which encourages us to seek the Reign of God in hope. There is thus in the eucharist a proper kind of play-acting involved. We are trying out the roles that will be fully ours in the Reign of God, as young children play 'let's pretend' games to get the feel of being mothers or fathers, or train drivers, or soldiers. And this is, of course, a vital mode of formation.

Worship As Liberating

The title of this chapter is intentionally ambiguous. It refers first to worship as liberating, the freedom to which Christian worship points us and into which in part we enter in worship, of which worship is the sign. And, in the second place, it refers to the freeing of worship so that it may be authentically Christian, and therefore liberating, worship, an expression of the freedom of the Spirit.

Come with me to the remote little village of Muthialapad in the Andhra country of South India. There is as yet no road suitable for cars, and we must approach either on foot or by bullock-cart, a sign that this is far from being a prosperous part of the country. The little Christian community is entirely composed of converts, one or two generations back, from an Untouchable caste, the Malas. Poverty-stricken, oppressed and despised for centuries, the change of religion has brought little visible change in the social and economic condition of the community. Their ramshackle huts are crowded together in the *cheri*, a damp hollow a little distance from where the higher caste people live. And there, totally incongruously, stands a tidy little gothic church.

The building and – far more important – the worship which takes place within it are of profound significance for that little group of poor and oppressed people. To us at first this comes as something of a surprise. The building has no architectural or artistic merit and jars with its social and physical setting; but to the Muthialapad Christians it is a constant visible reminder that the God and Father of our Lord Jesus Christ dwells with them, and that they have here no abiding city. No outsider would think of calling their worship glorious; on the surface it is rather humdrum and too westernised in form. But to these Christians, despised by their neighbours as irremediably polluting, ostracised and subject to daily indignities, petty or more severe, worship is a constant assurance that they are the beloved children of God, forgiven and endowed with dignity and regarded as of infinite worth by the God who is no respecter of persons.

Until thirty-five years ago, the Christians of Muthialapad were compelled to perform the traditional role of the Malas in the annual village festival. When the buffalo had been sacrificed, its entrails were draped around the necks of the Christian Malas who, thus attired, had to go in procession, dancing and playing drums and tambourines, through the main streets of the village. Here was worship which confirmed their degradation, which legitimised the social order of the village, which expressed a totally different message from that of the worship in the little

Mala church. Under duress they had to continue to participate in this repulsive idolatry, until a teenage boy, now a leading Christian academic, led the Mala Christians in refusing to take part in the traditional Hindu festival. The Christians' huts were burnt and there was violence; the police had to be called in to maintain a fragile peace.

But finally the point was won. There were two kinds of worship in Muthialapad. The one sanctified injustice and oppression, confirmed the social order of the village and condemned many to bondage and degradation. The other was the worship of free men and women, who found in it a human dignity denied to them in village society and a vision of justice and liberty.

Now we change continents, going to North America to listen to James Cone speaking of the significance of worship for American Blacks:

> The eschatological significance of the black community is found in the people believing that the Spirit of Jesus is coming to visit them in the worship service each time two or three are gathered in his name, and to bestow upon them a new vision of their future humanity. This eschatological revolution is . . . a change in the people's identity, wherein they are no longer named by the world but named by the Spirit of Jesus . . . The Holy Spirit's presence with the people is a liberating experience. Black people who have been humiliated and oppressed by the structures of white society six days of the week, gather together each Sunday morning in order to experience a new definition of their humanity. The transition from Saturday to Sunday is not just a chronological change from the seventh to the first day of the week. It is rather a rupture in time . . . which produces a radical transformation in the people's identity. The janitor becomes the chairperson of the Deacon Board; the maid becomes the president of Stewardess Board Number 1. Everyone becomes Mr and Mrs, or Brother and Sister. The last becomes first, making a radical change of self and one's calling in the society. Every person becomes somebody, and one can see the people's recognition of their new-found identity by the way they walk and talk and 'carry themselves'. They walk with a rhythm of an assurance that they know where they are going, and they talk as if they know the truth about which they speak. It is this experience of being radically transformed by the power of the Spirit that defines the primary style of black worship. This transformation is found not only in the titles of Deacons, Stewardesses, Trustees and

Ushers, but also in the excitement of the entire congregation at worship. To be at the end of time where one has been given a new name requires a passionate response with the felt power of the Spirit in one's heart.[5]

Other examples could be multiplied from various contexts around the world. In worship we receive a new identity, we are called and shaped for the practice of discipleship. By encountering God we learn how to be disciples. We learn to love by being loved; we learn to forgive by being forgiven; we learn generosity by being treated generously. The ability to love and do justice is released in us when and as we are loved. The experience of the joy of freedom in worship stimulates a passion for liberty, especially for those oppressed by inner and outer constraints. For in Christian worship we receive an appetiser for the authentic liberty promised for all the children of God.

Freeing Worship

'What', asked the history teacher, 'were the Four Freedoms?' Promptly the boy replied: 'Freedom from want, Freedom from fear, Freedom from thought, and Freedom from religion'. His answer, although wrong, was revealing, for many people, particularly in the secular West, see religion and worship as the opposite of emancipating. They are held to be things that bind, that limit, that enslave – the opium of the people. Freedom and maturity alike involve freedom from religion, leaving worship behind as something childish and enslaving, unworthy of an emancipated adult. Worship is outgrown, like playing with dolls or Hornby trains. We may well point out that modern people, having proclaimed that there is no need for worship, invent a multitude of surrogates and devote a remarkable amount of time and energy to the worship of strange gods – the pomp of civic religion, the ritual of the demonstration or the football match, the fertility cult that is denounced as pornography and countless other substitute forms of worship. We may go on to say that false worship is indeed a popular opiate; that it often disguises strong yet subtle forms of social

---

[5] James Cone, cited in Geoffrey Wainwright, *Doxology: The Praise of God in Worship, Doctrine and Life*. London: Epworth, 1980, p. 419.

control; that it discourages the asking of awkward questions; that it frequently conceals injustice and exploitation under a pall of sanctimoniousness.

But when we have said such things we still have to face the problem that many people, including many Christian and intelligent people, find what passes as Christian worship dull, irrelevant and totally remote from the great issues of freedom and human dignity with which we found Christian worship to be properly and necessarily linked all round the world.

Those who have dealings with young people these days must have become sadly accustomed to young Christians, brought up in good Christian homes, who abandon the public worship of God and put all their enthusiasm, commitment and concern into the work of Amnesty International, Anti-Apartheid, or the like. If you talk with them you quickly discover that they have been unable to find any connection between the worship which they have experienced and the great causes and concerns of justice and liberty. They have come to feel, as Reinhold Niebuhr did, that if the churches were realistic about their own worship they would remove the crosses from their buildings and put on the holy table instead the three little monkeys, who hear no evil, see no evil and speak no evil.

Is it possible for our worship to recover what once it had, when every conventicle on the hillsides was an act of protest, an affirmation of the crown rights of the Redeemer and a laying hold of the freedom with which Christ makes us free? Could the day come again when people could say of Christian worship in Europe something like this comment of a Latin American theologian? 'Every truthful and consciously celebrated eucharist can be regarded as the most radical act of protest,' proclaiming and showing forth the rule of Christ,

> the only saviour and liberator, the only Lord of history and of man . . . His rule excludes every other rule which seeks to dominate man and . . . in him all men are made free. By celebrating the Eucharist, we commit ourselves to the work of removing all forms of political, social and ideological oppression that are incompatible with what we have proclaimed.[6]

---

[6] S. Galilea, 'Les messes de protestation', in *Parole et Mission*, 14 (1971), p. 334.

But first, our worship must be freed from the distortions and limitations which make it so much less than Christian worship ought to be. Worship must be freed, if it is itself to be liberating.

How easy it is for worship to become domesticated and tamed within a particular culture and expression of the national spirit, a custodian of one people's ethos – and nothing more. There is, of course, a sense in which Christian worship must find itself at home in every age and culture, just as the language of worship should be language understood by the people. There is no case at all for worship being entirely uniform in every age and place.

But Christian worship may be tamed if it is confined too closely within a particular culture and society and ceases to be aware of itself as a specific expression of the constant worship of heaven and of every age and nation upon earth. Sometimes worship, which should be catholic in the truest sense, seems instead to have been imprisoned in the kailyaird, incapable of seeing over the fence or sharing in the worship of the whole Church of God. A baptismal certificate which some years ago was on sale in church bookshops in Scotland bore at the top a bold design, unambiguously tartan, the outline of which may be seen equally well as a thistle or a dove descending. The tartan thistle/dove suggests and encourages a dangerous confusion between what it means to be a Scot and what it means to be a Christian, a confusion which sometimes penetrates deeply into worship. The integrity of worship demands its liberation from provincialism and ethnic captivity, together with the realisation that Christian worship is a challenge, a questioning, a disturbance to all cultures and all social orders. For it points to, and is already the anticipation of, the Kingdom of God.

Our problem is not simply that so often in worship the kailyaird triumphs over the catholic; it is also that worship is so often seen as a middle class activity: a kind of 'bourgeois captivity' of worship. An experienced minister in a great housing estate says this:

> The mass of Protestant working people do not believe that the Church is on their side . . . It is obvious to the working class community that the Church does not belong among them, and that it

is not in solidarity with them in their lives. It is always a visitor from the outside.[7]

In one sense, of course, the Church and her worship must always be a 'visitor from outside'; or, to put the point more clearly, the Church is a pilgrim people, exiles and strangers seeking their true homeland, and worship is nourishment and direction for the way. But if worship is to speak of Christian freedom to ordinary folk it must be nourishment for *their* pilgrimage, it must relate to *their* hopes and fears, to *their* condition, rather as Christian worship relates to the Mala Christians of Muthialapad. The remarkable renewal of the Church in Latin America in recent decades arose largely from the discovery that it was impossible to worship God in the horrendous slums without sharing at the deepest level in the hopes and the despair of the poor and the oppressed. Christian worship lost its integrity if it became either isolated from the realities of life, or an escape from the implications of oppression. It is impossible to keep company with Christ if we refuse to accept the company he has chosen to keep. Following the patristic principle *ubi Christus ibi ecclesia*, where Christ is, there is the Church, it is necessary to go to find Christ and therefore the Church among the poor he loves, to listen to them and learn afresh from them how to worship God in Spirit and in truth. If we were to realise this, it could well ignite a revival of the Church and a new vitality in worship.

Our worship needs to be freed from its obsessive wordiness if it is to recover a vital awareness of the Word of God which is living and active. Only too often the Reformers' insistence on the complementarity of Word and Sacrament, so that each interprets and confirms the other, has been lost. Instead we have unease about symbols, signs, actions, movement, silence and indeed all forms of non-verbal communication and expression. Sacraments become regarded as little more than visual aids and worship sinks into a dry didactic exercise reminiscent of school classrooms prior to the advent of modern pedagogical method, with its emphasis on participation and learning by doing. There is more truth than we might care to

---

[7] John Miller, *Problems of the Ministry and Mission of the Church in New Housing Areas and Other Working Class Parishes*. Glasgow: privately published, 1976, p. 2.

admit in the words of that great Scottish Christian poet, Edwin Muir, writing of his motherland:

> The Word made flesh here is made word again,
> A word made word in flourish and arrogant crook.
> See there King Calvin with his iron pen,
> And God three angry letters in a book,
> And there the logical hook
> On which the Mystery is impaled and bent
> Into an ideological instrument.[8]

From this there flows the extraordinary passivity of the people in worship. We cannot expect to have an active, living Church which lives out its royal priesthood in responsible involvement in the life of the world if in worship, the throbbing heart of Christian love and care, the people of God are taught to be passive. In much of our worship the priestly activity of the People of God is hardly in evidence; instead the minister does and says practically everything. The symbolism is powerful – and terrifying. It runs directly counter to the doctrine of the corporate priesthood of believers and confirms a disastrously inadequate understanding of the nature and mission of the Church. We need to recover the sense of worship as an activity in which the whole People of God participate and which involves the whole person, not just the eyes, or ears, or brain. And in so doing we shall also find a truer understanding of the wondrous mystery of God and of Christ in our neighbour, a mystery which must be worshipped, loved and served, which must not be 'impaled and bent into an ideological instrument'; a mystery which constantly spills over into common life, calling into being fellowship, sharing, justice and hope.

Worship separated from the great issues of liberty and justice has become idolatry, an instrument of ideological manipulation, a way of hiding from God rather than encountering him. The prophets teach that it is not acceptable to God:

> What are your endless sacrifices to me? says Yahweh.
>
> I am sick of holocausts of rams and the fat of calves.

---

[8] 'The Incarnate One', in Edwin Muir, *Collected Poems*. London, 1963, p. 228. Grateful acknowledgement is made to Faber & Faber Ltd. for permission to quote this extract from the poem.

The blood of bulls and of goats revolts me. When you come to present yourselves before me, who asked you to trample over my courts? Bring me your worthless offerings no more, the smoke of them fills me with disgust. New Moons, sabbaths, assemblies – I cannot endure festival and solemnity, Your New Moons and your pilgrimages I hate with all my soul.

They lie heavy on me, I am tired of bearing them.

When you stretch out your hands I turn my eyes away, You may multiply your prayers, I shall not listen.

Your hands are covered with blood, wash, make yourselves clean. Take your wrong-doing out of my sight. Cease to do evil.

Learn to do good, search for justice, help the oppressed, be just to the orphan, plead for the widow.[9]

'My grandfather', a rabbi in one of Martin Buber's writings relates,

'was paralysed. One day he was asked to tell about something that happened with his teacher – the great Baalshem. Then he told how the saintly Baalshem used to leap about and dance while he was at his prayers. As he went on with the story, my grandfather stood up; he was so carried away that he had to show how the master had done it, and started to caper about and dance. From that moment he was cured.'[10]

That is an apt parable of the way in which Christian worship, the ritual representation of the story of God's liberation of his people, must be the authentic source of ongoing participation in the liberating activity of God himself.

Worship in Spirit and in truth is an encounter with the God who cares so deeply for justice and for those in bondage that he sent his Son in order that we might be free. And the joy of freedom which we find in the worship of the one true God is something which must flow out into the world, sustaining and clarifying the passion for liberty.

---

[9] Isaiah 1.11–17. Cf. Isaiah 58.6–8; Amos 5.21–24, etc.
[10] Cited in Edward Schillebeeckx, *Jesus: An Experiment in Christology*. London: Collins, 1979, p. 674.

SECTION THREE

PUBLIC THEOLOGY

8

Public Practical Theology

The Dual Accountability of Theology

In chapter 3 we said something about two 'publics' to which theology is often held to relate, the Church and the university.[1] Theology relates to a constituency outside the academy in a more obvious sense than does, say, philosophy. And many, but not all, theologians believe that it is important that theology is seen as accountable in some sense to the Church as well as to the university. Theology for them is seen as *church* theology, and such theologians understand themselves as simultaneously 'doctors of the church' and professors in the academy.

This dual sense of accountability sometimes leads to tensions. From time to time colleagues in other disciplines suspect that theology does not have a proper place in the university because it involves a faith commitment which impugns 'proper scientific impartiality'. And on the other hand, when Kierkegaard said, 'It is impossible for a professor of theology to be saved', he was suggesting that Christian truth is to be lived and loved on the way to salvation and is radically distorted if subjected to the detached, objectifying investigations characteristic of the academy. 'What I really lack,' Kierkegaard wrote,

---

[1] I have borrowed the notion of the publics of theology from David Tracy – see his *The Analogical Imagination*. New York: Crossroad, 1981, especially chaps 1 and 2.

is to be clear in my mind *what I am to do*, not what I am to know except in so far as a certain understanding must precede every action. The thing is to understand myself, to see what God really wishes *me* to do; the thing is to find a truth which is true *for me*, to find *the idea for which I can live and die*.[2]

Yet, at its best, theology which affirms this dual sense of responsibility to the Church and to the academy is able to show a proper combination of reverence and rigour, so that theology has something to offer both to the university and to the Church.

But what do we mean by the term 'church'? In a very general sense the Church is a community of faith, but this takes a great variety of forms. If we are thinking primarily of the institutional Church, the confessional family or the denomination, the Church often has a problematical relationship to its theologians, expecting them to concur uncritically in its teachings and its behaviour and taking it amiss when theologians ask hard questions or teach students to criticise church authorities. In recent times, for example, it has been interesting that the Roman Catholic Church has been willing to tolerate heterodox views on doctrinal matters, even very central ones, but has reacted strongly when theologians have raised questions about the authority structure of the Church and its hierarchical ministry. Churches of various traditions often expect 'their' theologians to be little more than channels for the authoritative teaching of the Church, disseminating rather than examining teaching delivered from on high, as it were.

It is, however, possible to have a sense of responsibility towards the Church which is not so tied to the present ecclesiastical institutional structures and systems. The ecumenical movement has already had a profound impact on the way theology is done and how theologians understand their task. Today the theological forum is thoroughly ecumenical and theological debate is not confined within confessional boundaries. In so far as theologians address a 'church public', that is usually understood in an ecumenical sense. They speak to and for an ecumenical Church which as yet has frail and provisional

---

[2] Alexander Dru (ed.), *The Journals of Kierkegaard 1834–1854*. London: Fontana, 1968, p. 44.

institutional expression, a Church which is the Church of the future, the coming Church.

Or again, there are theologians who see their churchward responsibility as focused on a Church understood in the light of the patristic adage, *ubi Christus ibi ecclesia*, where Christ is, there is the Church. This points towards a Church which is composed not only of believers or 'anonymous Christians' (in Karl Rahner's terminology), but of those for whom Jesus had a special care – the poor, weak, marginalised and forgotten. This adds an important dimension to the theologians' responsibility, as it does to the development of a proper ecclesiology.

There are, of course, dangers in the idea of a 'church theology', some of which have been identified in the South African *Kairos Document*, which denounced what it labelled 'church theology' almost as vigorously as it denounced 'state theology'.[3] The Kairos theologians accused liberal church theology, as they saw it in South Africa in the struggle against apartheid, of expressing itself in bland and inoffensive pronouncements which were sometimes no more than platitudes. These, they suggest, were never based on serious in-depth analysis of the situation, or sustained attempts to 'discern the signs of the times'. Above all, church theologians never said anything which would call down official retaliation on the Church, or endanger the interests of the Church; they 'rely upon a few stock ideas derived from Christian tradition and then uncritically and repeatedly applied to our situation'.[4]

The Kairos theologians rejected church theology for almost the same reason that Karl Barth embraced the idea of *church* dogmatics. For Barth the Church represented an alternative *Volk* and a different vision, totally opposed to the Nazi notion of the Germanic *Volk* and the Reich that would last for a thousand years. The Kairos theologians saw the liberal white churches as too deeply implicated in apartheid and too timid to denounce a false gospel or offer an alternative and inclusive community which would be a demonstration of God's will for

[3] The Kairos Theologians, *The Kairos Document: Challenge to the Church*. London: British Council of Churches, 1986.
[4] In Charles Villa-Vicencio (ed.), *Between Christ and Caesar: Classic and Contemporary Texts on Church and State*, p. 256.

all humankind. A similar point was made very strongly by Martin
Luther King Jnr, in response to white liberals who questioned
his forms of direct action as 'unwise and untimely'. In his *Letter
from Birmingham Jail* he wrote:

> I must make two honest confessions to you, my Christian and Jewish
> brothers. First, I must confess that over the last few years I have
> been gravely disappointed with the white moderate. I have almost
> reached the regrettable conclusion that the Negro's great
> stumbling block is not the White Citizen's Council-er or the Ku
> Klux Klanner, but the white moderate who is more devoted to
> 'order' than to justice, who prefers a negative peace which is the
> absence of tension to a positive peace which is the presence of
> justice, who constantly says 'I agree with you in the goal you seek,
> but I can't agree with your methods of direct action,' who
> paternalistically believes that he can set the timetable for another
> man's freedom . . . Shallow understanding from people of good
> will is more frustrating than absolute misunderstanding from
> people of ill will.[5]

There is another danger in church theology, that of becoming
the in-house language of a ghetto which has hardly any lines
of communication open to the outside world. When this
happens, as among the Amish people in America, outsiders
look to the Church as a quaint and irrelevant survival, a
fascinating museum-piece without broader relevance, whose
language and gospel are unintelligible outside. Ghettos can
sometimes be comfortable places, quite reconciled to being
different but no longer interested in mission, recruitment, or
the communication of a message which has relevance to
everyone.

Stanley Hauerwas has been accused of being a sectarian intent
on preserving the Christian message uncontaminated by contact
with the outside world.[6] He believes that faith must be embodied
in practice. The Mennonite, John Howard Yoder, taught him
that

[5] Martin Luther King, *I Have a Dream: Writing and Speeches that Changed the World*.
San Francisco: HarperCollins, 1992, p. 91. Cited in Ched Myers et al., *'Say to This
Mountain': Mark's Story of Discipleship*, pp. 156–7.
[6] Particularly by James Gustafson. A good discussion of the whole issue is in
David Fergusson, *Community, Liberalism and Christian Ethics*. Cambridge: Cambridge
University Press, 1998, pp. 64–7.

The most orthodox Christological or Trinitarian affirmations are essentially false when they are embedded in lives and social practices which make it clear that it makes no difference whether Jesus lived, died, or was resurrected.[7]

To cut a long story short, Hauerwas and his allies are endeavouring to ensure that a distinctive gospel message is addressed to the world. If they hesitate to embrace the world's agenda, or reject the use of the language of everyday secular life, it is because they believe they have something different and important to offer to public debate.

Turning to the academy as the site in which much theology is done and as a community to which many theologians feel a loyalty and have a sense of responsibility, the first thing to note is that theology is not the only discipline which relates to a community outside the academy. Medicine, law, social work and many other disciplines have a recognised responsibility to professional bodies outside the academy, while it is far less clear that other subjects like philosophy, classics or history have a distinct constituency outside to which they are accountable. But the academy as a whole has, or ought to have, a sense of being accountable to the broader society rather than simply carrying on some self-evidently justifiable activity. More and more often academics are being asked to explain and defend the usefulness and importance of what they do. And if they are wise they respond positively to such requests but resist the suggestion that every subject should be able to demonstrate its immediate usefulness. Church theologians would argue that theology can play a significant role in the university and, through them, the university can help the churches to operate in society with rigour and relevance.

In the past theology was often regarded as the Queen of the Sciences, the co-ordinating subject which was at the heart of the academic enterprise and held together the whole. In a secular, pluralist age this is no longer acceptable. The modern university has no central co-ordinating discipline, no Queen among the subjects. To have theology as the Queen of the Sciences was a very Constantinian assumption, which may have

---

[7] Stanley Hauerwas, *Dispatches from the Front: Theological Engagements with the Secular*. Durham, NC: Duke University Press, 1994, p. 23.

been acceptable while the idea of Christendom flourished, but is now obsolete. And this may perhaps free theology to fulfil its own modest servant role as it grapples with great questions: Can theology accept the standards and the tests of truth which are characteristic of the modern liberal university? Does it speak the language of the university, or does it have a language of its own? Can it speak Christian truth in the context of today's pluralist academy?

The Third Public

David Tracy argues that most theologians in fact seek to address three publics. We have already discussed two of these – the academy and the Church. The third public, and for our present purposes the most important, is the public of society. For Tracy this encompasses three spheres: first, the techno-economic structure which is concerned with the organisation and distribution of goods and services; second, the polity, concerned with the legitimate deployment of power, the implementation of justice and the control of conflict; and third, the sphere of culture, concerned with a huge variety of forms of symbolic expression.[8] Tracy is concerned to reaffirm 'the authentically *public* character of *all* theology',[9] while different branches of theology primarily address different publics:

> In terms of primary reference groups, *fundamental* theologies are related to the public represented but not exhausted by the academy. *Systematic* theologies are related primarily to the public represented but not exhausted in the church, here understood as a community of moral and religious discourse and action. *Practical* theologies are related primarily to the public of society, more exactly to the concerns of some particular social, political, cultural or pastoral movement or problematic which is argued or assumed to possess major religious import.[10]

Thus for Tracy the primary engagement of practical theology is with the public square and the debates and issues which arise there. This is not, of course, in any way a distinctively modern

---

[8] Tracy, *The Analogical Imagination*, pp. 6–7.
[9] Tracy, *The Analogical Imagination*, p. 55.
[10] Tracy, *The Analogical Imagination*, p. 57.

engagement. Lessons, positive and negative, can be learned from history for the appropriate form of theology's involvement in the public realm in the perplexing circumstances of today.

Confessional Public Theology

Theological contributions to public debate are, or ought to be, a way of confessing the faith, a part of the mission of the Church, a form of evangelism. Public debate, in other words, presents an opportunity and indeed an obligation to witness to the truth of the gospel and denounce false gospels; it is not simply a place where wisdom derived from the Christian tradition is offered to help resolve tricky issues on the public agenda. Christian public theology at its heart is gospel, precisely because it is Christian. And because it is confessional it must take the context in which it operates with profound seriousness.

Kierkegaard in a real sense anticipated a world that is as post-modern as it is post-Christendom. The condition of post-modernity is a pluralist society in which not only are many theories and world-views allowed and tolerated but there is a profound suspicion of grand theories and theologies, of systems which make claim to truth. These are essentially seen as coercive and inadequate to reality. Society, *pace* Rawls and others, does not need a consensus to survive, according to the post-modernists. Indeed, consensus can only be achieved by force or manipulation. It inherently involves a limitation of freedom, which in a fairly straightforward sense becomes the great central value of postmodernity. There is, in Lyotard's words, a profound 'incredulity towards metanarratives'.[11] The postmodern mind knows itself to be homeless; but it also recognises that no home exists. The mindset is melancholy and anxious, but it is also willing to come to terms with the fragmentation of reality and refuses to impose an artificial and fragile order upon it.

Postmodernists typically see the East European communist dictatorships that collapsed nearly a decade ago as both an exemplification of the Enlightenment project and its nemesis. Václav Havel would probably decline to call himself a

---

[11] Cited in Stephen K. White, *Political Theory and Postmodernism*. Cambridge: Cambridge University Press, 1991, pp. 4–5.

postmodernist, but his analysis of Czechoslovakia under the communists has a postmodernist flavour. Havel saw the death throes of the old communist regimes as indicative of a far more extensive and profound crisis that could perhaps be called the collapse of modernity, the Enlightenment project having run its course. The sad communist systems were 'a kind of warning to the West, revealing its own latent tendencies'.[12] The East holds up a mirror to the West; both are modernist societies in deep crisis. The system – and Havel clearly means both the old Marxist systems, where decay, decadence and demoralisation were easy to discern, and the societies of the West, where decline is more concealed – depends on ideology, whose function 'is to provide people . . . with the illusion that the system is in harmony with the human order and the order of the universe'. Ideology legitimates power and oppressive dictatorship, for it pervasively suggests that 'the centre of power is identical with the centre of truth'.[13] Ideology – overtly in the old Marxist regimes, more covertly in other modernist societies – is thus the main pillar of the system which effectively creates and internalises a false reality: 'It is built upon lies. It works only as long as people are willing to live within the lie.'[14]

Havel's diagnosis may be, at least superficially, postmodernist, but his response is not. He does not despair of knowing and living in truth, of witnessing to truth, either in unitary ideological despotisms or in conditions of pluralism and thoroughgoing relativism. He comprehensively rejects the modernist project of rebuilding the world according to some great rational scheme, especially a scheme that promises the overcoming of the human condition and a future contrived perfection. But Havel affirms the primary importance of 'togetherness', particularly that form which is 'being for' others.[15] And in this he reminds us of the unavoidable centrality of the Church in Christian theology.

Others, such as Alasdair MacIntyre, see the postmodern condition as a predicament. Modern society, for MacIntyre, is

[12] Václav Havel, *Living in Truth*. London: Faber, 1987, p. 54.
[13] Havel, *Living in Truth*, p. 39.
[14] Havel, *Living in Truth*, p. 50.
[15] See Zygmunt Bauman, *Life in Fragments: Essays in Post-modern Morality*. Oxford: Blackwell, 1995, pp. 44–55.

morally fragmented, since there are no generally accepted criteria for the resolution of moral disputes and conflicts.[16] No widely recognised moral framework exists; the situation is volatile, for behaviour lacks a rationale, or a place in a larger scheme which makes some claim to truth. The moral fragments that survive today were embedded and embodied in various traditions and practices which are, for the most part, dismissed as discredited and irrelevant survivals among deviant minorities. We cannot understand moral standards properly, MacIntyre believes, without situating these fragments in the context of the traditions of moral inquiry from which they originally came and from which they have become detached. Only if we take seriously the traditions of moral inquiry, he believes, will we be able to make progress towards resolving key issues of today.

Both MacIntyre and the postmodernists recognise that fragmentation is characteristic of the contemporary world. The postmodernists celebrate this fact; MacIntyre laments it as a grave predicament. I would argue that from the angle of the Christian mission we should recognise that fragmentation presents opportunities and challenges which are at the same time fresh and also have striking similarities to the situation in the ancient world when the Christian faith was born. We can learn from the early Church how to witness to the truth in a fragmented age. Whether fragmentation is a predicament or an emancipation, the gospel can be proclaimed in a fragmented age. That is the immediate task. Whether MacIntyre is right in suggesting that we should work towards a new Christian consensus on Aristotelian and Thomist foundations is a question we may leave aside for a while. My own inclination is that the establishment or restoration of some general consensus based on Christian foundations is inconceivable for the foreseeable future and probably, in the light of historical experience, undesirable. Today we have to witness to the truth in a world in fragments.

Disputes about justice and goodness which appear to be irresolvable represent not only academic difficulties but major problems of practice for people 'on the ground', as it were; hence they become pressing issues for Christian mission and

---

[16] Alasdair MacIntyre, *After Virtue*, pp. 104–5.

public theology. Politics and policy-making easily degenerate into, in MacIntyre's telling phrase, 'civil war carried on by other means',[17] an arena in which interest groups compete for control, using ideas as weapons rather than constraints and as justifications for volatile policy changes which in fact are little influenced by overarching moral considerations. Or the ideological pendulum swings from one extreme to another without the reasons for the change being clear or generally acceptable

Practitioners often feel that they are making do with fragments of moral insight which are frequently in unacknowledged conflict with other fragments, or are not recognised in the way the system or institution is run. And practitioners sometimes recognise that the fragments which are most important for them as insights into reality, as in some sense *true* and central to the sense of vocation which sustains them in their practice, are derived from a tradition which was and is nurtured in a community of shared faith to which they may or may not belong, and which is now a minority view in society. There is a widespread awareness that the foundations of practice have been shaken.

A fragmentary theology assumes that in this life we never see save 'in a mirror dimly', and only at the end 'face to face'.[18] This might make us more generally cautious about regarding theology as some grand coherent modernist theory instead of a series of illuminating fragments that sustain the life of the community of faith which nurtures them and claim also to be in some sense 'public truth'. After all, the gospels and even the epistles do not present a 'system'. Rather, they are full of parables, stories, epigrams, injunctions, songs – fragments, in short. The system-building came far later and it is still not easy to co-ordinate the material into a coherent, consistent system. Perhaps theologians should sympathise with the postmodernists' suspicion of systems and system building! Is it perhaps enough, with the man born blind, to know one thing with assurance: 'once I was blind; now I see' (John 9.25)?

---

[17] MacIntyre, *After Virtue*, p. 236.
[18] 1 Corinthians 13.12.

The Decay of Public Discourse

Many people are struck by the impoverishment of Western political discourse as revealed, for example, in recent election campaigns. Politicians operate in public almost entirely in terms of slogans and sound-bites. Issues believed to be sensitive, or likely to worry or alienate any group of voters, are sedulously sidelined and forgotten. Reforms, changes and improvements are presented as far as possible as involving no cost. Most politicians are afraid to suggest increasing personal taxation in order to benefit the community. Complex issues like poverty, world development, disarmament and redistribution seem to disappear from the agenda. There is precious little talk of visions of the future and hardly a suggestion that sacrifices might be required from some for the sake of others, or now for the sake of a better future.

In lack-lustre election campaigns two processes seem to come together. On the one hand, they suggest that Daniel Bell's 'End of Ideology' has in fact arrived after many premature announcements. The collapse of the Marxist regimes of Eastern Europe has left behind a profound distrust of ideology and grand overarching theories, partly for the very good reason that they are so effective at concealing what is really going on, disguising corruption and self-interest with 'the illusion that the system is in harmony with the human order and the order of the universe' (Havel). For the moment, at least, nothing has taken the place of the old comprehensive ideologies, which for all their defects and problems were at least sometimes able to constrain selfishness and locate political activity within a larger horizon than horse-trading.

The other, more immediate, reason for the decay of political discourse is the desperation of political parties to hang on to power. Ideological baggage that is uncongenial to any signifi-cant section of the electorate is jettisoned and in the process much of the vision that had elicited the deepest commitment in the past is also set aside. Lurking behind this is, of course, the deeper problem of how politics can be conducted in a radically secular society in which many people believe religious and theological views have no place or standing, while others fear that a society deprived of religion may quickly become inhumane and incoherent.

This is also the context within which we have to understand the strange renaissance of political religion and the powerful phenomenon of conviction politics which first emerged in Britain with Mrs Thatcher and is continued in rather different form by Tony Blair. There are people around once more in positions of influence who claim that Christianity is true and that it is necessary for healthy social life. We have today in Britain the resurgence of the Christian Socialist Movement and that redoubtable Anglo-Catholic MP, Frank Field, arguing that the fundamental defect of the welfare settlement of the 1940s was that it was based on a simplistic and over-sunny account of human nature. A Christian understanding of human nature, which takes both the *grandeur* and the *misère* of the human condition on board, would provide, he suggests, a far better, because truer, basis for welfare provision and policy.

In such a situation, the churches feel a special responsibility to contribute to public debate and to try both to enrich it theologically and to root it in the kind of realities which the Church as people knows at first hand. And the electorate now looks with almost unprecedented expectancy to the churches and to theology to make constructive and significant contributions to public debate.

Two Ways of Doing Public Theology Today

There are two broad and different ways in which a public theology may be articulated: the *magisterial*, in which the Church and theology claim to teach authoritatively, from above as it were; and the *liberationist*, in which the concrete message comes from below, arising out of real experiences and struggles on the ground. These two approaches correspond roughly to two quite closely related, but distinct, documents which appeared during the 1997 British election campaign as conscious attempts to influence the agenda and enrich the discourse of election-eering: the English Roman Catholic Bishops' paper on *The Common Good*, and the Conference of Churches of Britain and Ireland's report of an inquiry into *Unemployment and the Future of Work*.

The first is purely Roman Catholic in provenance, but consciously addresses a broader audience. It draws on a coherent and impressive body of social teaching which it believes to be public truth, capable of commending itself on strictly rational grounds to many who are not Catholics or Christians. The second is an ecumenical document which has its roots in a very much more complex, variegated and confusing tradition of social theology and draws quite extensively on insights from liberation theology.

Magisterial Public Theology

The Common Good is a magisterial document in every sense of that term. It takes very seriously the calling of the bishops to teach in social matters as well as in doctrine and personal ethics. It claims to draw on a coherent, incremental body of universally valid social teaching, believed to be accessible in principle to all, although the bishops clearly believe that the truth of this teaching is reinforced and exemplified in the Christian revelation. Drawing on this teaching, the bishops nevertheless recognise limits to their competence. Most specific issues and political and economic choices have in fact to be made by the responsible people within the authoritative horizon established by Catholic social teaching. What the bishops offer is more a framework for moral and political discourse than an engagement with particular details of policy. They set out emphases, principles and directions rather than specific policies.

If I am right in thinking that *The Common Good* essentially offers a framework or a method rather than policy conclusions, we can relate it to recent similar moves in the United States. A number of prominent US Catholic theologians, most notably Dennis McCann, Richard Neuhaus and George Weigel, are proposing a natural law framework for American public discourse. Their position draws heavily on the work of John Courtney Murray and is a response to a conviction that in pluralist America today political discourse is at the mercy of both special interests and ideological distortion. McCann in particular seeks to provide ground rules for public discourse in the face of ideologies and interest groups which threaten to fragment the conversation, reducing it to mutually incomprehensible sloganising, or turning the discourse into a battle in which (in MacIntyre's phrase) politics becomes civil war carried on by other means.[19] Catholics should, McCann suggests, offer the natural law approach of Catholic social teach-ing as a structural resource for public debate and adjudicating between the claims of various interest groups. The present fragmentation is acutely dangerous, these thinkers believe; theologians aware of this threat may act as 'facilitators who teach the rest of us the basic skills necessary for the intelligent use of the community's "moral language"'.[20] McCann, Weigel and others are deeply concerned at the danger of ideological domination of the public forum, so that the biggest battalions or those who shout loudest always win and justice becomes (in Thrasymachus' phrase) the interest of the strongest. A natural law framework as in Catholic social teaching might offset this danger, they believe, by providing a resource for rational resolution of issues in the light of first principles. American society, Weigel and Neuhaus believe, is at a 'Catholic moment' in which coherent ethical discourse based on Catholic understandings of natural law might give the Church a leading role in public moral discourse.

McCann and his colleagues are thus rather like Chesterton's monk, insisting that there should be a return to first principles.[21] And they believe that there is such a depth of concern at the quality and the consequences of contemporary public debate that people might now at last be ready to hearken to the monk.

The process of discussion which led to the drafting of the US Catholic bishops' earlier pastoral letters on war and peace and the economy[22] is suggested by McCann as a model of the kind of public discourse that he advocates, precisely because it allowed both the influential and the powerless to contribute to the discussion. For McCann, 'to keep everyone, including persons of influence, on board dialoguing, is deliberately to

---

[19] Dennis McCann, *New Experiments in Democracy* (London: Sheed & Ward, 1987) and (with Charles R. Strain), *Polity and Praxis: A Program for American Practical Theology*. Minneapolis: Winston, 1985. My discussion draws on W. D. Lindsey, 'Public Theology as Civil Discourse: What Are We Talking About?' *Horizons*, 19/1 (1992), 44–69.

[20] McCann, *New Experiments*, p. 96.

[21] G. K. Chesterton, *Heretics*, pp. 23–4; see above, p. 22.

[22] More recent pastoral letters are much less interesting, both in terms of method and content.

cultivate forms of solidarity and participation that could be just as much "covenantal and eschatological" as they are truly Catholic'.[23] He is right to suggest that such dialogue is extremely rare. More usually,

> The influential talk among themselves, assuredly, observing carefully the protocols of well-insulated hierarchies; and the marginalized share their egalitarian dreams, if at all, only in cries and whispers that even social activists have trouble deciphering.[24]

W. D. Lindsey, in a fascinating and polemical article, sees McCann's proposal as the imposing of a framework which claims neutrality and objectivity. It thus, he argues, must become 'a strategy of management that will "orchestrate" dissonant voices so that their unique tonalities will be muted and their specific textures suppressed'.[25] The structure of the argument, Lindsey claims, has pretensions of being disinterested and claims a kind of objectivity; but in fact it is intended to discipline all dissident voices, all positions which unashamedly claim to represent special interests, all other approaches which claim to be privileged. Both a 'preferential option for the poor' and a Niebuhrian understanding of the task as the balancing out of competing claims to reach a proximate and temporary settlement are excluded. McCann's position, claims Lindsey, is 'first and foremost *managerial* – a strategy for disciplining and silencing difficult Others'.[26]

The assumption that all positions are equally self-interested, and that Christianity comes in to provide a neutral framework within which competing claims can be adjusted, disguises, according to Lindsey, a managerial strategy, a longing to be at the heart of things. The Church and theology appear as legislator and law enforcer, the body, like the MCC or the Royal and Ancient Golf Club, which makes the rules and the referee or umpire who enforces them. It does not have interests of its own, or so it pretends, nor does it promote the special interests of any group. Its task is emphatically *not* attending to, incorporating, privileging or responding to the voice of the

---

[23] McCann, *New Experiments*, p. 141.
[24] McCann, *New Experiments*, p. 142.
[25] Lindsey, 'Public Theology as Civil Discourse', p. 51.
[26] Lindsey, 'Public Theology as Civil Discourse', p. 52

disempowered, the voiceless, the Other. It regulates the game magisterially, with authority, from the heart of things not from the margins, arbitrating from on high on the ebb and flow of the disputes in the public square.

Liberationist Public Theology

Lindsey underlines the problem and the difficulty in attending to, incorporating and responding to the voice of the disempowered, the voiceless, the Other. These voices are conspicuously absent from most of our theologies and only, I fear, heard rather *sotto voce* in *Unemployment and the Future of Work*, to which I now turn. This is unfortunate, for one of the main tasks of theology is surely to attend to and articulate the voice of the other, to give them a hearing when so much else, particularly in academic life, conspires to deny them a voice. Bishop David Sheppard spoke of the Working Party hearing a 'cry of pain' arising from 'a deep wound in the body, dividing those who are left out of decent opportunities from the favoured majority'.[27] And the report starts by recording that

> From our year of visiting all the countries and regions of Britain and Ireland, north and south, we have returned shocked and saddened by the sharpness of contrast we have found everywhere between a favoured majority on the one hand and those on the other who are left out.[28]

But the actual voice of the unemployed is rather rarely heard and then only when the terms of the discussion have already been clearly established, starting with general theological principles and then proceeding to careful social and economic analysis in which the voice of the expert, the policy-maker and the academic come across loud and clear.

For some of the members of the inquiry, visiting areas of high unemployment and encountering the human reality of worklessness was 'a mind-changing experience'.[29] The testimony of an unemployed man in South Wales is perhaps the most

---

[27] *Unemployment and the Future of Work*, p. v.
[28] *Unemployment and the Future of Work*, p. 1.
[29] *Unemployment and the Future of Work*, p. 54.

powerful passage in the whole report.[30] More of this sort of material would have immeasurably strengthened *Unemployment and the Future of Work*, especially if it had been allowed to set the terms of the discussion.

The general style of the report swings between a Royal Commission and a book of theology – two powerful and effective forms of discourse, which are also discourses of the powerful, although here presented in a quite popular and accessible form. Yet it speaks to the head rather than the heart. I don't think it was sufficiently calculated to promote empathy, to help us to *feel* that we belong together within the Body, to make us feel angry. I think I know why this was so. Confused, emotional, angry voices are disfranchised by the rules both of politics and the academy.

But within the Church there is occasionally a dynamic which I would like to have seen figure more prominently in the Report, because it is an important gift to society. I have seen that dull, respectable, middle-class body, a presbytery of the Church of Scotland, become angry as they listened to their fellow Christians from areas of deprivation speak about housing conditions, transport, health care, education, vandalism, and poverty in their parishes. And the presbytery's anger was a sign not only that they were listening, but that they were sharing emotion, that they were feeling accountable to one another, responsible for one another, members of one another. And I have seen academics in theology almost physically draw back, their body language proclaiming that this is no concern of ours, when angry, muddled, poor people interrupt serious, informed and well-intentioned debate about poverty, unemployment and homelessness and say first of all, 'You don't know what you're talking about'. In saying that, they were telling an uncomfortable truth which academics for the most part do not want to hear. And then they told their stories, usually in fragments, for, as Rilke said, 'The story of shattered life can be told only in bits and pieces'. It is a pity if the telling of these stories is left to the novelists (for Scotland one might instance James Kelman's *How Late It Was How Late* or Irving Welsh's *Trainspotting* as examples); for this surely is one of the tasks of theology and in particular

---

[30] *Unemployment and the Future of Work*, pp. 41–2.

of church theology: allowing the marginalised to tell their stories and relating them to the gospel story.

In many ways *Unemployment and the Future of Work* moved beyond the older middle axiom approach to public theology in the direction of liberation theology. In particular, like *Faith in the City* and *The Church and the Bomb*, it does not draw a sharp and impermeable curtain between middle axioms or principles and matters of application – specific policies and their implementation – considering the latter to be technical matters which can and should be left to the 'experts'. This is an important move for various reasons, two of which seem to me to be particularly significant. The first is expressed particularly effectively by R. H. Tawney when he said that to state a principle without its application is irresponsible and unintelligible.[31] The second is this: the press and indeed the general public read church and other similar reports backwards. If the conclusions and recommendations are striking, distinctive, controversial and constructive, they then read the rest to discover if these conclusions and recommendations come from an interesting source and line of argument. Filing cabinets are full of church reports that were arduously produced and raised not a ripple of interest because they were believed to be vacuous and over-cautious. *Unemployment and the Future of Work* is not one of these. It will continue to be discussed seriously for a long time to come and will then find its place in the history books. Its bold specificity is an important part of its value.

Unemployment and the Future of Work, if it does not highlight to any great extent experience, emotion and voices from the margin, does follow the older tradition of Christian social ethics by taking social science and 'the facts of the case', particularly as presented by the economists, with a seriousness amounting to reverence. My secular social scientist friends who specialise in issues of work and unemployment think very highly of *Unemployment and the Future of Work*. They find its approach and its conclusions and recommendations congenial. But I do not get the impression that they feel that the *theology* of the report is either particularly gripping or particularly illuminating.

[31] R. H. Tawney, *'The Attack' and Other Papers*, p. 178.

Which brings me directly to the theology of *Unemployment and the Future of Work*. I am an advocate of church theology, believing that theology is rooted in the community of faith as much as in the academy. There is theology, and church theology, in the report, particularly at the start, in the chapter on what the churches can do, and in the appendices. I like what I read. But it is not much, and if one compares the theology of the report with its economics it is hard to conclude that the theology is as thorough, serious or focused as the economics. It would not be easy to argue that theology provides the framework for the document. This is, of course, more a criticism of the state of British social theology than of the theology of *Unemployment and the Future of Work*. It is sad that we seem to have made so little progress in social theology since *Faith in the City*. I hope other theologians will join me in saying *mea culpa*!

Unemployment and the Future of Work is an ecumenical report, by far the most significant such report for many years. It is to be warmly welcomed as such. But it is a little disappointing that the ecumenical nature of the inquiry does not seem to have opened up the broad range of neglected possibilities – perspectives from the Continent, the WCC, Africa and Latin America – to enliven the still slightly cosy British scene, asking fundamental theological questions about the nature and the dangers of work, about our global responsibilities for one another and accountability to one another, about dignity, creativity and identity, about the power of the powerless and the privilege of the marginalised. Some of this is there in *Unemployment and the Future of Work*, sometimes in rather embryonic form. More would have been welcome.

What we have here is a distinguished contribution to public debate and public theology, worthy to be set alongside *Faith in the City* and *The Church and the Bomb* as major landmarks in the churches' exercise of their responsibility in and for British society today. It moves in a liberationist direction, but falls short of being a liberation theology contextualised in Britain.

9

The Public Church Reborn

What do we mean when we talk about *public* theology?

It is easiest perhaps to say what public theology is not. It is not the in-house chatter or domestic housekeeping of a sect, concerned above all with its own inner life and with little interest in what goes on outside. It is not a form of discourse which is obscure and inaccessible except to initiates into some arcane mystery. It is not technical language which may be quite sophisticated in its own terms, but which fails to communicate in any significant way to people outside a charmed circle. It is not a self-justifying academic jargon, opaque to all except specialists. It does not generate its own agenda and proceed as if nothing of importance is happening in the public realm. It is not obsessed with keeping a particular ecclesiastical system 'on the road', without change or challenge. It is not the ritual incantation of ancient formulae. It is not defensive, eager to hide or obscure processes that are happening in the depths; nor is it consciously exclusive of those who are outside the circle of initiates. It is not domesticated and tamed within a particular class or community.

No – public theology is rather a theology, talk about God, which claims to point to publicly accessible truth, to contribute to public discussion by witnessing to a truth which is relevant to what is going on in the world and to the pressing issues facing people and societies today. It does not generate its own agenda, nor does it simply take over the world's agenda. Indeed, an important part of its task is to identify and address the deep underlying issues that are often too painful or awkward for politicians and others to address in public debate, and to identify the coming agenda, the issues that people will be wrestling with in a few months or years. It takes the public square and what goes on there seriously, but it tries to articulate in the public square its convictions about truth and goodness. It offers convictions, challenges and insights derived from the tradition of which it is a steward, rather than seeking to articulate a consensus or reiterate what everyone is saying anyway.

Public theology is thus confessional and evangelical. It has a gospel to share, good news to proclaim. Public theology attends to the Bible and the tradition of faith at the same time as it attempts to discern the signs of the times and understand what is going on in the light of the gospel.

Discernment

But what is the discernment of which I am speaking?

The signs of the times discussed in the gospels[1] are manifestations of a new order latent in the disorder of the day, ready to emerge from the womb of the past. The scribes and Pharisees wanted a sign authenticating Jesus and the message of the Reign of God which he preached. They wanted all doubt removed. They sought certainty before they decided how to respond. They were not willing to take a risk. They wanted a sign so that they could be sure beyond a shadow of a doubt that the Jesus movement was the manifestation of the Reign of God before they responded to Jesus, before they did anything, before they joined the new community, before they committed themselves. They wanted proof, certainty, before they decided how to respond to this strange, compelling teacher and his call to discipleship.

And in the narrative, those who seek for a sign at the beginning, before they chance their arm, before they respond to the needs and sufferings of the world, are condemned by Jesus as an evil and adulterous generation. This generation is on the make, looking after its own interests, putting number one first, because its affections are free-floating and unattached.

---

[1] Matthew 12.38–42 and 16.1–4; Luke 11.16, 29–32; Mark 8.11–12.

It cries out in a childish way for certainty where no certainty is to be had. It calls for a sign. But no sign will be given it, except the sign of Jonah.

What is this sign? Jonah was one who witnessed to the new order despite himself. He tried to avoid the call of God; he ran away. And finally he reluctantly and dyspeptically denounced the Ninevites and their ways and settled down under a bush to witness their deserved destruction, which would be, he thought, a clear sign of the vitality of the divine justice. But to his chagrin, the Ninevites attended to the proclamation of the Reign of God. They repented and Nineveh was spared: a sign of the mercy and the love of God that infuriated Jonah. He was rather like the scribes and Pharisees who had asked for a sign: stewards of a true message, but treating it in a mechanical way as if it were a possession; refusing to recognise that the call to repentance is addressed to them in their self-righteousness first of all.

The Ninevites repented and thus embraced the Reign of God, having discerned the sign in penitence and hope. Is penitence perhaps the condition for true discernment? Is it only when we admit our own implication in suspicion, misunderstanding, prejudice, hostility and violence that we become able to discern the signs of the times? Are penitence and humility the path to insight, and arrogance and self-righteousness the way to lies? Hypocrisy and self-centredness, individual or collective, impede discernment. Pride stops us from discerning in events God's ever-renewed offers of judgement and opportunity. Humility is the key to discernment. Only in the penitent joy of encountering the God of history do we find that discernment is a gift of grace.

The other side of the sign of Jonah, is of course, the not very plausible analogy between the strange and incredible story of Jonah in the belly of the whale and the no less strange and far more disturbing story of the death and resurrection of Jesus. Here we find the great central sign of the Reign of God, given afresh to every generation and reflected again and again in human history, to be discerned whenever life emerges from death, hope from despair, joy from sadness. Although the Queen of the South came seeking wisdom and discerned it from afar, an evil and adulterous generation is too proud and fickle to focus its attention on this sign and discern the signs of the times in the light of the Jesus-event. Here is the new order growing secretly in the midst of the chaos and violence of the world, a reality which is only to be discerned by faith, not by formula.

Strangely and ominously, the gospel narratives stress that the scribes and Pharisees, for all their inherited scriptural wisdom and knowledge of God's people's experience of God's activity in history, were unable to read the signs of the times. The signs require a different sort of discernment from that of the scribes and Pharisees. It is not easy for intellectuals, for people of status and position, to discern that the emperor has no clothes on, and that a new and different order, the Reign of God, is breaking in. But sometimes discernment happens.

How then do we discern the signs of the times? Discernment is certainly not a mechanical process, the application of simple clues, principles or guidelines from Scripture or elsewhere. Intellectuals, theologians and ecclesiastics probably have special difficulties in discernment, because they have so often lost simplicity of vision and fallen into the grip of systems or ideologies which conceal at least as much as they reveal, so that they are not open to the radically new. To discern we need to recover true simplicity. Discernment means putting the events, choices and responses of today within the frame of eternity, taking the long view, with attitudes and understanding shaped by faith and imbued with hope.

And such discernment can lead to new and challenging insights in the public realm.

Public Theology and the Church

I would suggest that the discernment which we call Christian public theology is inevitably ecclesial, a church theology which is rooted in the life of the Church and cannot be severed from the Church without losing its integrity and authenticity. But it is not an *ideology* of the Church, in the sense of a theory justifying the life and the structures of the Church as they exist today. It relates not simply to the Church as it is here and now, but to the future Church, the Church as God wills the Church to be. It is highly critical of churches that are concerned for themselves and their own interests rather than for the Reign of God and the cosmos that God loved so much that he sent his Son for its salvation. It is a theology in critical solidarity with the Church, a theology which helps the Church to open out to the world in love and service. A classic account of sin is being *incurvatus in se*, turned in on oneself. This is as true of institutions as it is of individuals. A faithful public theology helps the Church to escape from its faithless self-obsession and seek once more to fulfil its mission in the world.

Public theology as I see it understands the Church, even in its weakness and faithlessness, as a sign and instrument of the Reign of God, as a kind of working model to which we can point in fear and trembling. Even allowing for all its defects and inadequacies, the Church is a strange, unique community extended in space and time, extraordinary in its inclusiveness and calling, nurturing expectation, hope and reconciliation.

And the Church, of course, takes different form in varying ages and cultural contexts. Sometimes it has been at the heart of things, exercising immense power over people's lives, determining the shape of the community and the standards by which people live, itself possessing great wealth and owning vast lands. The Constantinian Church was a very ambiguous sign. For the centuries from Constantine until the nineteenth century, this was the common shape of the Church. But the early Church was different. It was a small minority which saw its message and its role as public, which was taught to see itself as existing for others, as the salt of the earth, the leaven of the lump, a servant community gathered around a servant Lord.

And the public sphere is constantly changing too, as we shall see shortly. Simultaneously, and paradoxically, it has become globalised and fragmented. An increasingly secular and pluralistic public sphere is commonly hostile or uncomprehending towards public theology and the Christian Church. And theology, for its part, finds it hard to know how to confess the faith in this new world, how to discern its opportunities and responsibilities in witnessing to truth in the modern age. Sometimes today theologians are positively intimidated by the challenges and uncertainties facing them at every turn.

I for my part wish to argue that Christian contributions to public debate are, or ought to be, a way of confessing the faith,

a part of the mission of the Church, a form of evangelism. Public
debate, in other words, presents an opportunity and indeed an
obligation to witness to the truth of the gospel; it is not simply a
place where wisdom derived from the Christian tradition is
offered to help resolve tricky issues on the public agenda.
Christian public theology at its heart is gospel, precisely because
it is Christian.

In order to develop this theme I start with some history. My
assumption is that modern political culture has become highly
fragmented and that this fragmentation leads to both difficulties
and opportunities in theory and practice; it provides the context
within which a 'challenging and constructive enculturation' of
the gospel is possible today.

Augustine and Pagan Public Theology

In the twilight of the ancient world, confronted with the
charge that Christianity, the 'new religion', was in some sense
responsible for the collapse of the Roman *imperium* in face of
the barbarian onslaughts, Augustine developed a public
theology which was also a theology of history, or at least a set of
guidelines for discerning the signs of the times, and an emphatic
repudiation of the pagan public theology of the empire.
Augustine's *De Civitate Dei* was, in Peter Brown's words, both 'a
deliberate confrontation with paganism'[2] and a major effort of
theological construction which amounted to a specific
confession of the faith in a particular historical context. Pagan
public theologies and their Christian reflections and imitations
saw the development of the Roman Empire as being the subject
of history; they could not accommodate the possibility that the
empire might degenerate and collapse and that such an event
might be in any sense a judgement of God. Augustine, in
contrast, affirmed that the Roman Empire was, and always had
been, corrupt. It had been founded by a gang of robbers led by
Romulus, demonstrating the general truth that earthly states
without justice are bands of robbers and robber bands are states
in miniature.[3] It is not legitimate, Augustine suggested, to

---

[2] Peter Brown, *Augustine of Hippo – a Biography*. London: Faber, 1967, p. 312.
[3] *De Civitate Dei* III:4.

sacralise the empire or any other political system for that matter. Even the best of existing systems are provisional, partial and defective. The earthly city has no claim on our ultimate allegiance; only God and the heavenly city deserve unconditional loyalty. The gospel is not the good news of the *Pax Romana*.

Augustine's public theology refuses to deify any temporal order, even that of the Church visible, as it strives to interpret the signs of the times in the light of God's purpose to bring the heavenly city into which the elect will be gathered, and in which people are bound together by sharing the highest love, the love of God. Only in the heavenly city, the city of God, are true justice, peace and fellowship to be found. Thus Augustine affirms in the strongest terms the spiritual significance of the temporal order, while excluding it from the sphere of the sacred. Public life in the temporal city needs to be challenged, illumined and nourished by the gospel. Only in relation to the heavenly city can the earthly city be understood aright as either a gang of robbers held together by their love of power and riches, or as a band of pilgrims lovingly seeking the city whose builder and maker is God. Challenging the adequacy, justice and finality of the earthly city is in fact for Augustine a way of proclaiming the gospel.

Augustine unhesitatingly rejects the three kinds of theology presented by the Stoic Varro – mythical, natural (or philosophical) and political. He claimed that classical mythical and political theologies made no serious claim to truth, but were regarded as indispensable forms of social control, ways of legitimating the established order and ensuring loyalty and obedience. Natural or philosophical theology made an attempt to reach beyond the limits of the city to seek a more general truth, but it was commonly regarded as inherently seditious, something to be kept from the ears of the common people. Because it did not attend to revelation and confused nature with nature's God, philosophical theology, despite its pretensions, was doomed to futility.

In rejecting classical public theology Augustine was not rejecting public theology as such. Indeed, his own project in *De Civitate Dei* was the inauguration of a new style of public theology which related to the political order in a more subtle and

complex way than classical public theology because it saw its
task as speaking truth to power and interpreting history in the
light of the gospel, rather than explaining and justifying the
existing order. And the truth that is spoken to power can be
nothing other than the gospel, which is, for Augustine,
inescapably in the public square even when it concerns itself
with the soul and subjectivity. Augustine saw public theology as
speaking truth to power, as public confession of the faith, an
essential aspect of the mission of the Church.

The Christendom Project

Whether Christendom was the establishment or the subversion
of Christian faith is an issue that is still much debated.[4] In a
powerful book Oliver O'Donovan has recently sought to rehabilitate 'that centuries-long engagement with government
which we call "Christendom"'.[5] Christendom involved an
enlargement of the theological agenda. No longer was it
possible to avoid the dilemmas facing those who exercised
power. There was now a sustained and strenuous effort to shape
society by the gospel, for 'Those who ruled in Christendom
and those who thought and argued about government believed
that the gospel was true. They intended their institutions to
reflect Christ's coming reign.'[6] O'Donovan is right in suggesting
that in the Christendom era, when the truth of Christianity was
taken for granted as public truth, both church and the public
order were seen as witnesses to the Reign of God.

The conscious or stated intention of Christendom was the
proclamation and manifestation of the truth of the gospel. But
the reality was often very different. Often Christian public
theology came to perform the same functions in the same way
as the ancient pagan public theologies; old practices of
sacralising politics were revived and the political and
ecclesiastical orders (regarded as interdependent) were
absolutised. Old ways of thought about power, politics and

---

[4] See, for example, Alasdair Kee, *Constantine or Christ?* London: SCM Press, 1982.

[5] Oliver O'Donovan, *The Desire of the Nations: Rediscovering the Roots of Political
Theology.* Cambridge: Cambridge University Press, 1996, p. 193.

[6] O'Donovan, *The Desire of the Nations*, p. 194.

public life were reintroduced and often sat very uneasily alongside the worship of a crucified God.[7]

In both its forms, Byzantine and Western, Christendom meant the definitive entry of Christianity into the public realm, there to fulfil functions unthought of in the early days of the Church. These went far beyond prayer for, and obedience to, the authorities, the demystification of power and the claim that the great central images of the Christian faith – the Kingdom, the Lord, the City, and so on – have a public bearing on earth. Now the Church itself was a powerful institution and was looked to for support and guidance by the rulers, who repeatedly saw it as the ideological wing of government, and little more. Church leaders had to learn how to be chaplains to the powerful, not merely pastors of little flocks of the weak.[8]

If the intention of Christendom was faithfulness to truth, the reality was often ambiguous and contradictory. But this has been characteristic of mission and theology down the ages. And it ill becomes us, after the century of two world wars and the Holocaust, the Rwanda genocide and the horrors of Bosnia and Kosovo, to despise the Christendom project. And yet, in recognising that Christendom was never a monolithic uniformity, but comprehended a diversity of often conflicting impulses, it becomes difficult either to endorse Oliver O'Donovan's attempt to rehabilitate Christendom or to denounce Christendom as unqualified apostasy after the style of Alasdair Kee. Christendom in fact was both a project noble in its conception, something that was almost inevitable as Christianity became the majority faith, and also a drastic adulteration of the gospel. We must not forget that under Charlemagne whole tribes were forced to convert at the point of the sword, and were baptised by hosepipe as it were. The history of Christendom was punctuated with pogroms against the Jews, bloodthirsty crusades against the Muslims and massacres of Albigensians.

And when Christendom began to expand across the Atlantic the record was even more ambiguous. 1492 represents in a sense the apogee of Christendom. Columbus sailed the ocean blue

---

[7] See my *Theology and Politics*. Oxford: Blackwell, 1988, p. 58.
[8] D. B. Forrester, op. cit., pp. 28–9.

in order to conquer and convert the new world, absorbing it into Christendom. In 1992, while some people celebrated 'the evangelisation of the Americas', others denounced the genocide of native American peoples and the prolonged plunder of the Americas for the sake of Europe. The Conquistadors, extending the bounds of Christendom, read this royal *Requerimiento* to the chieftains of the tribes they encountered:

> I ask and require of you . . . that you recognise the Church as sovereign over the entire universe, in her name the Supreme Pontiff called Pope, and the King and Queen . . . as your superior lords . . . to consent and permit the priests to preach to you. If you do this, you do well and their Royal Highnesses and I will receive you with all love and charity. But, if you do not do this . . . with the help of God I will enter powerfully against you and will war against you everywhere and in every way that I can. And I will subjugate you in obedience to the Church and their Royal Highnesses. I will take you, your women and children, will enslave you and as such will sell you . . . and I will take your belongings and will do unto you all the harm and evil that it is in my power to do.[9]

Also in 1492, it was finally decreed that all Jews and Moors must leave the territory of Spain. Ethnic cleansing is not an invention of the twentieth century. Internally the Inquisition maintained the semblance of orthodoxy.

Many saw Christendom as a glorious vision, but with hindsight its awful ambiguity is only too obvious. At the heart of the ambiguity of the Christendom project regarded as an expression of the mission of the Church lay the question of the relationship between the gospel and power, an issue which is still omni-present in the practice and discussion of mission. If mission is very centrally concerned with speaking truth to power and announcing the good news that the powers have been subjected to Christ, what happens when mission is subtly transformed into speaking truth *from* power? This unavoidable issue is at the heart of the discussion of public theology today. And with the collapse of Christendom in the sense of a social and political order which claims to be founded on Christian truth and

---

[9] Quoted in two sixteenth-century documents: Fernandez de Oviedo, *Historia natural y general de las Indias* and Fr Las Casas, *Teoria y leves de la conquista*. See Luis N. Rivera Pagan, *Evangelizacion y Violencia: La Conquista de America*. Puerto Rico: Ediciones SEMI, 1991, p. 53. Translation by Guillermo Cook.

recognises to some extent Christian constraints on the use of power, Christian public theology faces new problems and fresh opportunities.

Universalising Modernity

The disintegration or fragmentation of Christendom in the sixteenth and seventeenth centuries – although the Western world remains full of potent remnants and relics – laid the foundations for a new scheme of order. The Enlightenment project of building a tolerant, liberal and rational world was on every count impressive both in its conception and its achievements. The West has been deeply marked by the Enlightenment in a way that many other parts of the world have not. A fundamental assumption of the Enlightenment intellect was that society can get along perfectly well – indeed far better than in unenlightened times – without particularistic religion in the public realm, or with religion firmly relegated to the private and domestic sphere. Kant, for instance, argued in his *Perpetual Peace* (1795) that the peace of the social and political order must be established on ahistorical and universal rational moral principles. These may be 'affirmed and ennobled' by religious beliefs, but the beliefs themselves have a marginal role and in the last analysis are dispensable. In the Enlightenment, public theology for the most part became an embellished form of political philosophy capable, for instance, of accommodating Adam Smith's economics as a department of natural theology. Despite the avowedly secular nature of the discourse, the tendency was increasingly to sacralise existing orders. A note of prophetic challenge and critique was rarely heard. Christianity gradually became, in Metz's words,

> an extremely privatized religion that has been, as it were, specially prepared for the domestic use of the propertied middle class citizen. It is above all a religion of inner feeling. It does not protest against or oppose in any way the definitions of reality, meaning and truth, for example, that are accepted by the middle class society of exchange and success. It gives greater height and depth to what already applies even without it.[10]

[10] J.-B. Metz, *Faith in History and Society*, p. 45.

There is not here a gospel to be proclaimed, a challenging truth to be witnessed to.

Enlightenment public theology had other problems too. A universal disembodied rationality showed itself impotent against the primordial loyalties which are so central to all of us. The tendency of Enlightenment rationality to disregard or deplore all particularist tendencies limits its ability to relate effectively to a world in which particularism is always powerfully present. It seems powerless to curb or channel nationalist fervour in the Balkans today. It deplores ethnic cleansing with the rest of us, but it finds patriotism barely comprehensible. It is incapable of understanding and affirming what is good in particularism and has repeatedly shown itself impotent in the face of upsurges of nationalistic fervour.

The critique of Enlightenment modernity, of course, goes much further. The desire to recognise, create and celebrate an orderly, systematic world finds its ultimate *dénouement*, it has been argued, in the Holocaust. Universalising abstract systems of thought are inherently oppressive according to postmodernist critics. And by ironing out difference they end up strangely unreal and unrelated to concrete experiences. Kierkegaard makes the point effectively: he was a resolute opponent of the grand theorists and systematisers of his day, of whom Hegel was the chief. Hegel had distanced himself from the Aristotelian tradition which saw philosophy's task as unveiling the order and rationality of the universe so that human life could conform to reality. Both Hegel and Marx developed systems based on a conviction that the world is full of defects which must be put right if it is to be intelligible. Marx differed from Hegel in rejecting the notion that thought had the power to transform; for him a material radical transformation was required, in which human agency plays a major part.[11] But both, in their varying ways, were grand theorists, subject to Kierkegaard's strictures. 'In relation to their systems,' Kierkegaard wrote,

> most systematisers are like a man who builds an enormous castle and lives in a shack close by; they do not live in their own enormous

---

[11] N. Lobkowitz, *Theory and Practice: History of a Concept from Aristotle to Marx*, pp. 340–1.

systematic buildings. But spiritually that is a decisive objection. Spiritually speaking a man's thought must be the building in which he lives – otherwise everything is topsy-turvy.[12]

Kierkegaard's suspicion of systems and grand theories was well-grounded. He knew that in its magnificence the castle of theory often serves to conceal what is actually going on, disguise an often unpalatable reality and even legitimate awful practices. He understood thought, and above all thought about God, as something which must be *dwelt* in, relate to experience and expose untruth and injustice wherever they are found. The castle of theory needs to be cut down to size, demystified as it were, so that humans can live and flourish there. Accordingly, Kierkegaard saw his role as a theologian as like that of Socrates, asking questions, exposing falsehood and, gadfly-like, stinging people into awareness of the truth. He wrote in parables and epigrams and meditations which were deliberately *un*systematic. He wrote *Philosophical Fragments*, followed by an immense volume, playfully entitled *Concluding Unscientific Postscript*. And in communicating thus, Kierkegaard perhaps gives us clues to effective theological communication in the modern, or postmodern, age at a time of moral fragmentation. Truth is not something to be comprehended, controlled, used, or appropriated. It is rather to be indwelt, lived out in action and witnessed to. And that is what Christian public theology is about today.

The Church in Crisis

It seems little more than a cliché to say that the Church is in crisis today, in the West at any rate. Numerical decline, the flight of younger people from the congregations, the growing gulf between the culture and ethos of the Church and that which surrounds it, the failure of nerve to be found even in the leadership of the Church – all these factors suggest that we are in the midst of a crisis of the Church which is also a crisis of the Christian faith in our land.

People react in different ways. Some wallow in wistful self-delusion, pretending either that nothing has really changed,

[12] Alexander Dru (ed.), *The Journals of Søren Kierkegaard*. London: Oxford University Press, 1938, 583. Cf. 582.

or alternatively that everything will be fine if we go back to the old ways. Others pin their faith on instant therapies and simple solutions: 'Get back Billy Graham, and everything will return to "normal"'! There is in fact a lot of panic around, usually disguised behind glib sloganising. And many church leaders have settled for managing decline, sometimes in ways which actually accelerate the process.

What is clear is that we are facing a new and unprecedented situation which few people understand and which church people in general find menacing and frightful. Many responses are ill-considered panic reactions. Too few people try seriously to analyse the Church's situation and ask what God is doing in our time and what he is calling us – as individuals and as church – to be and do. At its roots, the crisis of faith in the Church is the fact that we no longer attempt to discern God's judgement, God's opportunity and God's initiative in what is happening in our day. It is an indication of the weakness of our faith that we find it so hard to see that small, declining and relatively powerless churches may have a distinctive servant role to play in our kind of society, that the Church may be reborn in our age, that God continues to take the initiative if we have eyes to see.

Birth and Rebirth

The birth of the Church, whenever we locate it, was depicted in the Bible as an unambiguously public event. It is properly regarded as a birth, for the Church is not a society or community that people, however saintly and committed, devise or construct. It is a divine initiative, a fellowship called into being by God, shaped by God rather than designed by human beings. The Church is not an institution that we make, shape, devise or control. It is a gift which comes, like any birth, as a wonder and a miracle. The human task at this birth is that of midwife; there are ways in which we are called to assist at the birth of a new life, long nurtured in the womb, and care for it in thriving or in weakness.

The foundation narratives are at pains to suggest that the birth of the Church, unlike most other births, takes place in public and is already of public and political significance. This birth from the womb of Israel may be located in the nativity of Jesus or at Pentecost; the two tales of the origin of the Church, which is the Body of Christ, are in fact complementary.

The birth of Jesus, the gospel writers are at pains to suggest, did not take place quietly, in private, in the bosom of the family. There is public dislocation and disturbance from the beginning. The settled home at Nazareth must be abandoned for a temporary shelter in Bethlehem because of a Roman injunction. Shepherds hear angels singing in the open fields, while Magi journey for many miles of foreign land, following their star to seek a promised king. And the birth that caused this dislocation of the Magi also shakes the throne of Herod, so that the disturbed and threatened ruler slaughters the innocents in the hope that he might thereby destroy and kill the new-born king. This public birth was a public disturbance to received certainties and familiar patterns of life and understanding. T. S. Eliot's Magi, on coming to Bethlehem, discover that birth and death were intertwined in the nativity that was the goal of their arduous journey and quest. The birth of Jesus was for them 'a hard and bitter agony', which changed them totally and made them ever after restless and disturbed, incapable of being at ease and content with the old dispensation.[13] They had become aliens and strangers, seeking a better country.

That other, complementary birthday of the Church, the day of Pentecost in Jerusalem, was no more a private, hole-in-corner affair. The experience of the disciples caused a public disturbance. 'Devout Jews drawn from every nation under heaven' were called together by the unruly spectacle, and were amazed and perplexed at hearing in their own languages the great things God has done. The message of the gospel and the outpouring of the Spirit were from the beginning for all humankind, not for a little pious sect. The story finishes with the incorporation into the new-born Church of some three thousand people drawn from this cosmopolitan and curious crowd. Through public communication in many tongues the Church is portrayed as *oikumene,* as recruiting from, and therefore present in, 'every nation under heaven'.

---

[13] T. S. Eliot, 'Journey of the Magi' (1927).

The New Testament understanding of *rebirth* pivots on the story of a private, almost surreptitious, visit to Jesus by Nicodemus, representing the best of the old Israel. Even the most faithful of the old require rebirth, a new beginning, if they are to enter the Reign of God. Only those who, though old, become as little children can enter the kingdom. And rebirth, like birth, is not something we devise, decide, achieve or earn, but a gratuitous act of God. The devout old Nicodemus needs rebirth, change, a new direction, needs to be embraced and challenged by a divine initiative. An old man, not far from death, still needs rebirth. He comes in private, but rebirth, like birth, is a public matter.

If birth and rebirth are at heart divine initiatives, what is the role to which believers are called? Could it be, following the thought of Socrates and Kierkegaard, that of a midwife? What then is our task? A midwife does not make or shape the baby, nor does she herself give birth. She knows the process, she discerns what is happening, she comforts, fortifies, encourages and assists. Through her experience and training, she can discern and understand what is going on; and on this basis give help and encouragement as required.

This, then, is our task in relation to the Church: to discern, even when the hand of death seems to be upon the Church, where the seeds of new life are, to attend to what God is doing in the world and in the Church, to be expectant and responsive to what is going on. A church reborn is a church that is aware of its public identity and its public responsibilities and is constantly attentive to its calling to witness to the truth in the public realm, to speak truth to power. The challenge, in short, is a call to faithfulness amid the turbulence, uncertainties, and opportunities of the new millennium.

10

The Public Theology of a Servant People

If the Church in Britain has the courage and confidence to overcome nostalgia for a past when the Church was at the centre of things and, setting wistfulness aside, realise that even a church depleted in numbers and power still has a calling from God, then, and only then, it can set about its proper tasks of service and confession in today's world. I have said that the task is service and confession, but the two are rarely distinct from one another: we confess the faith in service and encounter God in the neighbour, as the story of the sheep and the goats in Matthew 25 reminds us. In such a situation, what service can public theology render today? I would like to say a little about three modes of public theology which seem to me to be particularly significant today: vision, prophecy and what I call 'theological fragments'.

Vision

There is profound truth in the familiar, and probably mis-translated, text: 'Where there is no vision the people perish' (Proverbs 29.18). The people perish because without vision they are locked in their past and present and incapable of imagining a future that will be better, because they have lost hope. Politics in such a situation becomes mere 'business', horse-trading, squabbling about power with little sense of the ends to which power is the means. Gaining and holding on to power become ends in themselves. For vision is what generates purpose for a society. Without vision public life becomes a battle of interests, unconstrained by a larger horizon of meaning; 'civil war carried on by other means', to use Alasdair MacIntyre's telling phrase, a civil war in which the prizes all go to the victors, and woe to the losers, the powerless and the vulnerable.

But what do we mean by vision? A distinguished American political theorist, Sheldon Wolin, published a book in the early 1960s entitled *Politics and Vision*. It attracted my attention because at that time many political philosophers were saying that the great debates about politics and society in the past were based for the most part on fairly elementary logical or linguistic confusions, or were simply emotional outpourings without deeper significance. Wolin's book took the tradition of thought about society very seriously and paid detailed attention to what theologians in the past had said about society and the state.

Wolin distinguished two senses of the term 'vision'. On the one hand, vision is used for a description of an act or an event. This type of vision, which claims a degree of objectivity, was long believed to be at the heart of scientific method. This kind of vision is very close to what is meant today by 'theory'.

Theory, as I argued in *Christian Justice and Public Policy*, has a variety of uses or functions. When properly used, theory, in David Garland's words, 'enables us to think about the real world of practice with a clarity and a breadth of perspective often unavailable to the hard-pressed practitioner'.[1] That is, it puts practice and 'the real world' in a broad perspective within which both understanding and practice can be deepened. But when I was involved in work on prisons and punishment, we also became embarrassingly aware of how easy it is for theory to disguise what was actually going on beneath high-sounding aspirations. A prison, for instance, which presented itself to the outside world as a place controlled by the theory of rehabilitation, preparing prisoners to be useful citizens contributing to the good of society, might none the less be an institution in which much violence and brutality were in fact the dominant features of experience for many within the perimeter fence.

---

[1] David Garland, *Punishment in Modern Society: A Study in Social Theory*. Oxford: Clarendon Press, 1990, p. 277.

But the outside world felt comfortable in the false belief that good was being done on society's behalf within the prison, while the prisoners and the practitioners felt that 'theory failed to illumine and clarify so much of their experience; theory was unable to explain a great deal that went on in the system, including many of the most important things' that had the deepest influence on people and behaviour.[2] Theory *can* be a flight from reality, or a disguise for what is actually going on. But some kind of theorising is necessary if understanding and practice are to be interpreted and improved within a broader horizon than that of a particular moment in a specific context. Some kinds of theory are so narrow and so frightened of value and critique that they end up as little more than a way of describing what is going on and ordering the data in such a way that they subtly accord finality to the present. Such understandings of theory hardly deserve Wolin's title of vision.

But there is for Sheldon Wolin another use of the term 'vision' which is more imaginative, as in an aesthetic or religious vision. It is now commonly accepted that this conception of imaginative vision plays a large part even in the scientific enterprise.[3] In thought about community, society, politics and the public realm, Wolin argues that this imaginative overall vision has a key role to play:

> An architectonic vision is one wherein the political imagination attempts to mould the totality of political phenomena to accord with some vision of the Good that lies outside the political order ... The vision may take its origin in a view of history like that of Hegel, where the phenomena of politics acquire a temporal depth, an historical dimension, as they are swept up into an overriding purpose that shapes them towards an ultimate end.[4]

Both Wolin's senses of vision are combined in a Christian understanding of social vision. Here the imagination is shaped and resourced by the symbols, narratives and imagery of the Christian and biblical tradition. An imaginative vision which encompasses the purpose and sweep of history, is open to the future and hence not at ease in the present; is also shaped by a

---

[2] Forrester, *Christian Justice and Public Policy*, p. 67.
[3] On this see especially Michael Polanyi, *Personal Knowledge*.
[4] Wolin, *Politics and Vision*, pp. 19–20.

descriptive yet critical vision of the present; and is not afraid to name oppression and injustice and ugliness and lies – all that distinguishes the present from the Reign of God.

A concern with vision should serve to remind Christians that theology is not exclusively engaged with 'academic' questions, or with particular problems, policies and ethical conundrums. It is at least as concerned with the visions that provide a horizon of meaning within which a society exists, policies are formulated, actions are taken and vocations are fulfilled. Visions generate and sustain Utopias, if you prefer that language. And, as Rubem Alves has suggested, 'When utopias are not imagined, ethics is reduced to solving problems within the established system' and we are at the mercy of an absolutising of a present which is deprived of any eschatological hope. Without vision, people give up seeking a better future because, in the absence of goals, social life loses meaning and becomes the arena for unbridled self-interest. A society without vision is petty, selfish and cruel.

The American theologian, David Harned, stresses that the way we see things and the way we make decisions are shaped by the stories that give us our identity. Indeed, the stories shape us as people and give us the resources for vision:

> Seeing is never simply a reaction to what passes before our eyes; it is a matter of how well the eye is trained and provisioned to discern the richness and the terror, beauty and banality of the worlds outside and within the self. Decisions are shaped by vision, and the ways that we see are a function of our 'character', of the history and habits of the self, and ultimately of the stories that we have heard and with which we identify ourselves.[5]

Visions have the ability to constrain selfishness and enable altruism, reaching out to the neighbour in love. Visions can open us to God's future and motivate us to seek the Reign of God. Visions generate hope and disturb and challenge us, especially when we are comfortable or complacent in the present. Indeed, it is usually people who are weak, marginalised and forgotten, despised people and suffering people who generate visions, who respond to visions, who live by visions.

---

[5] David Harned, *Faith and Virtue*. Philadelphia: Pilgrim Press, 1973, pp. 29–30.

Not all visions are equally good and desirable, of course. The communist dictatorships in Eastern Europe that collapsed more than a decade ago reminded us how a vision that was in some ways admirable could lead to dehumanising dictatorship and then decay rapidly, eroded by its own inadequacy. And Hitler's dream of the thousand-year Reich represented a vision that was devastatingly evil. In these recent days of 'tumult and trampling and confusion in the valley of vision' (Isaiah 2.5) there are many visions on offer which are exclusive, petty and even dehumanising. Other visions are simply individual pipe-dreams, ways of escaping from reality rather than engaging with the coming Reign of God. In many situations, as in Northern Ireland, there are powerful polarised and blinkered visions, dominated by bitter and partial memories of the past.

We are in an age when many visions are on offer and they are often in contention with one another. Different visions compete for people's allegiance. Christians today must learn how to assess visions, how to discriminate between visions. These are great issues of which academics (mainly theologians and social scientists) have to an amazing extent steered clear for many decades, preferring to concentrate on details rather than the broad picture, on description rather than evaluation, on the past and the present rather than God's future. Visions, the kind of visions which generate goals and horizons of meaning, have been left to 'visionaries', religious people, fanatics. But others too have responsibilities in these matters. At such a time, Christians have a special need to test visions, our own and others'. This means that they constantly measure their vision against reality: does it help us to see more clearly the world as it is and (even more important and, for Christians, more real) as it might be? Does it enable and encourage hopeful, courageous, just and loving behaviour? Does it help us to see evil, oppression, meanness and injustice for what they are and respond to them with faithful steadfastness?

The term *social* vision has an important in-built ambiguity. It can mean a vision of the future of a society, or a vision shared by many or most people in a community, or both. Social vision is necessarily incompatible with the kind of individualism so influential today, and also with the common assumption that the best that can be hoped for is some kind of balance of power.

Social vision speaks to us of our interdependence, our accountability to one another and our responsibility for one another. It
constrains and disciplines individuals and groups in their
pursuit of their interests in the light of a higher and more
comprehensive good.

Social vision as *shared* vision has peculiar problems in a
modern plural society. How can a sectarian vision, or a vision
held by a minority, commend itself to a whole great society as
something that can generate goals and give cohesion? Imposed
visions quickly destroy freedom and become vicious – so much
we must have learned from the last fifty-five years in Europe.
Pluralism can provide goods we would not wish to lose – openness and a degree of freedom for all, for instance. But some
contemporary supporters of pluralism commend a thoroughgoing pluralist society which is neither cohesive nor caring,
where vision is discounted, perhaps because history is believed
to be at an end (Fukuyama) and we have nothing left to hope
for.

Modern pluralism thus presents a direct challenge to social
vision. For F. A. Hayek, as a typical protagonist of pluralism,
only small, simple, face-to-face societies are capable of seeking
a common goal, of being held together by a shared vision.[6] In
large, complex societies a social vision can only be *imposed*, so
that what Hayek calls 'teleocratic' societies are inherently and
inescapably dictatorial. The 'great society' that Hayek desires
because it provides the conditions for liberty and prosperity
is one in which a multitude of individual and group interests
are bound loosely together without any overarching or constraining notion of the common good or a shared vision. The
operations of an invisible hand to bring about some kind of
balance between competing interests and scatter unantici-
pated goods, or make them 'trickle down', makes some kind of
moral sense of the pursuit of individual and specific goals as
a poor approximation to society. It rests on an impoverished
idea of community as simply an arena of conflicting interests,
where the nearest approximation to justice is some kind of

---

[6] F. A. Hayek, *Law, Legislation and Liberty*, 2nd edn, London: Routledge, 1982.
For fuller discussion and references see my *Christian Justice and Public Policy*.
Cambridge: Cambridge University Press, 1997, chap. 6.

equilibrium and the observance of some simple rules of fair dealing.

The inadequacy of such abandonment of the need for a shared vision and common goals is neatly demonstrated by the present turmoil in three social institutions which, like many, cannot be fully integrated into the market or regarded as simply arenas for the pursuit of private goods: the criminal justice system, the National Health Service and education. Each of these was shaped in the past by a social vision, often deeply influenced by Christianity. But when vision is eroded, such central social institutions are in danger of becoming harmful, under-resourced, divisive or even demonic.

Social vision, even the most forward-looking, is always a reading or a rereading of the past and the narrative canon which presents that past to us – for Christians around the world, the Bible. As such, social vision may lock us into a wistful and maudlin nostalgia, or it may fuel social conflict by excluding the other from our story and making the past a simple conflict between darkness and light. Social visions can be divisive, demeaning and bitter, let there be no doubt about that. They can make us captives of the past, incapable of responding to the challenges of today or the opportunities of tomorrow. But unless we can possess our past in a proper, realistic and responsible way we will never be able to cope with the future. And without an authentic vision we are hardly likely to be open to the neighbour and alert to the opportunities and responsibilities which lie to hand.

A Christian vision is inescapably social, precisely because all the great images of salvation and the future in the Christian tradition are models of conviviality, living together in mutual delight and responsibility – the Reign of God, the New Jerusalem, the city, and so on. It is a vision of a community of neighbours, remembering the expansive and rich content that the Bible gives to the term 'neighbour'.

In Britain in the past, crises and conflicts acted as catalysts for social vision, and religion usually provided the imagery and the language. Thus Scottish Chartists in the nineteenth century demanding fundamental citizenship rights marched to their meetings bearing Covenanters' banners and singing metrical psalms! It is my conviction that intellectuals and academics do not often generate social vision. But when vision emerges from situations of conflict, suffering and pain, from the deep and often dangerous places where vision is renewed, theologians and academics and clergy may articulate and criticise visions; indeed, they have a responsibility to do so.

Today in Britain, the Church declines numerically and religious language and symbols seem to many tired, jaded, jejune and esoteric. And yet it was in Edinburgh that Margaret Thatcher chose to deliver her 'Sermon on the Mound', and Tony Blair makes frequent reference to his commitment to Christian Socialism. Are these things perhaps reminders that religious language has not in fact lost its currency and, indeed, is not as devalued as is the language of political ideologies? Again and again we seem to be driven back to religious language and find even in Britain what Austin Farrer in a notable book on Revelation called 'the rebirth of images'. Are the symbols and the narratives of the Bible still capable of serving as vehicles for renewed and lively social visions of conviviality and hope? Can we rescue and renew a shared and hospitable Christian social vision, which is open to the future and generates goals and motivation for the twenty-first century? Can Christianity in today's Britain criticise and assess the visions on offer? Is Christianity still capable of pointing to a vision of the future which will draw people together in seeking justice, fellowship, truth and human flourishing?

Ultimately, for Christians, true vision is the vision of God and of fellowship in and with the Triune God. The Church is called to be a kind of preliminary manifestation, or earnest (*arrabon* = down-payment) of that vision. That does not mean that the Church or theology generates or devises the Christian vision. But they have a responsibility to discern, explore, manifest and proclaim it. In the New Testament the visions were not visions of the glorious future of the Church, but of a new heaven and a new earth, the renewal of the whole world, a New Jerusalem in which there will be no church or temple, but God will be all in all. Thus we are constantly reminded that judgement begins with the household of faith, the community that nurtures and commends the Christian vision. For we are stewards, not possessors, of the Christian vision.

Prophecy

Prophecy is the application of vision to a particular situation. It demonstrates as it were the cash-value, the relevance, of the vision, earths it in what William Blake called 'minute particulars'[7] and makes it operative in a specific situation and context. Without prophecy it is hardly possible to grasp the vision except as an escapist pipe-dream which has no bearing on the world, vacuous general statements rather than specific demands. True prophecy is disturbing because it challenges the dominant values and the conventional wisdom of the age. We constantly need to unpack the bearing of vision on specifics, for the concrete here means the actual points where people are hurting and the issues that press upon their reality. This is precisely what Martin Luther King did in the midst of the civil rights struggle when he proclaimed: 'I have a dream . . . every valley shall be exalted, and every hill shall be made low . . . we will be free one day.' And more recently in the century now drawing to its close, Archbishop Tutu, Oscar Romero and many another have proclaimed their Christian social vision with great courage and challenging relevance.

I find quite unconvincing the argument that while the generation and sustaining of vision and the pronouncement of general principles may be the proper function of public theology and the Church, prophecy and dealing with specific issues are not a responsibility of the Church as a whole, or of representative church leaders, but should be left to the occasional interventions of individuals. R. H. Tawney was surely right in criticising the vacuous generality of many church statements.[8] As the more recent *Kairos Document* from South Africa makes clear, such general statements rarely threaten the security or interests of the Church, or disturb politicians of whatever hue more than momentarily. But more important still, they rarely affect the way things go, or are tangible expressions of solidarity with the oppressed and forgotten.

---

[7] 'He who would do good to another, must do it in minute particulars. General good is the plea of the scoundrel, hypocrite and flatterer.' *Jerusalem*, chap. 3.

[8] Tawney, *'The Attack' and other Papers*, p. 178.

I do not wish to suggest that it is easy or uncontentious to attempt to unpack the bearing of vision on specifics. Far from it. But this is surely a central task of public theology which cannot be shirked. For without the hard and difficult endeavour to move from vision to the specifics of prophecy, what claims to be prophecy easily becomes a mere recycling of the favoured slogans of the moment without distinctive Christian, and therefore gospel, content or, at the other extreme, theological pronouncements which have no bearing on the specifics of the issue under consideration. Much that claims to be prophecy seems to have little if any theological content and to be hardly related at all to the Christian vision.

The worship of the Church is at least potentially prophetic, both a witness to the vision and a disturbing challenge to the specific injustices and untruthfulness of the context in which it is set. Stanley Hauerwas makes this point with his usual incisiveness:

> Because Jesus was who he was, Christians cannot help but be prophetic, since now their very existence is a prophetic sign of God's refusal to abandon creation. If the essential role of the prophet is to interpret the world in terms of God's providential care, then the church's very existence is prophetic, for without the church we would not know who we are or in what kind of world we exist.[9]

Prophecy is thus an unavoidable ecclesiastical and theological responsibility. A public theology which declines to prophesy is in a state of dereliction of duty.

Theological Fragments in Postmodern Times

The condition of postmodernity is a pluralist society in which not only are many theories and world-views allowed and tolerated but there is also a profound suspicion of grand theories and theologies, of systems which make claim to truth. These are essentially seen as coercive and inadequate to reality. Society, *pace* Rawls and others, does not need a consensus to survive, according to the postmodernists. Indeed, consensus

---

[9] Hauerwas, *Christian Existence Today*, p. 158.

can only be achieved by force or manipulation. It inherently involves a limitation of freedom, which in a fairly straightforward sense becomes the great central value of postmodernity. There is, in Lyotard's words, a profound 'incredulity towards metanarratives'.[10] The postmodern mind knows itself to be homeless; but it also recognises that no home exists. The mindset is melancholy and anxious, but it is also willing to come to terms with the fragmentation of reality and refuses to impose an artificial and fragile order upon it.

Postmodernists characteristically celebrate the fragmentation and pluralism of postmodern societies as a condition in which for the first time true freedom is possible. In postmodernity there is a new delight in feelings and emotion. Mystery and wonder are again in fashion, for the Enlightenment project of demystifying the world has been replaced with the re-enchantment of the world.[11] There is a new quality of concern with action and morals, a realistic acceptance of the ambiguities and uncertainties with which action is surrounded and a new respect for the concrete and the particular. Action does not necessarily call for justification or require to be fitted into some great scheme if it is to be authentic. 'Saints are saints,' writes Bauman,

> because they do not hide behind the law's broad shoulders. They know, or act as if they felt, that no law, however generous and humane, may exhaust the moral duty, trace the consequences of 'being for' to their radical end, to the ultimate choice of life or death.[12]

Indeed, commitment to great moral or political systems and ideals can sometimes conflict directly with an ethical attitude to the concrete other, as in Dostoevsky's doctor, who said:

> I love humanity . . . but I wonder at myself. The more I love humanity in general, the less I love man in particular. In my dreams . . . I have often come to making enthusiastic schemes for the service of humanity, and perhaps I might actually have faced crucifixion if it had been suddenly necessary; and yet I am incapable of living in the same room with anyone for two days

---

[10] Cited in Stephen K. White, *Political Theory and Postmodernism*, pp. 4–5.
[11] Z. Bauman, *Post-Modern Ethics*. Oxford: Blackwell, 1993, p. 33.
[12] Bauman, *Post-Modern Ethics*, p. 81.

together, as I know by experience . . . In twenty-four hours I begin to hate the best of men . . . But it has always happened that the more I detest men individually the more ardent becomes my love for humanity.[13]

In its concern with the concrete, with action, existence and freedom, and in its suspicion of grandiose and impersonal schemes and systems, postmodernity presents opportunities and challenges to the mission of the Church. Indeed, the recognition of fragmentation opens a whole range of evangelistic opportunities.

I have suggested the deployment of 'theological fragments' not because I buy into the postmodernist scenario (although I find it quite illuminating, particularly in its view of grand theories as oppressive), but because in a situation where most people are both ignorant and suspicious of Christian doctrine and practice there is really no other way forward than presenting or offering 'fragments' which may be seen as relevant and true, illuminating and helpful for just practice.

A theologian should not, I think, be ashamed of offering initially no more than 'fragments' of insight in public debate in the conditions of postmodernity. Postmodernists (and sociologists of knowledge) are, after all, right in affirming that systematic, carefully developed theories can sometimes conceal practices which are inhumane and brutalising. Ideologies can serve as the emperor's new clothes, so that the theologian's task, as a little child, is to cry out, 'But the emperor's got no clothes on!'. A fragment of truth reveals that to which most people have allowed themselves to be blinded. Truth-telling in a fragmentary way becomes even more important when the scheme to conceal the emperor's nakedness is something that is hurting people and destroying community.[14]

Moral and theological fragments come from specific quarries, or visions if you prefer that terminology. We know that theological fragments by which Christians live and which shape their practice have their home in a community of shared faith,

---

[13] F. Dostoevsky, *The Brothers Karamazov*. London: Heinemann, 1912, pp. 52–3.

[14] Notice that Z. Bauman characterises 'the post-modern perspective' as 'above all the tearing off of the mask of illusions; the recognition of certain pretences as false and certain objectives as neither attainable or, for that matter, desirable'. *Post-Modern Ethics*, p. 3.

the Church, which, if it is true to its calling and its mission, does not look back wistfully to an unrecoverable past, but looks forward with expectation to God's future, and meanwhile offers its fragments as a contribution to the common store and seeks to embody its insights in its life.

When a fragment is recognised as in some sense true, one should expect an interest in its provenance, its embeddedness in a broader truth. Is one of today's compelling tasks and opportunities the bringing together of 'theological fragments' which have been illuminating, instructive or provocative in grappling with issues of practice 'on the ground', reflecting on them and their embeddedness in the structure of Christian faith, and enquiring whether this gives clues to a constructive contribution in the public realm? This may well be the way towards the renewal and recovery of Christian social vision in the conditions of today.

By 'fragments' I mean a wide range of things – the importance of forgiveness in any decent criminal justice system, confessional statements such as the 1934 Theological Declaration of Barmen which established the German Confessing Church in opposition to Nazism, Frank Field's recent suggestion that a 'Christian' view of human nature is necessary for a viable welfare system, and many others. Fragments may be irritants (the grit in the oyster that gathers a pearl?), stories/ parables, the Socratic questioning of received assumptions, even the 'road metal' for straight paths.

Fragments, of course, come from somewhere; they have been quarried. My purpose in talking this way is partly evangelical: some people who recognise a Christian fragment as true may trace it back to the quarry from which it comes. But I am also increasingly aware that fragments detached from the quarry are particularly liable to be abused, misunderstood and distorted. Thus the theological task is, I believe, twofold: injecting or offering theological fragments in public debate and, simultaneously, labouring in the quarry or mine – work that may be largely invisible and regarded by most as irrelevant, but which is in fact essential. This, I believe, is precisely how Barth behaved in the 1930s: hard, unrelenting work on the *Church Dogmatics* 'as if nothing had happened' (his phrase), and simultaneously bombarding the Nazis and the German Christians with a fusillade of fragments which for many people provided a strong discernment of what was actually happening and how a Christian should respond. What I am profoundly opposed to is a facile presentation of idealistic commonplaces as if they were theological fragments!

Another parallel analogy which in some ways is a corrective to the fragments and quarry image and far more deeply rooted in Christian thought and liturgical practice, is that of the loaf and the crumbs or grains. The separate grains are ground and kneaded and baked into bread, the one loaf which is the sign of the Body of Christ, both the body broken on the cross and the body of believers who gather and are dispersed in the world to bring forth fruit. For the work of salvation, the work of God in the world, the body/loaf must be broken into crumbs, only to be gathered together into one at the end of time. At the heart of Christian faith and action is the breaking of the bread for the nourishment of God's people. The crumbs, the fragments, are food for a pilgrim people.

This all boils down to a conviction that ways of doing public theology which seemed to work in earlier times, when Christian assumptions were widely shared and many people were well acquainted with the 'quarry' and approved of it, are irretrievable. And I am also increasingly uneasy about any suggestion that a secular theory can do service as a surrogate for public theology. I am also uneasy about early liberation theology's over-eagerness to baptise Marxism, and the Vatican's (and Christian Democracy's) presentation of an alternative *system* of social doctrine, true everywhere and for everyone. Reality is too messy and too confused for either.

The question of how a fragmentary approach can avoid theory obscuring what is actually going on intrigues me. I certainly do not want to say that *all* theory obscures what is going on. On the contrary, I am sure that theory is indispensable. But theory must constantly be scrutinised with suspicion and subjected to Socratic questioning. What I think is quite essential – and terribly seldom done – is to attend to the 'victims' and the reflective practitioners and how they view the situation. I have been much shaken by poor people denouncing leading liberal or left-wing experts on poverty, saying, 'You don't know what you are talking about'. And I have heard similar complaints in other contexts. Often it is precisely at this point that a theological fragment could be offered which just might make some sense of a muddled and ugly situation, help reopen communication and encourage people resolutely to do justice. I've seen it happen. But not often.

Some fragments are like pieces of glass or gems that catch the light and display its wonderful colours, or generate a vision that many can share – glimpses into another world. It is perhaps better that visions and hopes of utopias should be generated in this way than by one of the huge ideologies that seem now to have collapsed. People and societies need to be liberated from being confined in the prison of 'the real world', unable to dream the dreams which will shape the practice of tomorrow and become ultimately the practice of the Reign of God. The point is made very powerfully by F. A. Hayek in a 1949 essay:

> The main lesson which the true liberal must learn from the success of the socialists is that it was their courage to be Utopian which gained them the support of the intellectuals and therefore an influence on public opinion which is daily making possible what only recently seemed utterly remote. Those who have concerned themselves exclusively with what seemed practicable in the existing state of opinion have constantly found that even this has rapidly become politically impossible as a result of changes in public opinion which they have done nothing to guide. Unless we can make the philosophic foundations of a free society once more a living intellectual issue, and its implementation a task which challenges the ingenuity and imagination of our liveliest minds, the prospects of freedom are indeed dark.[15]

So back to the quarry, to obtain the fragments that give us road metal, provoke the oyster to make pearls, concentrate the light into visions, generate utopias, build up jigsaws of meaning and nourish the activity of truthfulness, love and justice which is the practice of the Reign of God!

---

[15] Hayek, *The Intellectuals and Socialism*, p. 26.

SECTION FOUR

DIVERSITIES OF PRACTICE

11

Reformed Radical Orthodoxy: Can It Be Retrieved?[1]

There is in Scotland a theological tradition which at its beginning was probably the most radical strain in the mainstream
Calvinist movement. In certain ways it was markedly too radical
for Calvin himself![2] Down the centuries this radical theological tradition has been tamed in a variety of ways, but again
and again there have been at least partial retrievals of the
Scots tradition of interlocking theological, ecclesiastical, social
and political radicalism combined with a strong confessional
orthodoxy. One of these partial revivals may be taking place
today, with the coming of devolution and all the hope and
excitement this has engendered. In this chapter I want to
examine Scottish radical orthodoxy by way of some forays into
history and ask how far it is alive today, or can be retrieved. Is
the distinctive 'radical orthodoxy' of Scottish Calvinism relevant
and recoverable in the circumstances of the early twenty-first
century?

A recent, high profile and very lively, largely Anglo-Catholic,
theological movement led by John Milbank, which labels itself

---

[1] I am very grateful to my friend, Professor William Storrar, for helpful and
constructive comments on this chapter.

[2] See, for example, Quentin Skinner, *The Foundations of Modern Political Thought:
Vol 2: The Age of Reformation*. Cambridge: Cambridge University Press, 1978, pp.
302–3: 'So we find Hotman writing to Calvin in December 1558 to assure him that
"everyone was pleased with your letters in which you openly indicated that you
were outraged" by the inflammatory writings of Goodman and Knox.'

'Radical Orthodoxy', has emerged and is sending shock waves of excitement throughout the Anglo-American theological scene. The orthodoxy that they affirm is 'credal orthodoxy', apparently very much that of the high Middle Ages. On this basis, they have the ambitious project of 'recovering and extending a fully Christianised ontology and practical philosophy consonant with authentic Christian doctrine'.[3] The radicalism they espouse involves going back to the roots, particularly the patristic and early medieval roots, of the theological tradition, 'and especially to the Augustinian vision of all knowledge as divine illumination', thus hoping to overcome destructive modern dualisms.[4] They claim to be radical also in that they believe that the tradition needs to be rethought, because its 'collapse' at the end of the Middle Ages betrayed serious weaknesses which must now be remedied. They are in revolt against 'the self-conscious superficiality of today's secularism'. Indeed, they stand in conscious opposition to the modern world and the modernist or liberal theology which they believe makes fatal compromises with modernity, almost after the style of the First Vatican Council. What I do *not* see in this movement of 'radical orthodoxy' is a serious social, political and economic radicalism understood as direct implications of an orthodox theology.

That was the kind of radical orthodoxy which was at the heart of the Scottish Reformation and also had deep pre-Reformation roots in the Scottish tradition. At the time of the Reformation, it was generally assumed among Calvinists that the confession of the Lordship of Christ demanded through-going reform of church, society and state, as well as personal conversion of the individual. Christian orthodoxy was seen as inherently radical, neither a pietist retreat into individualism nor a liberal compromise with the powers, but a serious project to reshape church, society and the individual in accordance with Christian truth. The Scots Reformers set out to change the world as well as the Church in the light of the gospel. And that is exactly what they did.

---

[3] John Milbank, Catharine Pickstock and Graham Ward (eds), *Radical Orthodoxy*. London: Routledge, 1999, p. 2.

[4] Milbank et al. (eds), *Radical Orthodoxy*, p. 2.

This chapter is an essay in contextual theology, attempting to trace in broad outline the changing contours of the radical theological tradition in Scotland. But it also addresses the question whether this tradition in modified form can be retrieved not just in Scotland, but more widely, as an important resource for 'doing the truth' in today's world, with its very different challenges and opportunities from those of the past. The question with which I end will also be seen, I hope, as a challenge.

The Scots Reformation

To a far greater extent than in England or in most continental European countries, the Scottish Reformation was a popular movement, a Reformation from below rather than a religious change imposed from above by the Crown on a puzzled and sometimes resistant populace. The Scots Reformers were able to ride a mood of extreme disenchantment with the old Church and a profound questioning of the social, political and economic orders, so vividly portrayed in Sir David Lindsay's drama *Ane Satyre of the Thrie Estaites* (1540), wonderfully revived at the first Edinburgh Festival.[5] At the turning point of this drama, John the Common-weal, the ordinary poor Scot, supported by Gude Counsel and Divine Correctioun and grasping the book of the gospels, denounces in turn the oppression and exploitation of the nobles, the burgesses and the Church, and calls for a purification of church and state which will be both a reformation of the Church and the establishment of justice for the poor and the weak in Scottish society.[6] At the end, poor John is vindicated as representative of all the poor and forgotten in Scotland:

> Give John the Common-Weal ane gay garmoun,
> Because the Common-Weal has been owrelookit,
> That is the cause that Common-Weal is cruikit.

[5] Sir David Lindsay, *Ane Satyre of the Thrie Estaites*. Rev. edn, Edinburgh: Polygon, 1985.

[6] Peter Matheson gives an account of similar Reformation street theatre in Berne in 1522. Its anticlericalism and adoration of Christ resulted in 'formidable transformations in patterns of deference, concepts of honour and hidden assumptions'. *The Imaginative World of the Reformation*. Edinburgh: T&T Clark, 2000, p. 5.

With singular profit he has been sae suppressit
That he is baith cauld, nakit and disgysit.[7]

The Reformation, which was already beginning when *The Thrie Estaites* was first performed in 1540, quickly developed into a populist movement which the Reformers did not find hard to harness to their purposes and make into a 'reformation from below'.[8] This movement was as much about justice for the poor and liberation for the oppressed as it was about the reform of the Church and its doctrine; radical Reformed orthodoxy was regarded as a total package, in Peter Matheson's words, 'less a shopping-list of demands than the choreography for a new dance'.[9] Humanists such as George Buchanan were attracted to Calvinism because it seemed to offer the possibility of realising their Utopian hopes and it blended easily with their humanism. There was also the fact that the Scots Reformers drew heavily on a particular strand of late medieval conciliar and nominalist thought, particularly as mediated by the influential Scots theologian, John Mair, who taught mainly in the University of Paris and is believed to have taught both Calvin and Ignatius Loyola. There was thus an earlier Scottish radical and democratic tradition which easily fed into 'Reformed Radical Orthodoxy'.

The monarch, remaining thirled to the old faith, was at odds with a multitude of her people, led by a section of the middle nobility and Reformers who were on the radical wing of the Genevan Reformation. The Crown in Scotland fairly consistently opposed the Reformation, but was never capable of effective resistance or of restoring Catholicism, as happened in England under Mary Tudor.

In this context it was not, perhaps, surprising that the Scots Reformation actually affirmed a *duty* of resistance to tyranny. In the *Scots Confession* we find among the 'Warkis reputit gude befoir God' the saving of innocent lives, the defence of the oppressed and 'to represse tyrannie', while obedience to

---

[7] *The Thrie Estaites*, four pages from end – pages are unnumbered!

[8] The similarities with the Czech Reformation are impressively explored by Jan Milic Lochman, *Zeal for Truth and Tolerance: The Ecumenical Challenge of the Czech Reformation*. Edinburgh: Scottish Academic Press, 1996, pp. 1–4.

[9] Matheson, *The Imaginative World*, p. 9.

superiors is only enjoined when it is not repugnant to God's commands and when the authorities do not 'passe over the bounds of their office',[10] and are 'doing that thing quhilk appertains to [their] charge.[11]

This is developed by Knox into a positive duty of resistance to tyrants and unjust rulers. Calvin himself had made a cautious concession in affirming that in closely circumscribed cases the elected magistrates might legitimately resist a tyrant;[12] this was now extended immeasurably by Knox when he affirmed that the people at large have a duty to support magistrates in resisting a tyrant and may also themselves initiate resistance. On the basis of a covenantal understanding of society, Knox is able to appeal first to the nobility and then to the populace of Scotland in general to resist the despotic rule of Mary Stuart.[13] Resistance to tyranny and oppression was an obligation, for failure to oppose unrighteousness in the covenanted community involved complicity in injustice and placed the citizenry, along with their rulers, under the judgement of God. A sacred duty is laid on each citizen who is part of the covenanted community to take part in resisting and removing idolatrous and tyrannical authorities. And as in many places in the Bible, idolatry is closely linked to oppression and the doing of injustice.

This idea that the civil community was bound to God in a covenantal relationship implied, of course, that the whole life of the community was to be shaped by God's commands and should reflect the divine purpose of justice and love. Thus the second foundational document of the Scottish Reformation alongside the *Scots Confession* was *The First Book of Discipline* of 1560.[14] This was a blueprint for church and society in Scotland, outlining the organisation of the new Reformed Church, and how it would exercise what the *Scots Confession* saw as a third mark of the True Church, 'Ecclesiastical discipline uprightlie

---

[10] *Scots Confession*, Art XIV.

[11] *Scots Confession*, Art XXIV.

[12] Calvin, *Institutes* IV.xx.31.

[13] See *The Appellation to the Nobility and Estates* and *The Letter to the Commonalty* in *John Knox on Rebellion*, Roger A. Mason (ed.), Cambridge Texts in the History of Political Thought. Cambridge: Cambridge University Press, 1994.

[14] *The First Book of Discipline*. With Introduction and Commentary by James K. Cameron. Edinburgh: St Andrew Press, 1972.

ministred', from which no one in Scotland was to be exempt.[15] And it was so at the beginning: ecclesiastical discipline was exercised in cases of cheating merchants or oppressive landlords as well as in cases of fornication, adultery and sabbath-breaking. Among the offences that *The First Book of Discipline* regarded as the concern of church courts were 'oppressing of the poore by exactions' and 'deceiving of them in buying and selling by wrang met and measure'.[16] In the terms of the day, there was here a preferential option for the poor. Everyone in the realm, rulers and preachers as well as the poor, were to be subject to discipline. Through discipline, broadly understood, society with its social, political and economic structures was to be reformed.[17]

Knox was not afraid to emphasise human equality in the most emphatic terms. The poor have as much responsibility before God as the powerful for the spiritual and moral state of the nation because they have equal worth in the eyes of God.[18] The nation as a whole in solidarity is responsible to God:

> And if ye think that ye are innocent because ye are not the chief authors of such iniquity, ye are utterly deceived. For God doth not only punish the chief offenders, but with them doth He damn the consenters to iniquity; and all are judged to consent that knowing impiety committed give no testimony that the same displeaseth them. To speak this matter more plain, as your princes and rulers are criminal with your bishops of all idolatry committed, and of all the innocent blood that is shed for the testimony of Christ's truth, and that because they maintain them in their tyranny, so are you (I mean so many of you as give no plain confession to the contrary) criminal and guilty with your princes and rulers of the same crimes, because ye assist and maintain your princes in their blind rage and give no testimony that their tyranny displeaseth you.[19]

It is not inappropriate to see in these emphases on human equality and the collective responsibility of the community, roots of modern democratic politics.

---

[15] Art XVIII.

[16] *First Book of Discipline*, pp. 166–7.

[17] On this see Donald C. Smith, *Passive Obedience and Prophetic Protest: Social Criticism in the Scottish Church, 1580–1945*. New York: Peter Lang, 1987, pp. 11–20.

[18] In *The Letter to the Commonalty* in *John Knox on Rebellion*, pp. 118–26.

[19] *The Letter to the Commonalty*, pp. 124–5.

For both theological and prudential reasons, the Scots Reformers from the beginning rejected the idea of royal supremacy over the Church. They appealed to and mobilised the nobility and the common people to carry forward the work of reformation in church and society. Yet they were also eager for a 'godly prince', and in James VI and I they believed for a time they had found such a one. But although the godly prince had, they affirmed, clear duties to assist and support godliness and true religion, the prince could not possess spiritual authority within the Church and should not be regarded, after the fashion of many Lutheran principalities on the continent, as *primus episcopus*. Nor was the prince to be seen as supreme as much in ecclesiastical matters as in temporal affairs, as in England.

Once again the Scottish Reformation is shown to be more intrinsically radical than the English Reformation which found its theological rationale in Richard Hooker's *Laws of Ecclesiastical Polity*. Nor is it similar to the situation in Lutheran polities, which recognise a sharp distinction between the two kingdoms. It is determined to preserve the prophetic freedom of the Church. It even radically revises Calvin's own account of the two kingdoms and their relation:

> Let us observe that in man government is two-fold: the one spiritual, by which the conscience is trained to piety and divine worship; the other civil, by which the individual is instructed in those duties which as men and citizens we are bound to perform. To these two forms are commonly given the not inappropriate names of spiritual and temporal jurisdiction, intimating that the former species has reference to the life of the soul, while the latter relates to matters of the present life, not only to food and clothing, but to the enacting of laws which require a man to live among his fellows purely, honourably, and moderately. The former has its seat within the soul, the latter only regulates the external conduct. We call the one the spiritual, the other the temporal kingdom.[20]

Thus for Calvin both kingdoms are expressions of God's care and love for human beings, and in a sense they are complementary. Calvin agrees with Luther (if rather less emphatically!) that the two kingdoms must not be confused. They 'are always

---

[20] Calvin, *Institutes* III. xix. 15.

to be viewed apart from one another. When the one is considered, we should call off our minds and not allow them to think of the other'.[21]

But in Scotland a rather different account of the relation between the two kingdoms was there from the time of the Reformation. Theology and the gospel are not the concerns of the spiritual realm alone; they are the basis for a *confessional* politics and a *confessional* economics, based on an unashamedly christological foundation. The *Scots Confession* is thus in interesting ways comparable to the Theological Declaration of Barmen of 1934. Perhaps this is what attracted Barth to it in 1937.

The working out in Scotland of the theory of two kingdoms in terms of church–state relations is also distinctive and radical. The basic position is that the power of the Crown may be, and sometimes must be, confronted, even while honouring and respecting the office. Andrew Melville, the leader of the Second Reformation who, in an encounter with James VI at Falkland in 1596, called the king 'bot God's sillie vassall', typified the early relationship between church and state. Melville sees his task at a time of crisis for church and crown to speak truth to power and clarify what he sees as the true Reformed relationship of church and state. He addresses the king:

> And thairfor, Sir, as divers tymes befor, sa now again, I mon tell yow, thair is twa Kings and twa Kingdomes in Scotland. Thair is Chryst Jesus the King and his kingdome the Kirk, whase subject King James the Saxt is, and of whase kingdome nocht a king, nor a lord, nor a heid, bot a member! And they whome Chryst hes callit and commandit to watch over his Kirk, and governe his spiritual kingdome, hes sufficient powar of him, and authoritie sa to do, bathe togidder and severalie; the quhilk na Christian King nor Prince sould controll and discharge, but fortify and assist, utherwayes nocht fathfull subjects nor members of Christ.[22]

Here is a strong affirmation of the sole Lordship of Christ, and a powerful suggestion that this is mediated to the civil authorities by the Kirk, which in a special sense is the Kingdom

---

[21] *Institutes*, III. xix. 15.
[22] Robert Pitcairn (ed.), *The Autobiography and Diary of Mr James Melville*. Edinburgh: The Wodrow Society, 1842, p. 370.

of Christ. This distinctively Scottish version of the two kingdoms theory may from time to time have been open to the opposite dangers to those latent in the Anglican Reformation's affirmation of the royal supremacy.[23] It certainly involved a claim on the part of the Church to spiritual independence, which was seen by royalists in the sixteenth and seventeenth centuries as an unacceptable limitation on royal power. Because in the seventeenth century they were used as agents of royal control, bishops were – and are often still – seen in the Presbyterian mind as infringing both the freedom of the Church and its populist, democratic polity as a folk-church. As a consequence Scotland had four and a half centuries of controversy about the authority of the Crown, parliament and the civil courts over the Church of Scotland.

Thus the sixteenth-century Reformation period established a sharp distinction between the spheres of church and state, yet spoke of the mutual responsibilities that they had for each other. Scotland was to be a Christian commonwealth in which the activities of church and state were to be complementary. The Church was to be responsible for education at all levels, the relief of poverty and the maintenance of moral standards, as well as the worship of God and the preaching of sound doctrine. The state had the responsibility for defence, most serious matters of law and order and legislation in temporal matters. Much depended on smooth co-operation between church and state in their separate roles.

All this depended on a particularly strong christological emphasis in the early Scottish Reformation documents. The universal lordship of Christ, or 'the crown rights of the Redeemer', are constantly affirmed. At the heart of the 'Action Prayer' in the Book of Common Order of 1564, commonly called 'Knox's Liturgy', worshippers come to his table

> to declare and witness before the world that by him alone we have received liberty and life; that by him alone thou dost acknowledge us as thy children and heirs; that by him alone we have entrance to the throne of thy grace; that by him alone we are possessed in our

---

[23] On the development of the idea of royal supremacy in the early English Reformation, see especially Diarmid MacCulloch, *Thomas Cranmer*. New Haven: Yale University Press, 1996, especially pp. 278, 349, 364, 576f., 617.

spiritual kingdom to eat and drink at his table, with whom we have our conversation presently in heaven, and by whom our bodies shall be raised up again from the dust, and shall be placed with him in that endless joy which thou, O Father of mercy, hast prepared for thine elect before the foundation of the world was laid.[24]

A National Covenant

If the sixteenth-century Reformation Settlement suggested that the Church of Scotland was more a folk-church than a state church, the seventeenth century, through the development of ideas of covenant expressed especially in the National Covenant of 1638 and the Solemn League and Covenant of 1643, saw Scotland as a nation under God, bound together in faithfulness to God's covenant, with a national Church at the heart of its life. The two covenants were understood also as a protest by the nation particularly against policies which limited the freedom of the Church. The Revolution of 1688 recognised and affirmed the Church of Scotland's understanding of itself as a national Church and a folk-church which had a sphere distinct from that of the state within which it was and must be free. Church and state had responsibilities towards one another, responsibilities that could only be exercised if there was separation.

The radical populist and democratic emphasis continues close to the heart of seventeenth-century Scottish theology and political theory. The christocentric biblical theology of the earliest Reformation documents such as the *Scots Confession* is now replaced with a more scholastic Calvinism, and the new form of federal Calvinism expressed in the Westminster documents of the 1640s is on the face of it apparently less radical. But Samuel Rutherford, the pre-eminent covenanting theologian of the seventeenth century, is unambiguously radical in social and political matters and combines this with an emotional and passionate Calvinist piety, particularly as expressed in his immensely influential *Letters*. His *Lex Rex* (1644) was one of the most significant seventeenth-century works on political theology, which aroused intense antagonism particularly after the Restoration because it was interpreted as

[24] John Cuming (ed.), *The Liturgy of the Church of Scotland, or John Knox's Book of Common Order*. London: 1840, pp. 84–5.

an anti-royalist diatribe. In fact *Lex Rex* developed systematically, and in relation to radically changed circumstances, the theological and political radicalism we already found in Knox. The underlying theology was, however, significantly different. In almost medieval style it was assumed that there was a large overlap between Scripture and natural law. 'The Scripture's arguments,' he wrote, 'may be drawn out of the school of nature'.[25] No trace here of Barth's rejection three centuries after of natural law and natural theology! But on this basis, Rutherford affirms popular sovereignty. Kings do not rule by divine right, but have delegated power mediated from God through the people. Although he teaches that the people have 'irrevocably made over to the king' the powers of government, it still remains true that in the exercise of executive power the king is highly circumscribed. Indeed in Rutherford we find a quite clear form of the separation of powers, a constitutional theory which has more Calvinist roots than is sometimes acknowledged.[26]

Rutherford develops systematically, and in dialogue with continental thinkers, particularly Calvinists and Jesuits, what had been more cautiously suggested in the early Scottish Reformation documents – that there is a positive duty to resist an unjust and oppressive tyrant. This duty is normally (as Calvin himself suggested) laid on the subordinate magistrates and the estates; only in really extreme situations may a private citizen resist the established authorities. The argument, as Coffey points out, is based on natural law and Roman law almost as much as upon Scripture, and Rutherford is at pains to combat suggestions that passages of the Bible like Romans 13 are in fact admonitions to passive obedience.[27]

Rutherford also develops the radical Scottish tradition through what Coffey calls his 'genuine passion for social justice'.[28] The central role of the monarch and the judges is to

---

[25] Cited from *Lex Rex* in John Coffey, *Politics, Religion and the British Revolutions: The Mind of Samuel Rutherford*. Cambridge: Cambridge University Press, 1997, p. 153.

[26] See Coffey, p. 173.

[27] The latest discussion of Rutherford on resistance is in Coffey, *Politics, Religion and the British Revolutions*, pp. 175–83.

[28] Coffey, *Politics, Religion and the British Revolutions*, p. 170.

do justice, particularly to the poor. In order to do this they must live near the poor and appreciate their condition. As in the sixteenth-century Scots Reformation documents (and indeed in the Old Testament), the oppression of the poor and weak is closely linked to idolatry, which it is the duty of those in authority to extirpate.

Establishment and Disruption

With the establishment of Presbyterianism in Scotland as part of the Revolution Settlement of 1690, the Church of Scotland became a very central part of the power structures of the nation. The General Assembly assumed a role which it is only now relinquishing – that of a quasi-parliament, articulating the voice of the Scottish people on a variety of issues, not exclusively theological and ecclesiastical. A radical prophetic voice was heard less frequently and the political authorities and the landowners successfully established control over the appointment of many ministers. The literati of the Scottish Enlightenment such as Adam Smith sang the praises of the Presbyterian polity and the virtues of the Presbyterian clergy. These they saw as foundational to a lively, intellectual and open society. But clearly they did not expect the Kirk or its ministers to provide radical prophetic criticism of the social and political order. In *The Wealth of Nations* (1776) Adam Smith declared that 'There is scarce perhaps to be found anywhere in Europe a more learned, decent, independent, and respectable set of men than the greater part of the Presbyterian clergy of Holland, Geneva, Switzerland and Scotland.'[29] These are not wild radicals, Knoxes or Rutherfords. Rather, they commend themselves to their 'superiors' by 'their learning, the irreproachable regularity of their life, and by the faithful and diligent discharge of their duty'. The ministers 'have more influence over the minds of the common people than perhaps the clergy of any other established church'. For 'the common people look upon him with that kindness with which we naturally regard one who approaches somewhat to our own condition, but who, we think,

---

[29] Adam Smith, *An Inquiry into the Nature and Causes of the Wealth of Nations*. R. A. Campbell and A. S. Skinner (eds), Oxford: Oxford University Press, 1976, p. 810.

ought to be in a higher'.[30] The radical prophets of the
Reformation and covenanting times had become pillars of the
community!

The Scottish Enlightenment did not, however, uniformly
oppose the Scots radical tradition. Influential teachers and
savants like Frances Hutcheson and Millar presented a theologically informed philosophy which was full of radical
implications. Their disciples often enough maintained the
radical tradition, particularly outside Scotland; in America, for
instance, several of them were stirrers up of revolutionary
fervour. At home in Scotland, most energies went into church–
state disputes, rather than social reform.[31] Ecclesiastically there
was more tension in the Church about the people's right to call
their minister than Adam Smith recognised. The Secessions of
the eighteenth century were not only about the people's right
to call their ministers but about the democratic structure of the
Church, human equality and the need to preserve independence from the state and indeed the landed gentry.

The populist, radical tradition thus survived, if with some
difficulty, in the eighteenth century. One may argue that
this was less true of Scotland than among the radical Irish
Presbyterians who, inspired by the French Revolution, supported the 1798 Uprising, or in the American Revolution under
the influence of John Witherspoon and others.

Theologically, a modified scholastic Calvinism was almost the
foundational premise of the Scottish Enlightenment, which in
its main thrust was certainly not hostile to the Church or to
Christian faith.[32] But the philosophy and the theology of the
Scottish Enlightenment preserved little of the radical impulse
of the sixteenth and seventeenth centuries.

Among the faithful the radical tradition survived here and
there. It began to come alive in the Highlands when landlords,
usually strongly supported by the ministers they had appointed
to 'their' parishes, began to clear the people from their estates
to make way for sheep and other 'improvements'. The
widespread sense of outrage at what was happening led to a

[30] Smith, *The Wealth of Nations*, p. 810.
[31] I am indebted for these points to Professor Storrar. See also James Mackey,
Power and Christian Ethics, pp. 121–8.
[32] The least sympathetic was probably David Hume.

considerable proportion of the people of the Highlands joining the Free Church when the Church of Scotland split in 1843 on the issue of relations to the state. In the Free Church there was a cautious revival of the radical tradition, the belief that Calvinist orthodoxy had prophetic things to say in relation to the social order and the broader community.

It was, as I say, a *cautious* revival. Thomas Chalmers and the other leaders were almost obsessed with the dangers of public disorder arising from ecclesiastical disputes, and Chalmers' life-long defence of Establishment was an assertion that the established Church should provide the sinews of the social order through the parish system, which in a way was a con-tinuation of the tradition of *The First Book of Discipline.*

Chalmers' own social thought was conservative; he saw the social as well as the economic system as part of the divine ordering of things and thus beyond theological question.[33] At the laying of the foundation stone of New College, Edinburgh, he declared:

> We leave to others the passions and politics of this world, and nothing will ever be taught, I trust, in any of our [theological] halls, which shall have the remotest tendency to disturb the existing order of things, or to confound the ranks and distinctions which now obtain in society.[34]

Chalmers was as significant in his day in political economy as in theology; he was one of the leaders in what Boyd Hilton calls 'the baptism of political economy',[35] and he even received the accolade of being denounced by Marx as 'the arch-Parson Thomas Chalmers', a pupil of 'Parson Malthus'.[36] Chalmers taught political economy as a branch of natural theology, just as Adam Smith taught natural theology as part of moral philosophy.[37] For Chalmers, natural theology was so closely

[33] A. M. C. Waterman, *Revolution, Economics and Religion: Christian Political Economy, 1798–1833.* Cambridge: Cambridge University Press, 1991, chap. 6.

[34] Cited in Hugh Watt, *New College, Edinburgh: A Centenary History.* Edinburgh, 1946, pp. 3–4.

[35] Boyd Hilton, *The Age of Atonement: The Influence of Evangelicalism on Social and Economic Thought, 1785–1865.* Oxford: Clarendon Press, 1988, p. 56.

[36] Karl Marx, *Capital,* Vol. 1. Moscow: Progress Publishers, 1965, p. 617.

[37] The best modern study of Chalmers is S. J. Brown, *Thomas Chalmers and the Godly Commonwealth in Scotland.* Oxford: Oxford University Press, 1982. And an incisive discussion of Chalmers' social policy is Donald Macleod, 'Thomas

associated with classical political economy as to be almost indistinguishable from it. The clear implication of this was, of course, that the market (and perhaps, behind that, the social order as a whole) was a kind of divine ordering and therefore to that extent beyond human critique or control. 'The whole science of Political Economy', he wrote, 'is full of those exquisite adaptations to the wants and the comforts of human life, which bespeak the skill of a master-hand, in the adjustment of its laws, and the working of its profoundly constructed mechanism.'[38] The workings of the market point to a beneficent God who gives good gifts to his children through market transactions, which harness human self-interest to the achievement of the common good. Thus the selfishness of human beings results in 'cheapening and multiplying to the uttermost all the articles of human enjoyment, and establishing a thousand reciprocities of mutual interest in the world'; accordingly it displays 'the benevolence and comprehensive wisdom of God'.[39] The market, as part of the providential ordering of a just and loving God, is beyond critique and should be left undisturbed to pursue its benign course.

In addition to this sacralising of economic processes, Chalmers was also one of the leading figures in commending a way to combat what people at the time called 'pauperism'. The term is significant. It suggests that the problem is *poor people*, who develop in an industrial society communities and cultures and patterns of behaviour which actually perpetuate and exacerbate poverty. Essentially, Chalmers taught, pauperism is caused, not by society, economic structures or injustice, but by interference with economic processes. By 'trying to mend the better mechanism which nature had instituted', evils such as the multiplication of pauperism are engendered.[40] The Poor Law taking the place of private and ecclesiastical charity, Chalmers believed, simply makes the situation worse, as do

---

Chalmers and Pauperism' in S. J. Brown and Michael Fry (eds), *Scotland in the Age of the Disruption*. Edinburgh: Edinburgh University Press, 1993, pp. 63–76.

[38] Thomas Chalmers, *On the Power, Wisdom and Goodness of God as Manifested in the Adaptation of External Nature to the Moral and Intellectual Constitution of Man*. Vol. 2. London: William Pickering, 1834, p. 36.

[39] Chalmers, *On the Power, Wisdom and Goodness of God*, p. 36.

[40] Chalmers, *On the Power, Wisdom and Goodness of God*, p. 30.

common patterns of behaviour and attitudes among poor people themselves. The solution to pauperism is also largely in the hands of the poor themselves; charity and government intervention often do more harm than good. Official policies of relief, which usually ran counter to 'economic laws', make the situation worse. In Malthusian tones, Chalmers declared:

> There is no possible help for them [the poor] if they will not help themselves. It is to a rise and reformation in the habits of our peasantry that we look for deliverance, and not to the impotent crudities of a speculative legislation . . . This will at length save the country from the miseries of a redundant population – and this we apprehend, to be the great, the only specific for its worst moral and its worst political disorders.[41]

'The remedy against the extension of pauperism', he declares elsewhere,

> does not lie in the liberalities of the rich; it lies in the hearts and habits of the poor. Plant in their bosoms a principle of independence. Give a high tone of delicacy to their characters. Teach them to recoil from pauperism as a degradation.[42]

The state and the broader community are not responsible for 'pauperism', nor is its solution in their hands: 'Neither government nor the higher classes of the state, have any share in those economical distresses to which every trading and manufacturing nation is exposed', for 'the high road to the secure and permanent prosperity of labourers, is through the medium of their own sobriety, and intelligence, and virtue'.[43]

Paupers have no claim in justice; only on the compassion of their neighbours, most desirably expressed in Chalmers' view through a revitalised parish system. The local community, best represented by the parishes of an established Church in which the rich and the poor are held together in mutual responsibility, was the most appropriate agency for *disciplining* and caring for paupers, for the local community knew the individuals and families concerned, as well as local conditions,

---

[41] Chalmers, *On Political Economy*, pp. 25–6, cited in Donald C. Smith, *Passive Obedience and Prophetic Protest: Social Criticism in the Scottish Church 1880–1945*. New York: Peter Lang, 1987, p. 131.
[42] Cited in Smith, *Passive Obedience and Prophetic Protest*, p. 117.
[43] Cited in Smith, *Passive Obedience and Prophetic Protest*, p. 88.

and could adapt their treatment appropriately. The Church, in Chalmers' thought, while it had close relations to the state, was in essentials a body independent of the state. In spiritual and moral matters it had its own proper sphere, in which the state should not interfere.

Pauperism and economic distress were caused by well-intentioned tinkerings with God-given systems, and the solution depended upon the character of the poor and a true, that is Christian, account of human nature, together with the moral paternalism of an established Church which was concerned with nurturing the poor in virtue and responding wisely and guardedly to the misery of the poorest.

We have in Chalmers an example of a kind of theology which was immensely influential in its day. It rested on an apparently Calvinist/Augustinian account of human nature, but it embraced and endorsed almost without qualification the dominant contemporary economic and social theories. Its central problem was identified by Barth a century later: a free-floating natural theology has an in-built tendency to sanctify existing orders and assimilate to secular theories and philosophies. Chalmers' social theology in fact owed as much to Adam Smith as to the gospel and it suggested behaviour towards the poor that was often callous and even cynical rather than generous. Perhaps Donald Macleod is right in suggesting that it is not theology at all, because Chalmers 'is merely lending the weight of his authority as a churchman to a purely secular economic theory'.[44] Certainly Chalmers' social theology has few links with the strong christological emphasis of the early Scottish Reformation. It also had very tenuous links with the populist strand in the radical Calvinist theological tradition in Scotland, except (and this is important) that it continued to put the issue of poverty high on the Church's agenda.

And yet the radical tradition continued in the nineteenth century. Chartists marched to their rallies singing metrical psalms, behind banners bearing the symbols of the Covenanters, and their speeches in Scotland were permeated with biblical imagery and symbols.[45] Keir Hardie, the leader of the

---

[44] Donald Macleod, 'Thomas Chalmers and Pauperism', p. 70.
[45] See Donald C. Smith, *Passive Obedience and Prophetic Protest*, p. 165, etc.

Independent Labour Party, frequently proclaimed that his socialism was founded on Christian insights. John Philip, Scottish Congregationalist, campaigned for the rights of 'natives' in South Africa. In America, evangelical Presbyterians were among the leading abolitionists, drawing on the anti-slavery lectures of the Scottish Enlightenment teachers in the ancient Scottish universities.

Two World Wars

My colleague, Stewart J. Brown, has done pioneering research on the Scottish churches in the years after the First World War and the lead-up to the Union of 1929 between the Church of Scotland and the United Free Church.[46] The aftermath of the war and the beginning of the Depression led to widespread disillusion with the Christian faith and the recognition that the economic and social problems facing British society were indeed very deep-seated. On the whole the Scottish churches were reluctant to engage prophetically with such problems, and their main response to the General Strike of 1926 was to remain 'impartial', help with relief and conduct evangelistic campaigns. The United Free Church Moderator that year, Dr George Morrison, after delivering an address on 'Revival', 'held the balance evenly, and . . . charmed everyone by the happiness of his remarks' when the Assembly was addressed first by the Prime Minister, Stanley Baldwin, and then by a delegation from the Union of Scottish Mine Workers.[47] Shortly afterwards, while the strike was still on, the Moderator took part in an evangelistic campaign in the Fife coalfields, where his lace and ruffles attracted a good deal of ribald attention![48]

Brown suggests that Presbyterian church leaders in the 1920s and early 30s were concerned that their relation with government should not be hampered by any intemperate or

[46] See S. J. Brown's, 'The Social Ideal of the Church of Scotland in the 1930s', in Andrew R. Morton (ed.), *God's Will in a Time of Crisis: A Colloquium Celebrating the 50th Anniversary of the Baillie Commission*. Edinburgh: Centre for Theology and Public Issues, 1994, pp. 14–31.

[47] Alexander Gammie, *Dr George H. Morrison: The Man and his Work*. London: James Clarke, 1928, p. 126.

[48] Gammie, *Dr George H. Morrison*, pp. 134–9.

one-sided statements, or a prophetic radicalism which might forfeit government support for the projected union. More ominously perhaps, the reunited Church of Scotland declared itself to be 'a national Church representative of the Christian Faith of the Scottish people'.[49] This often went along with strong feeling against Irish Roman Catholics as an alien importation into a racially and religiously unified Scotland. It was even suggested in an article in the Church of Scotland magazine, *Life and Work*, in 1934 that the Scottish church union of 1929 was the model for the union that the Nazis had forced on the German Protestant churches!

A major turning-point was the Oxford Conference on Church, Community and State of 1937. For some significant Scottish church leaders, this was their first real exposure to ecumenism and it gave them an opportunity to hear at first hand what anti-Semitism and racism were doing in Germany. Some who had colluded with the anti-Irish and anti-Roman Catholic policies came to their senses. Most from this time came to see Scottish theology and Scottish church life in a broader global frame and to understand themselves as in some sense accountable to the *oikumene*.

During the Second World War the General Assembly established an influential 'Commission for the Interpretation of God's Will in the Present Crisis', with Principal John Baillie as Convener. This marked a new turn to a more radical stance in the Church of Scotland. Baillie called himself a Christian socialist and was unhappy with the conservatism and caution of the Church's contributions to public affairs in recent years. The work of the Commission marked the start of a new-style reformism, closely associated with the liberal evangelical theology of John Baillie and his brother Donald.[50] The Iona Community, founded by George Macleod in 1937, combined a consistently radical stance on political and economic matters, particularly issues of peace, with a concern for the renewal of worship and an interest in the Celtic tradition. Among its more prominent supporters were most of the leading liberal

---

[49] *Articles Declaratory of the Constitution of the Church of Scotland*, Article III.

[50] On the Baillie Commission see especially, Andrew R. Morton (ed.), *God's Will in a Time of Crisis: A Colloquium Celebrating the 50th Anniversary of the Baillie Commission*. Edinburgh: Centre for Theology and Public Issues, 1994.

evangelical theologians of the time, such as John and Donald Baillie.

The liberal evangelical tradition which was dominant in Scottish theology from the late nineteenth century until the 1960s was in general reformist rather than radical in its social and political orientation. It was aware of its Calvinist roots, but tended to be rather uninterested in the theology which emerged from the Scottish Reformation, and to see itself primarily as a contributor to the emerging ecumenical theology which arose out of the German Church Struggle, the Second World War and the missionary movement, and which looked forward to a day when theology would be a common Christian enterprise rather than a series of separate confessional projects.

The fact that Karl Barth chose to base his 1937–8 Gifford Lectures at Aberdeen on the *Scots Confession* of 1560, by then almost forgotten in Scotland, came as a great surprise.[51] It had not apparently occurred to many Scots theologians themselves that their Reformation heritage might have something to offer to the crises of the mid-twentieth century. The only modern popular edition of the *Scots Confession* was published as a result.[52] In the 1950s to 70s liberal evangelicalism seemed to give way steadily to a Scottish Barthian movement led by Professor T. F. Torrance. In terms of its outworking in ecclesiastical, social and political matters, however, this Scottish Barthianism was for the most part cautiously conservative. It is symptomatic that the key point on which T. F. Torrance differed from the master was infant baptism. In the 1950s T. F. Torrance headed a Church of Scotland Special Commission on Baptism which vigorously defended infant baptism and implied a conservative, Christendom-style ecclesiology in radical conflict with Barth's own assumption that Christendom was over and the West was once again a field of mission in which the baptism of infants no longer made acceptable sense.[53] There was, to be true, a revival

---

[51] Karl Barth, *The Knowledge of God and the Service of God According to the Teaching of the Reformation*. London: Hodder & Stoughton, 1938.·

[52] G. D. Henderson (ed.), *Scots Confession, 1560 and Negative Confession 1581*. Edinburgh: Church of Scotland, 1937.

[53] See *The Biblical Doctrine of Baptism: A Study Document issued by The Special Commission on Baptism of the Church of Scotland*. Edinburgh: Saint Andrew Press, 1958.

of Calvin studies in Scotland around scholars such as R. S. Wallace,[54] and T. F. Torrance himself, but the political and social radicalism of early Scottish Calvinism did not figure prominently in this revival of Calvin studies, and Scottish Barthianism was in most respects cautiously conservative.

The aftermath of the Second World War found theology and church life in Scotland buoyant, as elsewhere in the West. The theological colleges were full, churches were packed with worshippers, new churches were being built in the housing estates, where the Sunday schools were full to overflowing, and the Church of Scotland membership reached an all-time high in 1957. Little of the disillusion that followed the First World War was in evidence. There was an almost universal conviction that the war had been necessary to destroy a great evil, and there was a widespread feeling that the churches and some theologians had played a significant role in the destruction of Nazism. In particular the dialectical theologians – Barth, Brunner, Bonhoeffer and others – had identified the evil early and courageously unveiled and denounced the Beast. There was immense confidence that the relatively new ecumenical biblical theology was a major resource for the renewal of the churches and their social witness. The new ecumenical biblical theology found support both from liberal evangelicals and from Torrance-style Barthians. But in Scotland as elsewhere it came to an end in the 1960s, partly as the consequence of the onslaught of James Barr and others on the received method-ological certainties of biblical theology, partly because of what Robert Jensen has called 'the implosion of its energizing institutions' such as the Student Christian Movement, and partly because of a kind of theological capitulation to the secular.

Possibilities of Retrieval

I share John de Gruchy's conviction that 'Reformed theology is best understood as a liberating theology that is catholic in its

[54] See R. S. Wallace, *Calvin's Doctrine of the Christian Life* (Edinburgh: Oliver & Boyd, 1959); *Calvin's Doctrine of the Word and Sacrament* (Edinburgh: Oliver & Boyd, 1953); and T. F. Torrance, *Calvin's Doctrine of Man.* London: Lutterworth Press, 1949. On T. F. Torrance's influence on British reception of Barth, see Alister E. McGrath, *T. F. Torrance: An Intellectual Biography.* Edinburgh: T&T Clark, 1999, chap. 6.

substance, evangelical in principle, and socially engaged and prophetic in its witness'.[55] This kind of theology should prophetically address the power structures and also expose the elements of alienation and false consciousness within the tradition itself.[56] My brief and sketchy history of Scottish theology suggests that this sort of radical orthodoxy has in the past flourished at times of crisis, political, social and ecclesiastical. Periods when the Church has been under attack and bereft of power and influence appear to be the times when the Church and theology have felt free to be prophetic and express the radical impulse, repossessing the tradition of the Scottish Reformation

There is little doubt that the Church of Scotland and its theological tradition are today in a state of crisis. Institutional decline has led in many quarters to a failure of nerve. A massive cultural change of seismic proportions has led in one generation to the legacy of Calvin and Knox, which was for centuries a matter of national pride, becoming a major embarrassment to many. In the Church and in theology there appears to be something of a failure of nerve.

But there are signs within the Church of a revival of radical Reformed orthodoxy. The contribution of the churches and theology to the long debate about devolution and the future of Scotland was remarkable, with a range of notable figures playing major roles, in particular, perhaps, Canon Kenyon Wright and successive conveners of the Church of Scotland Church and Nation Committee. William Storrar drafted the 1989 Church and Nation report on the Constitution, which argued impressively that there was a distinct Scottish constitutional tradition which was deeply rooted in the history we have been exploring in this chapter. Storrar also established Common Cause, which drew together a 'rainbow coalition' of Scots intellectuals and public figures in the campaign for devolution. And one could go on ... Not only are there already seeds of a renewal of radical Reformed orthodoxy, but some fruits are already appearing!

---

[55] John W. de Gruchy, *Liberating Reformed Theology: A South African Contribution to an Ecumenical Debate*. Grand Rapids: Eerdmans, 1991, p. xii.
[56] de Gruchy, *Liberating Reformed Theology*, p. 41.

In Scotland today a radical impulse and a sense of community which have clear roots in the Scottish Reformation continue to flourish and be influential in politics. This was evident at the opening of the Scottish Parliament in July 1999. The proceedings were markedly informal and started with a wonderful rendering by Sheena Wellington of Burns' great song, 'A man's a man, for a' that', a strongly egalitarian poem which pokes fun at a hierarchical ordering of society and appears to be a secular expression of Calvinist egalitarianism. This was followed by the singing of the hundredth psalm to the Calvinist Genevan 'plain tune', which had its origins in the Calvinist insistence that the people should play an active part in the music of worship as in the life of civil society.

Could this ecclesiastical and theological crisis and the turning point represented by the establishment of the Scottish Parliament be the moment of opportunity for retrieving and repossessing the Scottish tradition of radical orthodoxy? I think and hope that this may be the case. And if this time of crisis in Scotland is a moment of opportunity for retrieval, so now, as in the past, stimuli and resources from outside have their role to play. Liberation theology has clear affinities with the radical tradition we are discussing, and most of its roots are Roman Catholic. More often than is commonly recognised in Scottish history, Presbyterians and Roman Catholics have been at one in affirming the independence of the Church from the state and seeking to restructure society on a Christian basis. Perhaps retrieval of radical Reformed orthodoxy could also be a moment of ecumenical convergence. Nor is it irrelevant that Barth's retrieval of the radical Calvinist tradition has led a Dutch liberal Calvinist, H. M. Kuitert, to see Barth as the godfather of liberation theology and modern radical political theology in general.[57]

We can learn much from liberation theology about the issues that a radically orthodox Reformed theology should address, in Scotland or elsewhere. And addressing such an agenda can avoid the danger of a scholastic or universalising renewal of the tradition. Theology needs help in discerning the signs of the

---

[57] H. M. Kuitert, *Everything is Politics but Politics is not Everything – A Theological Perspective on Faith and Politics*. London: SCM Press, 1986.

times, although it must not neglect its own distinctive contribution to this process. It must be brave enough to name and
confront the idolatries of today. It must attend to the tradition
even as it listens to the cry of the poor, the weak and the
oppressed, the voice of John the Common-weal. And it must
have the courage, as did Knox, to address both the ordinary
people of Scotland and the powers.

12

Ecumenical Practice: Reflections on Ecclesiology and Ethics

The recent ecumenical concern with the relationship of ecclesiology and ethics arose immediately out of the Justice, Peace and the Integrity of Creation (JPIC) process. Here there was a mounting conviction that the issues of concern were not simply ethical but in fact impinged upon matters of faith and doctrine, and in particular the nature of the Church. Accordingly, a process was designed at the Vancouver Assembly of 1983 to culminate in the churches at all levels entering into a 'covenant in a conciliar process':

- to confess Christ, the life of the world, as the Lord over the idols of our times, the Good Shepherd who 'brings life and life in its fullness' for his people and for all creation;
- to resist the demonic powers of death inherent in racism, sexism, class domination, caste oppression, and militarism;
- to repudiate the misuse of economic organisation, science and technology, in the service of powers and principalities and against people.

The Assembly called for 'a clear covenanting commitment to work for justice and peace', and rejection of 'the heretical forces which use the name of Christ or "Christian" to legitimise the powers of death'.[1]

---

[1] David Gill (ed.), *Gathered for Life*. Geneva: WCC, 1983, p. 89.

This call eventually led to the World Convention on JPIC in Seoul, Korea in March 1990. The intention was that the world's churches should enter into a covenant, combining confessional statements with practical commitments to resist negative forces and support positive initiatives. The underlying conviction was that ecclesiology and ethics belong together, but the proceedings of the convention and its outcomes were so confusing and incoherent that it has, with some justice, been roundly criticised.[2]

The Search for Unity and Obedience

But the origins of the concern for ecclesiology and ethics are, of course, far older than JPIC. From its beginnings the modern ecumenical movement has wrestled with the relation between ethics and the being and unity of the Church. There has been a steady conviction that there *is* a relationship, but spelling out what it is has proved hard and controversial and continues to be so today. Some people have felt that the only way to progress towards unity must be to set aside ethical concerns which are so often divisive among Christians, or to pursue the two quests independently of one another. Others have found in ethical struggles a new and vital experience of unity and solidarity, even of what it means to be the Church. And others again have found fresh and challenging ethical insights emerging from the ecumenical movement's work and the new experiences of unity that this has brought.

The Ecclesiology and Ethics Study Project arose as part of a sustained effort to overcome this deep tension in the modern ecumenical movement, and indeed in the lives of the churches. On the one hand there were many who felt that the way to unity was through doctrinal agreement – the traditional Faith and Order approach. Doctrinal agreement, particularly in ecclesiology, it was held, would remove the real obstacles to Christian unity; ethical issues were secondary and here more diversity was allowable than in matters of doctrine. Thus some theologians, including a Scottish friend of mine, believed that

---

[2] There is a brief discussion of this in my *The True Church and Morality*. Geneva: WCC, 1997, pp. 40–3.

with the approval by Faith and Order of the immensely significant convergence document *Baptism, Eucharist and Ministry* (1982) the last real obstacle to reunion had been removed. These theologians were quickly disillusioned, as it gradually became obvious that unity required conviviality and a sense of needing one another and belonging together rather than simply formal confessional agreements, and that disunity was often the result of non-theological and institutional factors which had not been adequately addressed in the process leading up to BEM.

On the other hand, there were those who proclaimed that doctrine divides and moral struggle in the world unites, suggesting that the churches should work together and would then find more commonalities in action than in doctrine or worship. This was often regarded as the Life and Work or, later, Church and Society approach.

But the reality was, of course, more complex. On the one hand Christians were reminded, particularly by the German Church Struggle and the Theological Declaration of Barmen (1934) and more recently by the struggle against apartheid, that there was such a thing as 'moral heresy' (Visser t'Hooft), that certain types of practice were radically incompatible with Christian confession and that certain ethical issues at least were necessarily church dividing.

There was also a discovery that in ethical struggle alongside others there was often a real and profound new experience of what it is to be Church, that *ecclesiogenesis* (Leonardo Boff's term) often takes place in the struggle for justice and truth. The being and message of the Church are often at stake, it was realised, when it wrestles with great ethical issues.

This led the Rønde consultation of 1993, which produced *Costly Unity*, to distinguish 'cheap unity' which 'avoids morally contested issues because they would disturb the unity of the church',[3] from costly unity which is the discovery or recovery of the churches' unity in struggles for peace and justice, where witness and social praxis are linked inseparably together in a context of solidarity.

[3] *Costly Unity: Koinonia and Justice, Peace and Creation.* Geneva: WCC, 1993, p. 39.

The next consultation, at Jerusalem, reaffirmed that there can be no ecclesiology without ethics and no (Christian) ethics without ecclesiology,[4] and the Fifth World Conference on Faith and Order at Santiago de Compostela declared:

> The being and mission of the Church, therefore, are at stake in witness through proclamation and concrete actions for justice, peace and integrity of creation. This is a defining mark of koinonia and central to our understanding of ecclesiology. The urgency of these issues makes it manifest that our theological reflection on the proper unity of Christ's Church is inevitably related to ethics.[5]

In this discussion process it was, I think, clearly shown how ecclesiology and ethics mutually illumine, question and interpret one another. A good way of understanding the koinonia which the Church seeks to manifest for the sake of the world might be, I suggest, the Johannine idea of dwelling in truth and unity, where faith and action are two sides of the one coin and the truth is known and loved in the solidarity of costly unity, discipleship and obedience.

There were, however, obvious dangers in this process, particularly reductionism. There was a serious danger of the revival of the once common assumption that theology is simply a vivid way of speaking about ethics with no claim to truthfulness about reality or, alternatively, that ethics should lose its proper autonomy and integrity. In ecclesiology there emerged subtle suggestions that the Church should be regarded as no more than a moral community – or, even worse, as essentially a fellowship of the good, the moral achievers, or of passive victims. Sometimes the Church was regarded as primarily a political movement, with the gospel as a kind of manifesto for the elimination of poverty or the establishment of justice. Such dangers are perennially present. But the project of relating ecclesiology and ethics has been there from the beginning, and is in practice unavoidable.

---

[4] *Ecclesiology and Ethics: Costly Commitment.* Geneva: WCC, 1995, p. 65.
[5] Thomas F. Best and Günter Gassman (eds), *On the Way to Fuller Koinonia: Official Report of the Fifth World Conference on Faith and Order.* Geneva: WCC, 1994, p. 259.

Ecclesiology and Ethics in Scripture

The whole modern ecumenical discussion of ecclesiology and ethics has, of course, roots deep within the tradition of faith which provides resources and challenges for the contemporary debate. In the Bible moral and doctrinal teaching interweave in a subtle and significant manner, suggesting that you cannot have one without the other. The indicative and the imperative are inseparably bound together. The command is rooted in the story. The ten commandments are presented as given by the living God who proclaims 'I am the Lord your God who brought you out of Egypt, out of the land of slavery.'[6] The authority of the commandments arises from the fact that the people have been delivered by the God who has bound himself to Israel in covenant-love. In their dealings with this God the people hear God's command and discover what they ought to do. Because they have experienced the bitterness of slavery and the contempt that is often visited upon strangers and outsiders, and because they have encountered a God who cares passionately for the forgotten and hears the cry of the poor, they are to be hospitable and gentle towards the strangers in their midst and open-handed towards the poor.

Similarly in the New Testament, doctrine, story, moral teaching and membership of the community are woven together into a seamless web. In the epistles, ethics is not a mere postscript to doctrinal teaching but an inseparable part of what it is to be a believer. And in the gospels it is abundantly clear that being a disciple, following Jesus, involves a lifestyle, a discipline, a strenuous way, a wrestling with moral choices. Indeed, in and through the moral life we come to know God: 'Those who live by the truth come to the light so that it may be seen that God is in all they do.'[7] And the Letter of John declares that 'everyone who loves is a child of God and knows God, but the unloving know nothing of God, for God is love'.[8] Being a disciple, confessing the faith, involves a particular loving stance in relation to life and action.

---

[6] Exodus 20.2.
[7] John 3.21.
[8] 1 John 4.7–8.

But Christianity is not legalistic. The lifestyle for Christians is not cast in bronze, immutable and hard. Because they believe that the source of all good is the *living* God, Christians have to learn to attend to God's call and rely on God's grace and on God's forgiveness when they go astray. And since ethics is essentially a relationship to God, believers struggle to discern the signs of the times, to understand what God is doing and calling on his people to do.

Nor is Christian morality individualistic. We act and exist in solidarity with others, with a vast company of people bound to us by ties of mutual responsibility and accountability. Believers see themselves as part of the Body, working in harmony with the Body, sustained by the Body. The Body is steward of disturbing memories and hopes which put the present into a new perspective. In the Body the various members depend upon one another, support one another and forgive one another. They have different functions, tasks, callings and responsibilities, but within the Body the ranking and hierarchy of society is transcended or reversed; all are necessary, each is of infinite worth and dignity. And in the Body the conflicts, animosities and divisions of society are overcome in shared concern for one another, in mutual honouring: 'If one part suffers, all suffer together; if one flourishes, all rejoice together.'[9] And this Body is international so that it includes Iraqis and Americans, bound together in mutual accountability and concern even in the context of the Gulf War.

In itself, the existence of the Body is a moral statement, a demonstration and exemplification of the ethic which is integral to the gospel. The behaviour of the community confirms or questions the truth of the gospel that its members proclaim. Bishop Lesslie Newbigin tells of preaching in a South Indian village. The preacher stands in the open air, with the little Christian congregation gathered around to listen. But others are listening too – from a distance, through open windows, or with backs turned on the preacher, from the shade of a great banyan tree, non-Christian villagers also hear the preacher's words. They see, in front of them, their Christian neighbours. And if they know that these neighbours' lives are immoral or

---

[9] 1 Corinthians 12.26.

that the little village congregation is riven with animosities and hostility, it is hard for them to take the gospel seriously. But if their Christian neighbours, the little flock in that village, are visibly finding joy in believing, rejoicing in God's forgiving grace, struggling to express in their lives the love and justice of God, then the others are far more likely to hear and be attracted to the message which has shown that it can transform lives. The congregation, the Body, the Church is thus a kind of hermeneutic of the gospel. The message and the ethics are inseparable from the life of the Church.

Within the Body divisions of hostility, suspicion, competition are, if tolerated, pathological and can destroy its vitality and integrity. But the unity and harmony of the Body does not remove particularity, plurality and difference; indeed, it enhances and enriches these things and blends them into a common purpose. In Christ the old animosities and separations are overcome, as exemplified in the classic division between Jew and Gentile. The writer of the Letter to the Ephesians addresses the good news to the Gentiles:

> Once you were far off, but now in union with Jesus Christ you have been brought near through the shedding of Christ's blood. For he is himself our peace. Gentiles and Jews, he has made the two one, and in his own body of flesh and blood has broken down the barrier of enmity which separated them; for he annulled the law with its rules and regulations, so as to create out of the two a single new humanity in himself, thereby making peace. This was his purpose, to reconcile the two in a single body to God through the cross, by which he killed the enmity.[10]

Notice that God's purpose is to create a single new humanity – the unity of the Church is simply a sign and foretaste of the broader unity of humankind which is God's goal. The unity of the Church is therefore not simply for its own sake, a matter, perhaps, of streamlining church structures – although any community needs organisation if it is to survive and flourish. The New Testament teaches that the way the Church is structured and operates is to be at the service of the gospel and to confirm that gospel. The Church points to, and already expresses in a partial way, the coming unity of humankind.

---

[10] Ephesians 2.13–16.

Nor is the unity of the Church simply a prerequisite for the mission of the Church, although it is that: in the High Priestly Prayer in John's Gospel Jesus prays, 'May they all be one; as you, Father, are in me and I in you, so also may they be in us, that the world may believe that you sent me.'[11] Unity is the goal as well as the way.

The unity of the Church is therefore a vital expression of the gospel, a demonstration of the truth of the gospel. But there are true and phoney kinds of unity. Unity takes many forms. There is cheap unity as well as costly unity.

Church and Ethics in Early Centuries

This linking together of unity, the being of the Church and the behaviour of believers, continues in the early Church. Commonly the Fathers saw the being and unity of the Church as necessitating a peculiar lifestyle among believers. Ignatius of Antioch gathers together these themes as naturally belonging together when he writes to the Magnesians:

> When I heard of the disciplined way of life your Christian love has taught you, it gave me so much pleasure that I decided to address a few words to you in the faith of Jesus Christ. As I go about in these chains, invested with a title worthy of a god, I sing songs of praise to the churches; and I pray for their corporate as well as their spiritual unity – for both of these are the gifts of Jesus Christ, our never-failing life. May they be one in their faith, and one in the love which transcends all other virtues; but chiefest of all may they be one with Jesus and the Father, since it is only by enduring in him all the prince of this world's indignities, yet still eluding his clutches, that we can come to the presence of God.[12]

Early Christians continued for the most part to regard themselves as 'resident aliens' who belonged to a kind of counterculture and alternative community to the existing social orders which were hastening towards destruction. Within the Church, Christians lived by different standards from those

---

[11] John 17.21.
[12] *Epistle of St Ignatius of Antioch to the Magnesians*, chap. 1. From Maxwell Stanniforth (ed.), *Early Christian Writings*. Harmondsworth: Penguin, 1968.

of the world, nurtured a distinctive hope and represented an alternative pattern of community. The Church and the ethics it sustained offered another way of ordering life from that of the ancient world, the 'still more excellent way' of love that Paul commends in 1 Corinthians 13. But the church and the ethics it demanded and sustained were not to be nurtured in some self-sufficient ghetto; they simultaneously challenged and sustained the structures of the world, as Tertullian proclaims:

> We are a body knit together as such by a common religious profession, by unity of discipline, and by the bond of a common hope . . . We pray, too, for the emperors, for their ministers and for all in authority, for the welfare of the world, for the prevalence of peace, for the delay of the final consummation . . . Your citizenship, your magistracies, and the very name of your curia is the Church of Christ . . . You are an alien in this world, and a citizen of the city of Jerusalem that is above.[13]

Within the Church, Christians live by gospel standards, which are distinct from the ethics of the world and depend upon the expectation of the end for the delaying of which they pray so that the gospel may be preached to every creature. The Church is a kind of parallel community which represents a challenge to the secular order because it stands as an alternative possibility of ordering life.

It has been argued that it was this distancing from the world in order to sustain a fellowship of love without compromises with power which enabled Christianity to revitalise both community and social and political thought in late antiquity. The Christian community sometimes understood itself as the soul, giving life to the body politic and sustaining that body by its prayers. But it was also a challenge to the state and a source of new and much needed ideas for Western social thought.[14] It resisted assimilating its ethics to the dominant mores of the surrounding society and it endeavoured to witness in the way the community was structured and operated as well as in the words and actions of its members, to the truth of the gospel and the value of the way of love.

[13] Tertullian, *Apologeticus* 39; *De Corona* 13.
[14] See Sheldon Wolin, *Politics and Vision*, pp. 96–7.

Models of Ecclesial Ethics

In the long pre-ecumenical centuries of division, competition and hostility between the different Christian traditions, the various confessions have developed rather different understandings of what it is to be 'church', and of how church and ethics were properly related. These have related to differing understandings of the nature of the Church, and have grown up within specific traditions, often in relative isolation from other understandings. In more recent times the various models have begun to interact far more seriously and continuously with one another, and have often found that there are unexpected complementarities and convergences between them. I outline four of the principal ones, in broad-brush terms, almost as Weberian 'ideal types'.

Roman Catholic moral theology, as is well known, is rooted particularly in the activity of the confessional. From the time of the Irish Penitentials, starting in the sixth century, moral theology developed not so much as the ethical dimension of the Church's proclamation and being, but rather as an intellectual service of the activities of the priest as confessor, reflecting on how best to handle tricky issues of conscience and drawing up sometimes strangely specific tariffs of penalties for offences. This 'fascinating and repelling literature'[15] played a pivotal role in the rechristianisation of Europe, constantly emphasising, as it developed into a major tradition of moral reflection, that Christian faith cannot be separated from a distinctive moral stance.

For centuries, Roman Catholic moral theology was highly individualistic and legalistic, but the development of this tradition, so elegantly and authoritatively analysed by Jack Mahoney, provided the foundational resources for the magisterial social teaching of modern times and was, like so much else, refreshed and reinvigorated by the Second Vatican Council. Mahoney speaks of the task after the Council as finding for moral theology 'its most challenging and enriching programme for the future as an ethics of

---

[15] John Mahoney, *The Making of Moral Theology: A Study of the Roman Catholic Tradition*. Oxford: Clarendon Press, 1987, p. 5.

koinonia.[16] Moral theology, he argues, now becomes in a broader sense an ecclesial theology; it is no longer primarily a *clerical* discipline, focused on the guidance of confessors and concentrating primarily on individual behaviour. The Church is to witness as a fellowship of believers, in example as much as in words, to the truth of the gospel as it is found in Jesus Christ. Moral theology, in brief, is not just to service the confessional; it is to enable the Church to *be* the Church as a sign of the Reign of God.

But there remains, I believe, an unresolved tension as to whether moral teaching flows magisterially from the top, to be simply received by the faithful, or is generated in some sense from below, emerging from a *consensus fidelium*. This issue is central to controversies such as that between the liberation theologians and the Congregation for the Doctrine of the Faith, and between the US Catholic bishops and the Vatican about the mode and method of their moral teaching in their Pastoral Letters on war and peace and the economy. And it also highlights a contrast between the increasing centralisation of the Roman Catholic Church's moral magisterium (in apparent tension particularly with the official teaching on subsidiarity), on the one hand, and the World Council of Churches' stress on attending to the voice of the silenced and powerless and on participation, on the other.

For the Orthodox, disciples are made, morals and character are taught and the gospel is proclaimed primarily through the liturgy. Historically it is not hard to show that the moral content and bearing of the liturgy have often lain largely dormant for long periods of time, before being reborn, sometimes to dramatic effect. Alexander Schmemann, the Orthodox liturgical theologian, argues that authentic worship is 'the expression, creation and fulfilment of the Church'; but in practice, he suggests, churches have become 'cultic societies' whose worship is experienced as 'a departure out of the world for a little while, as a "vent" or break in earthly existence'. When the Church becomes a 'cultic society', its worship, life and being are evacuated of ethical content. Rather, Schmemann argues, the worship of the Church ought to be experienced 'as the love

---

[16] Mahoney, *The Making of Moral Theology*, p. 346.

of God directed towards the world, as a witness to the Kingdom of God, as the good news of salvation, as new life'.[17] The ethic that is expressed in and supported by the liturgy is an ethic for the world, not for a small sect living an enclosed life in a ghetto.

In worship the future for all is experienced and proclaimed; an *antepast* of the heavenly banquet is provided; divisions are overcome and the principles of true community are exemplified. To be honest, much of this has lain dormant for long ages, but liturgy has also frequently demonstrated its capacity for rebirth and return to relevant, challenging life.

An emphasis on the significance of liturgy as a resource for and an expression of ethics is now widely shared among non-Orthodox Christian churches. But other traditions have been more hesitant to emulate the Orthodox reluctance to make pronouncements on ethical issues, seeing this as more a by-product of the Caesaropapist tradition than an insistence on achieving a *consensus fidelium* before authoritative statements are made.

In the Reformed tradition, ecclesial ethics were manifested particularly in the systems of 'ecclesiastical discipline' which were considered so important that in many Reformed confessions discipline appeared alongside faithful preaching and the right administration of the sacraments as a mark of the true Church: 'Ecclesiastical discipline uprightly ministered, as God's word prescribes, whereby vice is repressed and virtue nourished', as the *Scots Confession* of 1560 put it.[18] This discipline is the way of forming disciples and maintaining the boundaries of the Church. It is assumed that the Church is and must be a moral community, that right belief is inseparable from right action and that the agent of discipline is the community acting collectively.

In a sinful, broken world the Church must be a community of grace and forgiveness, but also of growth in holiness and love. Discipline – in the New Testament, *paideia* – means education, socialisation, nurturing, moral formation, character-building, enculturation, the maintenance of community.

---

[17] Alexander Schmemann, *Introduction to Liturgical Theology*. Crestwood, NY: St Vladivar's Seminary Press, 1986, p. 31.
[18] *Scots Confession* (1560), chap. 18.

Discipline takes place in solidarity and restores the bonds of love and fellowship, as evidenced in these words of the minister to a penitent offender in a congregational gathering to receive him back into the community, according to a sixteenth-century Scottish order for discipline:

> You have heard also the affection and care of the Church towards you, their penitent brother, notwithstanding your grievous fall, to wit, that we all here present join our sins with your sin; we all repute and esteem your fall to be our own; we accuse ourselves no less than we accuse you; and, finally, we join our prayers with yours, that we and you may obtain mercy, and that by the means of our Lord Jesus Christ.[19]

Reformed systems of discipline originally emphasised solidarity in offence and mercy and spoke powerfully of grace. But structures of discipline in most Reformed churches gradually degenerated, becoming harsh, punitive and legalistic. The original conception was a striking demonstration of the necessity for a moral structure in the household of faith which in fact expressed the gospel and mediated grace.

A distinctive Lutheran emphasis, closely mirrored in major strands of Anglicanism, is on the doctrine of vocation.[20] All believers have a dual vocation – to salvation through the Church and to sharing through secular offices and callings in God's gracious work in the world. In their vocations people are drawn to serve God in serving their neighbours; whether knowingly or not, they become 'masks' or 'veils' of God, the instruments of his love. Sometimes this can be quite paradoxical in its outworking, as when the statesman or soldier in fulfilment of the responsibilities of his vocation is obliged to resort to force, coercion and violence: 'The hand that wields this sword and slays with it is then no more man's hand but God's, who hangs, tortures, beheads, slays and fights. All these are his works and his judgements,' declares Martin Luther.[21]

---

[19] Order of Excommunication and Public Repentance, in John Cumming (ed.), *The Liturgy of the Church of Scotland, John Knox's Book of Common Order*. London, 1840, p. 145.

[20] The classic treatment of Luther's understanding of vocation is Gustav Wingren, *The Christian's Calling*. ET Edinburgh: Oliver & Boyd, 1958.

[21] M. Luther, *Whether Soldiers, Too, Can Be Saved*.

The doctrine of vocation affirmed in emphatic terms the spiritual and moral significance of 'ordinary life', to use Charles Taylor's term, and also the autonomy under God of secular vocations. This relative autonomy of the secular can be understood in dangerous ways, as when, under Hitler, some church leaders saw themselves as disabled on principle from questioning or opposing the activities of the Nazis, because their mandate only ran in the sphere of church and not in the secular world. None the less it represents a sound and true moral insight: we serve God through serving our neighbours in the business of secular life, and although the absolute ethic of the Sermon on the Mount may not always be directly applicable, those who strive to serve God in the struggles of the world can constantly rely on the grace and forgiveness of God.

According to Max Weber and others, the austere Puritan version of this kind of ethics gave a definitive shape to modern society and in particular to the modern economy. But although the ethic of vocation was set in a sophisticated theological frame, it is an ethic for disciples fulfilling their callings in ordinary life rather than an explicitly ecclesial ethics, or an ethics which engages directly with social structures. The ethical role of the Church is hardly more than to encourage and support the faithful in their secular callings.

Models of Church and Their Ethical Expression

It is not only that different ecclesial traditions nourish differing ethical approaches, which are often seen as opposed rather than complementary; varying ways of being 'church' seem to predispose towards certain styles of ethical action, each of which on its own may seem to lack the ecclesial and ethical fullness which has become possible in a more ecumenical age.

Let me give an example of how different ecclesiologies led to different ethical expressions.

In Ireland at the time of the great Potato Famine of the 1840s three different expressions of what it is to be church – the established Anglican Church of Ireland, the Roman Catholic Church and the Quakers – responded in radically different ways to the horrors of the famine.

The established Church of Ireland was to some extent in the pocket of the government and the landlords. It had a highly privileged position, but in only a few places was it the church of the majority of the people. It was the church of the government, the landed gentry and the professionals. Often it found itself unable to criticise or oppose the fact that some Protestant landlords took advantage of the famine to turn their peasant tenants off their land and ship them off to America or Canada.

It also bought into the fashionable understanding of economics, which was commonly regarded in British Protestantism at that time as a branch of natural theology and carried with it a repressive and moralistic approach to the issue of 'pauperism', endorsing behaviour which on the face of it was sharply at variance with biblical attitudes to the poor. Charles Trevelyan, an evangelical brought up in the Clapham Sect, the permanent head of the Treasury and thus the British official most directly responsible for dealing with the famine, declared, 'The great evil with which we have to contend is not the physical evil of the famine, but the moral evil of the selfish, perverse and turbulent character of the people.' At every point he resisted outdoor relief, even while recognising the existence of a famine in which thousands would die. At the height of the hunger he warned: 'if the Irish once find out there are any circumstances in which they can get free government grants . . . we shall have a system of mendicancy such as the world never saw'.[22] There were honourable exceptions, of course, but the clergy and bishops of the Church of Ireland by law established found it difficult to be prophetic, or to question the purposes and policies of government. It looked to many observers at the time as if the Church of Ireland had become the ideological wing of government

The Roman Catholic Church in much of Ireland was the church of the people, and particularly of the poor, the main victims of the famine. Catholics had for long suffered from the Penal Laws, which excluded them from the army and navy, the law and almost every civic activity and educational opportunity.

---

[22] Cecil Woodham-Smith, *The Great Hunger*. New York: Old Town Books, 1989, pp. 156, 171.

In brief, there was a system of sustained discrimination against Catholics in force, by which means a largely alien minority maintained control. Priests and bishops frequently acted as the spokesman and representatives of the repressed Catholic peasantry. They regularly made protests and, as the famine bit more deeply into the fabric of society, they demonstrated that the best and most courageous prophets are pastors who know and share the condition of their people.

The Roman Catholic Church in Ireland was effectively a folk-church, and a church of the poor. Both its ecclesial reality and its ethical stance were deeply influenced by these facts. As a folk-church which was not an established church, it avoided, until the setting up of an independent Irish state, many of the ambiguities and tensions that go with the realisation of folk-churches, as witness the former Yugoslavia today, Germany in the 1930s, or many another case. The Church of Jesus Christ is certainly a people, a folk, but the relation of this people to the folk in the midst of whom it is set is a complex and sometimes volatile one.

The role of the Roman Catholic Church in Ireland since independence is another, and a different, story that we might wish to discuss. For it then became a recognised national church, virtually an established Church, and thereby a 'sign' of a rather different sort.

The most surprising and, to my mind, intriguing case was that of the Quakers. They were few in number, virtually all upper or middle class, mainly English or immigrants to Ireland a few generations back. Their theological and ecclesial lineage was similar to that of the Mennonites: unabashedly sectarian, ethically absolutist and yet committed to speaking truth to power. In Ireland, as Dissenters, the Quakers shared with the Roman Catholics in a long history of discrimination and persecution. During the famine the Quakers raised amazingly generous sums of money for relief in Ireland. They sent little delegations to distribute relief. And these delegations also collected and reported on the awful facts of the situation. Quakers in London and Dublin ensured that these carefully verified reports found their way to the desks of the most influential members of the government. The Quakers combined personal charity with a reverence for the truth and a courage in presenting it to those who were in a position to do something about it.[23] And then, with extraordinarily clear insight, the Quakers concluded that adequate relief could only be raised and administered by the government, and that the only real solution lay not in philanthropy, but in legislation to reform the Irish land system.[24]

The Quakers represented very accurately an ecclesiological model which has come to the forefront of contemporary discussion, particularly through the work of John Howard Yoder and Stanley Hauerwas. The Church, in this model, is a community of 'resident aliens' who are not frightened of being a minority and refuse to withdraw from the public square to the security and comfort of a ghetto. As such, they heed the words in Jeremiah, 'Seek the welfare of the city where I have sent you into exile, and pray to the Lord on its behalf, for in its welfare you will find your welfare'.[25] Ethical witness is essential to the being of the Church in this understanding, and ethical witness involves exemplifying at least partially the message that is proclaimed. In Yoder's words, 'the very shape of the people of God in the world is a public witness, or is "good news", for the world'.[26] Thus the Church is a 'paradigmatic community' which 'does not have, but rather is, a social ethic', seeking to embody as well as proclaim the truth that is in Jesus Christ.[27] This model of what it is to be 'church' and of the integral role of ethics in the being of the Church is widely attractive in the present discussion, and deserves to be examined closely and critically.

Each of these models of the Church and its ethical dimension has its strengths and its weaknesses. It is one of the glories of the modern ecumenical movement that churches with very different historical self-understandings and conflicting views of their ethical responsibilities now engage with one another in the common search for fuller ways of being the Church which

[23] See Woodham-Smith, *The Great Hunger*, pp. 157–9, 180, 241–6, 292, 309–10, 383.
[24] Woodham-Smith, *The Great Hunger*, p. 383.
[25] Jeremiah 29.7.
[26] John Howard Yoder, *For the Nations: Essays Public and Evangelical*. Grand Rapids: Eerdmans, 1997, p. 6.
[27] Stanley Hauerwas, *Truthfulness and Tragedy*. Notre Dame: University of Notre Dame Press, 1977, pp. 142–3.

does not have, but is, a social ethic. The modern ecumenical discussion of ecclesiology and ethics emerges from this remarkable convergence, conversation and conversion.

13

The Practice of Mission:
An Indian Case Study[1]

The pioneer Scottish missionary, Alexander Duff, in later life held the chair of Evangelistic Theology in New College, Edinburgh. His work in the establishment of Scottish missions in India, most notably in Calcutta, the particular emphasis he gave to these missions, together with the rigour of his reflections on the task and strategy of mission in a particular context entitle us to regard him as a notable contextual practical theologian, well in advance of his time. Wolfhart Pannenberg is right to affirm that 'the mission directed to all mankind is not simply the practice which originally created the church, but also the ultimate horizon on which the whole life of the church must be understood.'[2] In this chapter I explore an episode in the history of missions which has, I believe, profound implications for how we should understand and undertake the task of mission today. Reflection on the successes and failures of Duff's missionary project can yield insights what are still challengingly relevant.

Duff understood mission in a broad frame of historical development. It was directed at far more than the conversion of individuals, although these had their place. He took very seriously the 'Great Commission' to preach the gospel to the

---

[1] I have recently benefited from discussions on the theme of this chapter with Dr Sudhir Chandra, who is at present working on a study of nineteenth-century Indian converts to Christianity.

[2] Pannenberg, *Theology and the Philosophy of Science*, pp. 438–9.

nations, and he expected the gospel to have profound influence on culture and national life as well as on individual behaviour.

I am concerned here to examine the transmission and influence of certain specifically Christian ideas which, I argue, contributed to the embryonic development of Indian nationalist thought prior to about 1860. This will involve us in concentrating on a short period in which there was a strong Christian contribution to the intellectual formation of an emergent westernised élite, primarily in Calcutta and, to a lesser extent, in the other Presidency towns and large urban centres.

A Marginal Community

Throughout our period, the existing Christian community in India was a tiny and internally fragmented community whose social marginality was a factor in its size, its recruitment – which was largely of socially isolated individuals who were normally denied any status within the caste system and who were placed on conversion in a social limbo – and its dependence upon European patronage.[3] Indian Christians for the most part operated in small ghettos encapsulated within Hindu society. For our present purposes, however, it is more important to note what one might call the 'ideological marginality' of Indian Christians and, to a slightly lesser extent, missionaries. This was by no means a necessary product of social marginality, although to be sure communication between a marginal group and caste Hindus or Muslims of high status was in normal circumstances extremely restricted, as missionaries regularly found to their surprise and frustration on arrival in India. The obstacles to real communication between Christian and Hindu, especially on matters of theological and intellectual importance, were extremely strong, particularly outside the Presidency towns, and regularly frustrated hopes of entering into real dialogue across religious and community boundaries.

---

[3] The Abbé J. A. Dubois stated that of his two or three hundred converts of both sexes 'two-thirds were pariahs, or beggars; and the rest were composed of *sudras*, vagrants and outcastes of several tribes who, being without resource, turned Christians, in order to form new connections, chiefly for the purpose of marriage, or with some other interested views' (*Letters on the State of Christianity in India.* London, 1823, p. 134). Other missionaries and observers, both Protestant and Roman Catholic, made similar reports.

There had, of course, been a variety of earlier attempts to break out of ideological marginality and engage at depth with Hindu thought. Recognising that a church composed almost entirely of low status converts so dependent on Portuguese patronage that Christians were regarded as unclean foreigners ('Parangis') could not communicate in any effective manner with high caste groups, Roberto de Nobili in the early seventeenth century developed a new strategy. He set himself up as a holy man of high status, separated himself socially from Christians of low caste origin, mastered Tamil and Sanskrit, and gradually gathered around himself a body of high caste converts who were permitted to retain many of their social and religious practices after conversion. In particular, high caste converts were not obliged to have social or liturgical contacts with fellow-Christians who came from low caste backgrounds. In accordance with this policy of accommodation a clear distinction was made between conversion and westernisation, and Roman Catholic missions were for long discouraged from concerning themselves to any major extent with social reform, 'improvement', education, or the inculcation of Western values.[4]

This is not the place for an assessment of de Nobili's achievement and influence. Suffice it to say that by the start of the nineteenth century the Roman Catholic missions which retained something of the policy of accommodation were no less ideologically marginal than the new Protestant missions, and seemed to have little to offer to the ferment of ideas which marked the genesis of modern India. A nineteenth-century Protestant, such as Bishop Caldwell, could say of Roman converts that 'in intellect, habits, and morals' they 'do not differ from the heathen in the smallest degree',[5] thereby indicating not just a personal bias which certainly distorted reality, but the very strong emphasis which all Protestant

---

[4] On de Nobili see S. Rajamanickam, *The First Oriental Scholar* (Tirunelveli: St Xavier's College, 1972); *Roberto de Nobili on Adaptation* (Tirunelveli: St Xavier's College, 1971); and *Roberto de Nobili on Indian Customs* (Tirunelveli: St Xavier's College, 1972); D. B. Forrester, *Caste and Christianity* (London: Curzon, 1980, pp. 15–16); Vincent Cronin, *A Pearl to India* (London: Hart-Davis, 1959); Stephen Neill, *A History of Christianity in India: The Beginnings to 1707* (Cambridge: Cambridge University Press, 1984, pp. 280–300 and 414–17).

[5] Cited in C. F. Pascoe, *Two Hundred Years of the SPG, 1701–1900*. London, 1901, p. 541.

missionaries themselves put on changes of 'intellect, habits, and morals' within their own flocks. These Protestant ideas of social change, education and general uplift gradually found a ready response in certain sections of the Hindu community and opened up the way to the discussion of theological ideas as well as social and ethical notions with a small but increasingly influential urban élite. Shared social aspirations first brought Protestant missionaries into contact with Hindus who were eager for change and looking for allies in social reform. And this contact quickly opened up the possibility of more general intellectual interchange. But the possibility rarely became a reality. Modernising Hindus were frequently happy to enlist missionaries (but seldom their converts) as allies in seeking social reform; but commonly dismissed their theology and *weltanschauung* as extravagant, irrelevant and of little interest.

Varieties of Mission Strategy

We focus, however, on an important, if minuscule, interaction in which some Protestant missionaries and converts for a time broke out of ideological marginality and made a significant contribution to debates in which can be traced the origins of much later nationalist thought. The initiation of this dialogue was specifically the work of the Church of Scotland missionaries. The Scottish missions established in the Presidency towns in the 1830s, with their distinctive emphasis on English-medium education and a general intellectual position deeply influenced by the Scottish Enlightenment, recognised and seized the opportunity of making a challengingly relevant contribution to the ferment of debate in the 1830s, 40s, and 50s among the educated youth of the Presidency towns, now for the first time exposed in depth to the challenge of Western ideas.[6] Alexander Duff in Calcutta, John Wilson in Bombay and John Anderson in Madras, together with their colleagues and imitators, saw in this situation an opportunity both to make converts and to

---

[6] The authoritative account of the intellectual background of the Scottish missions to India is Ian D. Maxwell's unpublished Edinburgh PhD: 'Alexander Duff and the Theological and Philosophical Background to the General Assembly's Mission to Calcutta to 1840' (1995).

influence the mind of India in a Christian direction. The converts they made, though few in number, were rather different
from most earlier converts to Christianity: they came from the
higher castes; they were intelligent, restless and well-educated
men who in many cases made considerable material and social
sacrifices in order to become Christians; and a number of them
became influential and widely respected intellectual leaders in
the broader society. They were drawn from circles which had
already been deeply penetrated by Western ideas, so that traditional ways of thought had been undercut, and their adoption
of Christianity was clearly an intellectual choice. In particular
they rejected the social order of caste and embraced the
Christian Church as representing a new model of social order
and social relations. The significance of the interaction lay in
more than the acquisition of new converts. Christian ideas now
penetrated Indian society in a quite new way, either mediated
through the converts or directly from the missionaries.

Earlier Protestant missionaries had, it is true, put characteristic stress on education, but on the whole it was vernacular
education at an elementary level which they offered and for
various reasons this proved attractive only to low caste Hindus
and those who were already Christians. Thus Duff, on visiting a
number of the existing mission schools soon after his arrival,
reported that

> all the pupils who frequented Bengali mission schools were
> individuals of a very inferior grade in society, individuals who had
> been in no perceptible degree affected by those changes which
> were insensibly stealing into the higher circles – individuals over
> whom caste and its prejudices still hold absolute and undisputed
> dominion – individuals imbued from infancy with the notion that
> it was an indignity to ancestors, an impiety against the gods to
> change the profession of the caste in which they were born, or
> aspire to anything beyond the humble circumstances of their birth
> – in a word, individuals who, from the very circumstances in which
> they were placed, had no desire to seek after, or cultivate any of the
> higher branches of tuition, whether of native or of foreign growth.[7]

[7] Alexander Duff, *India and India Missions*, 2nd edn; Edinburgh, 1840, p. 539.
Cf. Michael Laird, *Missionaries and Education in Bengal, 1793–1837*. Oxford: Oxford
University Press, 1972, pp. 174–5.

Duff may well have exaggerated, but his conclusion that the existing mission schools were not acting as effective channels for Christian ideas because they were not attracting able pupils who were themselves open-minded and likely in due course to become leaders in society was solidly based.

Furthermore, there were significant differences in the content of the teaching of Duff and his colleagues as compared with that of earlier Protestant missionaries. The Lutheran missionaries, who first arrived in South India in the early eighteenth century, had been characterised by an individualist pietism which, together with their subscription to Luther's doctrine of the 'two kingdoms', made them regard most social, political and philosophical issues as quite beyond their proper concern as Christian missionaries.[8] Accordingly, the education they offered consisted of basic literacy and numeracy, together with biblical and doctrinal teaching, and did not in itself prove attractive to high caste Hindus. By the mid nineteenth century the Leipzig Society represented a brand of confessional Lutheranism which was deeply influenced by romanticism and, under its remarkable and scholarly Director, Karl Graul, developed a sophisticated theology of mission to the effect that the object of mission was 'the nations' rather than individuals. But he interpreted this in a very different way from Duff. Graul was a considerable Tamil scholar and vehemently criticised the Anglo-Saxon missionaries for a cultural arrogance which, he believed, distorted their gospel and made them a danger to the cultural integrity of the peoples among whom they worked. On the face of it, this theology could have mediated the German romantic understanding of nationalism to India. But its impact was highly circumscribed and such responses as it did arouse were more revivalist than contributing in any way to the mainstream of early nationalist thought.[9]

---

[8] This is not to deny that some of them became sympathetic and scholarly observers of Indian society, languages and culture – and even Indian religion. But such interests were not always appreciated back in Europe. B. Ziegenbalg's important *Genealogy of the South-Indian Gods* (1703) lay unpublished for 154 years in the mission archives in Halle! A modern edition was published by Unity Book Services in New Delhi in 1984.

[9] K. F. L. Graul's two most relevant works are: *Explanations concerning the Principles of the Leipzig Missionary Society with regard to the Caste Question* (Madras, 1851); and *Die Stellung der Evangelisch-Lutheranischen Mission in Leipzig zur Ostindischen Kastenfrage*.

Baptist missionaries had been at work in Bengal for almost forty years before Duff's arrival in 1830. Some of them had been identified with Jacobinism before their arrival in India and were suspected of continuing to nurture republican and egalitarian ideas.[10] The social origin of most of them was the class of 'skilled mechanics', and as Dissenters they had been excluded at home from most opportunities of advancement and exposed to radical political views. From time to time the British authorities in India made it clear that they regarded them as politically dangerous, and both in India and at home people of conservative inclinations saw the endeavour to convert Hindus to Christianity, particularly when engaged in by Dissenters of low social status and suspect political opinions, as inherently seditious and likely to lead to tumult and insurrection. Sydney Smith, for example, dismissed the Baptist missionaries as 'the lowest of the people . . . little detachments of maniacs', whose efforts would never be crowned with success but rather lead to 'the utmost risk of losing our empire'.[11]

The dangers anticipated as a result of the missionary work of the Baptists and others were greatly exaggerated. They did arouse some minor controversies on account of aggressive preaching and polemical pamphlets attacking the religious beliefs of Hindus and Muslims, but never enough to pose any serious threat to law and order or justify a charge of sedition. The Baptist missionaries both allied themselves with progressive Hindus such as Ram Mohan Roy on a number of issues of social reform, and also engaged in vigorous theological debates with them. They tended to distinguish between Hindu *religion*, which they wished to destroy as false idolatry; Indian *culture*, which they regarded as in many ways excellent; and Indian *society*, which they believed required radical reform to make it conform

---

Leipzig, 1861. There is a brief discussion of Graul's career in O. G. Myklebust, *The Study of Missions in Theological Education*, Vol. 1 (Oslo, 1955), pp. 93–103. See also Arno Lehmann, 'Karl Graul, the Nineteenth Century Dravidologist', *Tamil Culture* (1964), pp. 209–25.

[10] See E. Daniel Potts, *British Baptist Missionaries in India, 1793–1833.* Cambridge: Cambridge University Press, 1967, pp. 171f.

[11] Sydney Smith in *The Edinburgh Review,* Vol. XII (1808), pp. 151–81.

to their Christian ethic.[12] But the religious and social practices which attracted their wrath did so because they were reckoned incompatible with Christian faith, and not at all because they were impeding the development of a healthy nationhood. The Baptists had converts, some of them high caste, although hardly any from the restless emerging élite for whose sceptical and westernising notions they had little sympathy or understanding. Through their educational work centred on the College at Serampore, and in particular through their translations of the Bible, they contributed to cultural renaissance and the development of the Bengali language, but it is hard to see them as contributing in any significant way to the development of nationalist ideas.

Mission and the Scottish Enlightenment

The direct appeal to young intellectuals, already in revolt against much in the tradition, was left to Alexander Duff, and it was the contacts which he fostered and the highly distinctive content of his teaching which made possible a direct Christian contribution to the shaping of early nationalist ideas. Duff arrived in Calcutta in 1830 with instructions to found a school in a country town some safe distance from the supposedly corrupting influences of metropolitan Calcutta. Typical of Scotland at the time was an emphasis on education, enlightenment and civilisation as necessary preliminaries to direct evangelism. Dr. John Inglis, a leader of the moderate party in the Church of Scotland and for many years Convener of the Church's India Mission, believed that 'little could be expected from mere preaching to an uneducated and barbarous people', for 'till the human mind be, to a certain extent, cultivated and enlightened, it may be fairly regarded as, in one respect, incapable of entertaining the faith of the Gospels'.[13] Before revealed religion could be preached it was

---

[12] Potts, *British Baptist Missionaries*, p. 225; David Kopf, *British Orientalism and the Bengal Renaissance*, Berkeley and Los Angeles: University of California Press, 1965, pp. 80, 51–4.

[13] D. Mackichan, *The Missionary Ideal in the Scottish Churches*, London, 1927, p. 113. George Smith, *The Life of Alexander Duff, D.D., LL.D.*, London, 1879, Vol. 1, p. 34.

necessary that the mind and manners be prepared by teaching natural religion: 'the testimony furnished by the light of nature, to the existence, attributes, and moral government of God, and the duty and destiny of man'.[14] Duff and his colleagues and supporters at home emphatically rejected the view of Sydney Smith that 'in comparison to many other nations who are equally ignorant of the truths of Christianity, the Hindus are a civilized and moral people'.[15] And they found their view confirmed by discovering young educated Hindus who had already vehemently rejected their own tradition as inadequate, and by their alliance with the Anglicists, such as C. E. Trevelyan.

Duff's initial survey of Calcutta and its environs persuaded him that there was already a considerable demand for English education in the city and that his Institution should be established close to the Hindu College where, under the prodigious influence of the brilliant young teacher, Henry Derozio, a generation was being entranced by the very debates of the Scottish Enlightenment out of which Duff's own theology and strategy of mission had emerged.[16] Duff's attitude to the Hindu College and Derozio's influence was ambivalent. 'The more advanced of the young men', he claimed in 1830, 'have in reality, though not openly and avowedly, shaken off Hindooism, and plunged into the opposite extreme of unbounded scepticism.'[17] The situation was pregnant with possibilities for good or ill: he saw his task as that of reclaiming 'these wanderers, whose education and worldly circumstances invest them with such mighty influence among their fellow countrymen', an effort which must 'in some degree affect and modify the future destinies of India'.[18] Derozio had opened up an area of debate in which the Scots felt thoroughly at home; his work was not to be undone, but corrected and built upon.

[14] *Home and Foreign Missionary Record of the Church of Scotland*, Old Series, Vol. 1 (Aug. 1838), p. 61, cited in: Gavin White, '"Highly Preposterous": Origins of Scottish Missions', *Scottish Church History Society Records*, 1976, Vol. XIX, p. 124. Although some Hindus referred to their faith as 'natural religion', Duff would have none of it.

[15] Sydney Smith, *Edinburgh Review*, p. 179.

[16] The remarkable report on Duff's survey of mission possibilities in Bengal, compiled a mere six weeks after his arrival in Calcutta, is now housed in the National Library of Scotland.

[17] Letter of 15 October, 1830, National Library of Scotland, MS 7530.

[18] Letter, 15 October, 1830.

From 1830 onwards, in addition to the work of the school, Duff and his colleagues gave great attention to a series of 'lectures . . . in the English language, on the Evidences of Natural and Revealed Religion to a number of Heathen youth, whose minds were previously opened by an acquaintance with European literature and science'.[19] Derozio had inculcated patriotism into his disciples; the missionaries felt no need to question this aspect of his teaching, for they too felt they were assisting at the birth of a great nation.[20] But the missionaries were convinced that only Christianity, not Derozio's scepticism, could provide a secure foundation for true patriotism.

Christianity as the Midwife of the Nation

Duff and his colleagues believed that Christianity provided the only basis for sound and healthy social life, and that without Christianity India had no future as a nation. If India were to remain Hindu, no national consciousness could develop, they believed, for Hinduism (which Duff regarded as one, closely integrated, 'gigantic system') was a prison-house of the mind. In the short term, a Hindu India would always resist the 'beneficent effects' of British rule; and in the long term it was incompatible with the development of nationhood because its genius was to divide people from each other rather than binding them together by shared purposes and common aspirations.

The secularism and scepticism of the Derozians provided no firmer foundation for nationhood. Duff regarded the Derozians as rootless, egoistic sophists with no ultimate care save for their own interests. From their ranks, however, he hoped would come the leaders of the new India. But first they must replace their volatile scepticism with a more securely based commitment which, in Duff's view, could only be adherence to Christianity. Secular Western education such as had been given in the Hindu College, which many influential government officials wished to spread throughout India in preference to education based on Christianity, would, Duff

[19] Letter, 15 October, 1830.
[20] W. S. Mackay, *The Missionary's Warrant and the Church's Duty: A Sermon*. Calcutta, 1850, p. 15.

believed, produce infidels and rebels. The Revolt of 1857 was later presented as a demonstration of the dangers which flowed from government sponsorship of purely secular education. Separation between India and Britain might be inevitable and even desirable in the long run, but the inculcation of Christianity among the leaders of India would delay that separation and ensure that, when the day came, independent India would be based on sound foundations.[21]

Duff's strategy involved the direct confrontation and refutation of basic Derozian ideas, the conversion of key individuals and the gradual percolation of Christian ideas through these converts to society as a whole. Christianity would not triumph suddenly, and individual conversions were on the whole less important in his scheme than the gradual undermining of Hinduism through the reception of Christian ideas. The real need, to Duff's mind, was for a 'decided permanent change in the *national intellect*'.[22] W. S. Mackay, one of Duff's leading colleagues, put the appeal of the Scottish missionaries very clearly in his lecture on Deism to an audience of young men in Calcutta:

> And, if we long, and pray and glow with desire for the moral and spiritual enlightenment of India; if we would give our right hands or our right eyes, to see this nation rescued from superstition and misery and redeemed unto God can it be that there is no corresponding feeling among you? In the generous warmth and flush of youth, with floods of novel light and novel truth pouring into your minds, with fame to win, and blessings awaiting you, and opportunity and high and glorious enterprise beckoning you on – and the end the regeneration of your own beloved country it surely cannot be that the blight of Hinduism is upon you and that you will leave the work to strangers.[23]

Such appeals to share with the missionaries in the work of national regeneration led to the baptism of a number of leading Derozians and other young intellectuals in Calcutta, and also in connection with the Scottish missions in Bombay and Madras.

---

[21] Duff, *India and India Missions*, pp. 408ff., 456. Cf. his *Missionary Addresses*, Edinburgh, 1850, p. 40.
[22] Duff, *India and India Missions*, p. 317.
[23] W. S. Mackay, *Lecture V on Deism*, Calcutta, n.d., p. 4.

The most notable names among the Calcutta converts were Lal Behari Day, K. M. Banerjea, Michael Madhusudhan Dutt, Kali Charan Chatterjee, Gopinath Nandi, Mohesh Chunder Ghose and Ananda Chand Mozumdar. The converts were seen by Duff and his colleagues as destined to be the real leaders of the renaissance and reformation upon which the future of India depended. They were to be the Pauls, the Luthers, the Knoxes of their native land. Reformation and renaissance were regarded as virtually a single process which was the presupposition of progress, enlightenment and national maturity.

The emphasis placed upon religious reformation reflected how closely for the Scots missionaries the Reformation of the sixteenth century and their own national consciousness were bound together. Nor was it in any way absurd to see a connection between the European Reformation and the genesis of European nationalism, or to posit a similar religious reformation as a necessary precondition for Indian nationalism. In the context of the time there was nothing strange in seeing the replacement of Hinduism with Christianity as in no significant way different from the sixteenth-century reformation of the Church in Europe. Ram Mohan Roy and others who sought to reform Hinduism while remaining Hindus were characteristically dismissed as pusillanimous Erasmian equivocators. A reformation, the Scots missionaries believed, was always sparked off by outside influences (in the case of the European Reformation a prominent 'outside influence' had been the coming of the New Learning), but could only be carried through by indigenous reformers. Western learning understood as a coherent corpus of Christian truth was to be the outside stimulus for the Indian Reformation/ Renaissance; the converts, having drunk deeply at this well, were to be the Indian Reformers:[24]

> Some Indian Luther may be roused to give expression to the sentiments that have long been secretly, though it may be vaguely, indefinitely, waveringly, cherished in the bosoms of thousands. Whole districts may awaken from their slumbers. Whole cities may proclaim their independence. Whole provinces may catch the flame of liberty – all India may be born in a day.[25]

---

[24] Duff, *India and India Missions*, pp. 355–410.
[25] Duff, *India and India Missions*, p. 377.

The Outworking of the Vision

Here was a heady vision indeed. But in practice, of course, things did not work out as the missionaries had hoped. They recruited a small cadre of truly remarkable men who were very deeply influenced by the missionaries' teaching. But although Duff and his colleagues professed that their own role was modest and temporary, in practice they contradicted their own theories by refusing equality of status to the converts, who gradually in consequence either scattered as ministers in other denominations and parts of India, or entered secular employment. When they produced proposals for a national church, or claimed a share in control of the mission, they were met with uncomprehending and paternalist rebukes at the hands of the missionaries. Practice belied theory, and the missionaries showed themselves highly suspicious of their converts' attempts to relate their Christian faith to Indian culture and aspirations. It was quite acceptable for a convert to attack Hindu Reform movements such as the Brahmo Samaj, as did Lal Behari Day and K. M. Banerjea in particular, arguing that the 'new Vedantism' has never produced any practical change for the better in the institutions of the country, so that 'it will never regenerate India'.[26]

But endeavours to demonstrate that becoming Christian did not alienate one from Indian culture, and indeed that Christian faith was the true fulfilment of the Vedic tradition, more truly Indian than the Hinduism of the day, were frowned upon.[27] K. M. Banerjea's emphasis on religious continuity and Christian patriotism was not what the missionaries expected or approved. 'I have heard it said', he wrote,

> that we Christians have no feeling for our country or our race, and that our adoption of the Christian religion is an act of treachery to India and her institutions, both ancient and modern . . . I think I could prove to any jury of educated Hindus that the charge is utterly unfounded; that we Christians have never, in a religious

[26] K. M. Banerjea, *Lectures to Educated Native Young Men. Lecture IV on Vedantism.* Calcutta, 1851, pp. 28–30.
[27] See David Kopf, 'The Missionary Challenge and Brahmo Response: Rajnarain Bose and the Emerging Ideology of Cultural Nationalism', *Contributions to Indian Sociology*, NS, No. 8, 1974, especially pp. 17–18.

point of view, renounced any of India's institutions, which they themselves do not denounce as idolatrous ... [Indeed], we are better patriots than the Brahmos.[28]

The missionaries' belief that their converts were to be new Luthers was shown, among other things, in their encouragement of the converts to write. These writings, in English and the vernacular, are of considerable quantity and form a corpus of extremely interesting material, documenting in detail a fascinating phase of cultural and religious interchange. They range from essays directly sponsored by the missionaries and published in newspapers such as the *Madras Native Herald* and the *Calcutta Christian Observer,* to substantial and independent works of literature such as Lal Behari Day's *Bengal Peasant Life* or Michael Madhusudhan Dutt's poetry.

Our specific interest in these writings is, however, the nationalist ideas which they contain. On the whole they reflect fairly precisely the theology of the missionaries and suggest a willing acceptance of the reforming role for which the converts had been cast. But to this general acceptance of their mentors' views the converts add a far more detailed knowledge and more sensitive appreciation of things Indian, and they not infrequently notice and underline implications of the missionaries' positions which were not recognised by the missionaries themselves. Two instances of this arise in relation to the understanding of providence and the assessment of caste.

Providence and Nationalism

The notion of a divine providential ordering of history was a dominant theme in the Scottish missionaries' thought.[29] This

---

[28] K. M. Banerjea, *The Peculiar Responsibility of Educated Natives and their Duty thoughtfully to enquire into the Christian Scheme of Salvation.* Calcutta, 1865, pp. 14–16.

[29] On the relation of understandings of providence and the missionary movement see, G. Studdert-Kennedy, *Providence and the Raj: Imperial Mission and Missionary Imperialism* (Walnut Creek: Altamara, 1998), and *British Christians, Indian Nationalists and the Raj* (Delhi: Oxford University Press, 1991); J. G. Greenlee and C. M. Johnston, *Good Citizens: British Missionaries and Imperial States* (Montreal: McGill-Queen's University Press, 1999); and Brian Stanley, '"Commerce and Christianity" Providence Theory, the Missionary Movement and the Imperialism of Free Trade, 1842–1860', *Historical Journal,* 26/1 (1983), 71–94.

decisively shaped their understanding of their own task and that of their converts. Sometimes the missionaries suggest, in almost Hegelian or Marxist style, that prior to the Western and Christian impact India had been an ahistorical society which had only in recent times been brought within salvation history. But certainly the missionaries generally understood British rule as a providential ordering, a sign of God's care for India rather than simply an opportunity for the making of individual converts. The British in India are, consciously or unconsciously, agents of divine providence, but fallible agents, as their failures which contributed to causing the Mutiny demonstrated.

Almost, but not quite invariably, the missionaries stop with the veiled suggestion that British rule is in some sense the ultimate dispensation of providence for India. The converts, on the other hand, while accepting the missionaries' general understanding of history and agreeing that the British ruled by divine ordering, are far clearer and more unanimous in seeing and affirming that the Scottish missionaries' views logically lead to regarding British rule as a stage to national independence.

Caste and National Unity

It was similar with the missionary attack on caste. Protestant missionaries as a whole were peculiarly vehement and consistent in their onslaught on caste. The converts accepted and repeated all the main counts in the missionary indictment. Caste, they said, was an integral part of Hinduism and also its Achilles' heel. It was quite different from European concepts of class and rank and fundamentally incompatible with Christian ideas of social order. Caste impeded evangelism and forbade humane relationships and even acts of ordinary morality between those of different castes. It narrowly circumscribed the diffusion of knowledge and was responsible for the intellectual and social stagnation of India. But other charges are given pride of place in many of the converts' writings on caste. Narayan Sheshadri, one of John Wilson's converts in Bombay, argues that caste is responsible for the paucity of Indians who are 'like the patriots of Greece and Rome. This monster-system of caste, by extinguishing patriotism and other social feelings, has, in many ways, done much to lower the national character of the Hindus'.[30] K. M. Banerjea agreed that national character had degenerated as a result of caste, which was 'the principal cause of India's humiliation'. Caste not only discourages patriotism and weakens character, but it puts 'an end to unity and strength in the nation by setting caste against caste and fragmenting society'. Thus, he continues, 'a people divided and sub-divided like the Hindus, can never make head against any power that deserves the name. The Muhammadan conquest was the natural result of such national weakness.' By implication it was caste also which had laid India prostrate before the British. Then comes the exhortation which is the key to much of the thinking of Banerjea and other converts:

> If India is destined in the counsels of Providence to look up once more among the nations of the earth, it will only be by unlearning the institution of caste, and by adopting the religion of her present rulers with all its temporal and spiritual blessings.[31]

Furthermore, converts were quick to draw out of the missionaries' position on caste implications which were extremely uncongenial to their mentors. They enquired, for instance, what was the difference between the caste distinctions that were rejected with such vehemence and the denominational rivalries among Christians, and they suggested that the refusal of communion between the various churches was no different in principle from the prohibition of commensalism between Brahmin and Pariah. They realised that the egalitarianism on which the attack on caste was based also condemned attitudes of racial superiority, shown even by some missionaries. The Church, which they saw as central to a new Indian nationhood,

---

[30] In Narayan Sheshadri and John Wilson, *The Darkness and the Dawn in India: Two Missionary Discourses.* Edinburgh, 1853, p. 34. The same point is developed in B. A. Irving, *The Theory and Practice of Caste.* London, 1853, pp. 38–40.

[31] K. M. Banerjea, 'Hindu Caste', *Calcutta Review,* XV (1851), p. 70. A detailed discussion on caste in which four young converts took part in Madras in 1845 is fully reported in the *Madras Native Herald* and reprinted in Joseph Roberts, *Caste, in Its Religious and Civil Character Opposed to Christianity.* London, 1847, pp. 63–131. In later life Banerjea modified his opposition to caste. It remains an evil, but he fears that any attempt to eradicate it 'may produce a far greater evil than its own most malignant form, and the remedy may prove worse than the disease'. 'Origin and Development of Caste', *Transactions of Bengal Social Science Association,* Vol. VII (1878).

was both more Indian and more united than the denominations imported by the missionaries.

Conclusion

Christianity, for Banerjea and the other converts, was seen as providing the only adequate answer to India's problems and the only possible basis for true nationhood. They agreed with the Hindu reformers, as against the Derozians, that patriotism must have a religious basis, but denied that contemporary Hinduism was capable of sustaining healthy national feeling. Only Christianity, they believed, could provide the proper foundation for progress and nationhood. And they went on to argue that Christianity, so far from being an imported and alienating system, was more truly the heir of the ancient Indian tradition than was the decadence of contemporary Hinduism.[32]

Some of the ideas of the Scottish mission converts were peculiarly interesting and in the long run increasingly significant, particularly their insistence on concepts of providence and equality and on the need for religious change to undergird national revival. Yet most of the converts themselves returned after a time to social marginality and Christian ideas did not continue for long to feed as directly and impressively into the national awakening.

The dialogue out of which the converts arose, and to which they contributed, did not last long. Many of the converts held leading positions within some branch of the Church, but became rather isolated from the broader society. The Calcutta converts in particular were widely scattered, and within the churches the disturbance of their questioning was gradually effectively neutralised. Their central belief that without Christianity national renewal would be impossible was unrealised in the sense that few national leaders were to be Christians, and the Christian community, which remained small and uninfluential, played little part in the development of the national movement. Yet through the early converts

[32] See K. M. Banerjea, *A Review of the Moonduck Oopunishad, translated into English*, Calcutta, 1833; various comments in *The Enquirer* magazine, of which he was editor, in 1834 and 1835; *Lectures to Educated Native Young Men*, 1851; and *Hindu Caste*, 1851.

and through leading figures such as Keshub Chunder Sen and
P. C. Mozoomdar, who were sympathetic to Christianity but not
technically members of the Church, specifically Christian ideas
continued to have their impact on the early development of
nationalist thought.[33] But that is another story.

[33] See M. M. Thomas, *The Acknowledged Christ of the Indian Renaissance.* Madras:
CLS, 1970.

Epilogue

In order to be truthful
We must do more than speak the truth.
We must also hear truth.
We must also receive truth.
We must also act upon truth.
We must also search for truth,
The difficult truth,
Within us and around us.
We must devote ourselves to truth.
Otherwise we are dishonest
And our lives are mistaken.
God grant us the strength and the courage
To be truthful.
Amen.

(from Michael Leunig, *The Prayer Tree.* Sydney: HarperCollins, 1998. Reproduced with the author's permission.)

Index

223